# THE RIGHT STORY
## *at*
# THE RIGHT TIME

## Changing the Lives of Children and Adolescents
## One Story at a Time

by
Marianna deCroes

# DEDICATION

I dedicate this book to all who tell stories to children and adolescents and thereby pass on the traditions and values of their culture through storytelling.

# ACKNOWLEDGEMENTS

Child development as presented throughout this book is based on the work of Rudolf Steiner and my direct experience using Steiner's pedagogy (also known as Waldorf pedagogy) working with children as a teacher in Waldorf/Steiner schools for 15 years. Storytelling is an integral part of the Waldorf/Steiner curriculum from Kindergarten through High School. I am indebted to these individuals with whom I studied in my years of teacher training: Norman Davidson, Werner Glas, Eugene Schwartz, Barbara Renold, Barbara Glas and Sophia Walsh.

Many of the ideas about how to learn to tell a story are offered out of my experience in workshops at the International School of Storytelling in East Sussex, UK. Roi Galor, Sue Hollingsworth, and Ashley Ramsden have been my mentors and friends for 14 years.

This book would not have been possible without the loving support of my husband, Keith Patterson, who read drafts, edited redundancies, and smiled encouragement when that was truly what was needed.

# FORWARD

What is it like to be a child in the 21st century? How can our children manage to grow up physically, emotionally and spiritually healthy alongside the ever-accelerating speed of digital communication and streaming information bombarding them with images and news from the world they have inherited? What can we do to help them go to bed each night peacefully and wake up with joy, hope and courage as they become aware of, and exposed to the challenges of the difficult and sometimes dangerous world they must grow up in?

The passion to discover answers to such questions drove Marianna and I on individual quests through the years until our paths crossed at the International School of Storytelling in the UK where I teach. My colleague, Sue Hollingsworth, invited Marianna there and whispered in my ear that I MUST meet her for we had much in common. Intrigued by Sue's praises for Marianna, I was expecting to meet a great and wise alchemist – I was not disappointed!

The fruit of this meeting was the co-creation of a new body of work for groups of parents, teachers, youth workers, nature guides and many others from all over the world who wished to explore, through the art and craft of storytelling, how to help children and teenagers meet and overcome their challenges.

This journey led us to work with hordes of children in schools, classrooms, clubs and outdoor settings to find, develop and tell stories tailored for specific age groups from toddlers to adolescents. This labour of love led Marianna to create an object of deep magic. It is a combination of treasure box, packet of seeds, compass, guide map and a call for a great adventure in the form of a book. This book is the very one you hold in your hands right now.

In this remarkable book Marianna shares passionately and generously her life's work with children and educators. It will guide you on a well-mapped journey to help you learn how to support children to build a healthy body, develop social and emotional skills, expand their imaginations and strengthen their discernment, resilience and sense of direction in this world. This book will help you provide children with wholesome nourishment through the wisdom of stories and the gift of your presence, attention and personal warmth as a storyteller in a fun, practical and creative way.

I feel blessed to have met Marianna and shall forever carry with me the memory of watching her stand on top of a chair in front of a large group of teenagers, wave her arms in the air, and claim their attention and ignite their passion by repeatedly calling out with them, louder and louder in a fiery chorus, a Ralph Waldo Emerson quote:

"Nothing great was ever accomplished without enthusiasm!"

I shall delay you no further from beginning this book, this journey. For the sake of your children or students, some great work needs to be done to guide them, and you shall do this work with the help of Marianna and this golden book.

*Roi Gal-Or*

Co-Founder of the International School of Storytelling,
Forest Row, UK, father of Eliya (13) and Matan (1)

# Contents

## Part 1

## CHAPTER 8

## CHAPTER 16

## CHAPTER 17

# Part 3

# Part 4

# Story Water
## By Jelaluddin Rumi

From *The Essential Rumi* **by Coleman Barks\***

A story is like water
that you heat for your bath.

It takes messages between the fire
and your skin. It lets them meet,
and it cleans you!

Very few can sit down
in the middle of the fire itself
like a salamander or Abraham.
We need intermediaries.

A feeling of fullness comes,
but usually it takes some bread
to bring it.

Beauty surrounds us,
but usually we need to be walking
in a garden to know it.

The body itself is a screen
to shield and partially reveal
the light that's blazing
inside your presence.

Water, stories, the body,
all the things we do, are mediums
that hide and show what's hidden

Study them,
and enjoy this being washed
with a secret we sometimes know,
and then not.

*\*Reprinted here with the kind permission of Coleman Barks*

# ONCE UPON A TIME ...

In ages past, scattered about the mountains, hillsides, and seacoasts of the world, traveling storytellers called the people together to share the old wisdom, the time-honored stories of the dreams, adventures, hopes, joys, and sorrows of the people. Through these ancient tales, the history and ethics of the people were passed from one generation to the next generation. Amidst laughter and tears the children and young people were initiated into what it meant to be human and specifically what it meant to be a member of that culture.

As the storyteller spoke the invocation, a mood of expectancy and excitement filled the air. A pithy tale spiced with humor and surprise unfolded before the wide eyes of the audience as ancient and imaginative imagery was woven in the weft of words. The tale spun its way from heart to heart, drawing the community together.

Tellers tailored the tale to the audience taking on a bit of the local character of the place and the flavor of the folk present. The intimacy of the storytelling experience spoke deeply to each individual. The imaginations of the adults were nourished and inspired, and, in the case of the children and adolescents, *developed*.

The experience of shared storytelling served many purposes. It instructed the community regarding how to live together; it inspired them to feelings of compassion, understanding, and love; it offered explanations for catastrophes; it taught them about the community's history; it created a context for understanding the day-to day striving of the individual within the larger community.

As a teacher and parent, I am keenly aware of the challenges and problems faced by children and teens today. We all recall the transitions and passages that each child must traverse on the way to adulthood. Some are inherent to the process of growing up. Others are individual in nature like bullying, death of a friend or family member, adoption, divorce, lack of confidence, and fear of failure or the dark, to name a few.

In the power of children's and adolescent's imaginations lies the ability to change the way they experience the world. The metaphor a story delivers is a message sent straight to the imagination. It bypasses the conscious mind, the memory and the patterns of behavior on its journey to the interior world. The listeners are then free to respond to the call for change in their own unique way. Sometimes the change is "overnight". Sometimes it occurs over a period of days, weeks, or months. How is this possible?

Stories mirror inner problems, doubts, fears, frustrations, and situations common to the process of growing up. While children and adolescents may be stuck in a particular way of seeing themselves, or trapped in a repetitive behavior, once they have seen their dilemma reflected in a story it is as if an inner door opens and they walk through it into a new way of perceiving themselves and the world. The old behavior gently fades away.

Growing up is hard work. Stories can help, and you can be the teller of those tales for the next generation.

## HOW TO USE THIS BOOK

To use this book to best effect, you should first read all of the sections from the beginning through the chapter that deals with the child's or adolescents' age you are interested in. Information presented in earlier chapters has relevance to the later chapters. Especially note that often stories in an earlier chapter can be used with much older children.

The chapters by age group begin with an explanation of what is happening developmentally with the children at this stage of life, and provide half a dozen or more stories that are appropriate. Sources for additional stories are provided as well.

You will find helpful indices in Part IV of this book. For instance, if a child is challenged with a problem or life circumstance like boredom, dishonesty, adoption, friendship or any other number of concerns, there's an index that will help you pinpoint just the right story to help that child.

# Part 1

# Introduction to Storytelling

# CHAPTER 1

## Why Tell Stories to Your Children or Students?

### Telling a Story is Different than Reading a Story.

What happens when we sit with a child or group of children face-to-face and eye-to-eye and tell a story? When we put down the book a new way of story sharing unfolds. Because we are face-to-face, a new way of connecting with one another occurs.

Your eyes are on your children or students, not on the pages of the book. You know immediately when you need to adjust the way you are telling the story. In this intimate setting, the story can be told with warmth in a way that suits the age and circumstance of the child. The question in the eyes of the child inspires the storyteller to elaborate about a particular moment in the story. The gentle worry in the child's face shows the teller it is time to cut back on the drama and description and move on with the story.

The light glowing softly in the eyes of the child enkindles warmth in the adult and stimulates the adult's imagination further. The play back and forth between teller and listener becomes the co-creative world where the story lives. Your children or students also see *you* in a new light. You are no longer simply mommy or daddy or teacher, but also a storyteller: a shining example of the creative imagination at work.

There will be many times when you read to your child. This is important and not to be missed. I remember reading the *Chronicles of Narnia* to my sons and the great joy and wonder of that shared story! I challenge you to do both.

Is telling a story truly different than reading a story? Here's a quick experiment for you to experience the difference. Find a favorite poem that you know by heart. Then, in front of a mirror read the poem out loud from the book. Now, put down the book, and speak the poem into the mirror to yourself. Observe how it looks and feels different. Jot down some thoughts about your observations. They'll be useful as you learn to transition back and forth from reading stories to telling them.

## The Right Story at the Right Time Can Make a Difference in the Life of the Child

I have experienced over and over how the telling of a story at just the right time can have life changing effects for a child or a group of children at school. Let me give you two examples:

1. **At Home.** I remember listening to the stories my grandmother told about her childhood growing up on a farm in southern Indiana. I was amazed to find that her childhood was so utterly different than mine. For some years before she got married, she was a nanny and traveled widely around America with a family that she grew to love. I loved her stories and found them fascinating. Not only did I get to know my grandmother better but also I learned about a world that was different from the one I was growing up in. After having heard these stories, I felt more deeply connected to my grandmother. Telling the stories of our lives to our children gives them a sense of their roots and allows them to connect more deeply with their parents and grandparents. Give your children this gift. No matter how simple, tell them a story from your own childhood. But beware; once you start telling these stories, you may never stop!

2. **In the Classroom.** I once taught a group of children who played together very well. Whenever a new child joined the class, the children were excited and welcoming. However, once there was a child who joined the class who was very shy. This child spoke softly, smiled often, but did not join in any games at recess. The child stayed apart and played on the edges of the playground. After a while, the others gave up trying to engage the new student. The child lived in a world

that was focused on studying the caterpillars, ants, butterflies, and other creatures that played amongst the flowers and shrubs. I tried everything I could think of to help integrate this child into the class. Finally, during a study of Botany, I told a biographical story about a man who contributed to the science of botany and who, as a child, spent hours of his free time watching the way various insects lived and interacted in their specific environments. I crafted the biography to focus first on the gentleman's childhood, in which his behavior was similar to that of the young student's behavior. The children were very attentive as was the student. I noticed several children looking over at the student during the story and smiling, and the student smiled back! After that, the children talked to the student about the insects and other interests, and the student, in turn, talked to them. Slowly, the child became integrated into the social fabric of the class. This was a compelling confirmation of the power of a story for me as a teacher and also confirmed for me that biography is a great source of story material.

In the second example above, how did I choose the right story to address the situation wherein the child didn't "fit in" with the class? How does one discern which story is the right one to tell at a specific time? Together, we will thoroughly explore that process and I will provide appropriate stories for you to tell.

## Stories Nurture the Imagination

Stories unite us in our imaginations and carry us to other lands and times and bring us back home again forever changed.

As you tell the story, you observe your listeners' reactions, which increases your enjoyment of the storytelling process, and fires your imagination to create details of your own. As children enter into the different worlds your stories conjure, they experience your imagination at play, and it inspires and develops their own imaginations.

Why the emphasis on development of the imagination? A vivid imagination allows children to respond to problems in their lives and actively pursue ways to overcome them. Later in life, a well-developed imagination is the path to solving business problems, unraveling scientific mysteries and envisioning a better future. After all, what is a hypothesis but a possibility created in the fertile imagination of the seeker? Imagination is vastly important to individual development and societal improvement.

Children are striving to make sense of their experiences by using their imaginations to fill in the gaps of their understanding. Children often wonder where they came from and what they will do when they grow up. Stories piqué their curiosity and feed their dreams.

Building an active imagination is the work of childhood. If the imagination is not developed during childhood, it is hard to recapture later. Children thrive on imaginative exchanges with adults. It is important for children, especially under the age of nine that the metaphors we offer them are true to nature. This practice gives the young child confidence in the world she experiences around her every day. By creating a story that answers a child's question about the world that is in harmony with nature, you engage the child's imagination and also pique the child's curiosity about the world.

There will be years of "down to earth" scientific discussions about how things work as your child matures into adulthood. Childhood is precious and is the building ground of the imagination. I am reminded of stories of scientists who have given us so much through their research. They typically begin the solving of a problem or mystery by using their imaginations to create as many possible options to explore and test as they can envision. Through the exploration of just the right combination of insights, experiments, and problem solving, they come to a new discovery, concept, or scientific law. Such discoveries then require years of being put to the test before being recognized as true. Often, such people are described as having the curiosity and imaginative power of a child.

## Storytelling Connects Us More Deeply With Each Other

Telling stories to your children or students is a powerful and enjoyable way to connect with them. When you sit eye-to-eye at home or in a classroom full of students to tell a fable, folk tale, or myth, you share a quiet, focused, intimate moment. You feed dreams, inspire hearts, and build imaginations.

As you develop the skill of discerning the right story to tell at the right time, you will learn to select tales that speak deeply to growing minds and hearts: stories that will calm fears, create a sense of place and belonging, build confidence, support self-esteem, teach valuable life lessons, and help children find their way in the world as they tackle the challenges of growing up. It is an activity that connects you to your children or students in remarkable ways.

At the same time you are inspiring and nurturing them, you set your own imagination free to play and create. Storytelling done well connects teller and listener in a pas de deux. The teller takes the tale into herself/himself and lets if flow out again, building the world of the tale in the storytelling space. The children hear the story, the descriptions and words, take them in and react to them. The teller reads the listeners and adjusts the tale to fit this particular group, in this place, at this time. Thus, the story morphs as the teller and listeners feed one another in what I call a co-creative dance that calls the story into being in a way that is unique to this one telling.

As stories widen children's inner world, they develop their vocabulary and expand their vision of the past and the future effortlessly. Stories have been called the food of the ages. They explain the world as metaphor in language and imagery that has fed children around the world for countless generations. With storytelling, you can widen your children's or students' horizons in an intimate setting that will strengthen your connection to one another and feed their understanding of themselves and the world.

# Connections Made and Connections Lost
## Life Before and After the Advent of TV

I am old enough to remember life before television. I remember the day the TV arrived. Two men got out of a truck parked in front of the house and together carried a massive cardboard box up the steps to the front yard and then up the second set of steps onto the covered front porch where my mother stood with the front door open. My two sisters and I were standing aside on the porch watching the event. The box was then carried into the living room and unpacked. In that moment we ushered into our family life such classics as "I Love Lucy," "The Little Rascals," and "Father Knows Best," in black and white, of course. And in that moment, our life as a family was changed irrevocably

Prior to the advent of TV, we played outside until dark, ran home for supper when mother clanged the triangle (she had a metal triangle that she struck with a metal wand, and we could even hear it at the end of the block!). After supper, we sat together telling stories of the day's adventures, played games, and did homework. Once the TV arrived, little by little, we spent more time watching and less time talking and sharing together. I remember noticing how our lives were changing and experiencing an inner sadness that I could not give voice to or understand at the age of 11. Yes, I loved those programs, but I also missed the closeness of our family times and could not express clearly what had changed or how it had changed. A sense of loss was present as our time together diminished.

We were often read to before bed and my father told stories that he invented about riding across the ocean on the back of a whale. My grandmother told stories about her childhood on a farm in southern Indiana, growing corn and beans and picking fruit. She baked bread for us every week and lots of pies. Every Saturday I went with her to the local farmer's market to buy vegetables, fruits, and her special ingredient for the best pie crusts in the world: home-rendered lard! She also came to love the TV. The soap operas were her favorites.

My mother created daily and weekly rhythms for the family that changed with the seasons. One fond memory is getting up early on Saturday morning to the smell of frying chicken! I knew what that meant. After a quick breakfast, the picnic basket was filled with chicken, watermelon, potato salad, and lemonade. Then we were off to Lake Michigan for a day on the sand dunes and playing in the waves in the lake. Every summer the neighbors would organize a bicycle parade and all the children would decorate their bikes with streamers, flowers, whatever struck their fancy and ride down the streets of the neighborhood. Family traditions created a sense of warmth and a rich shared life experience between us. They also provided connections to the larger community and to our neighborhoods.

But these intimate times of storytelling, and these rich experiences of being present with one another for picnics and neighborhood events diminished over time as TV provided escape and entertainment and drew us into THAT world instead of sharing OUR world.

## Storytelling Improves Children's Emotional Intelligence

Howard Gardner in his book, *Multiple Intelligences*, talks about the importance of emotional intelligence (EQ) in the lives of children and adults. It is an important ability that includes being able to read other people's facial expressions accurately as you problem solve and work towards solutions with another human being or in a group.

According to Gardner, less that 20% of success in the workplace is due to one's IQ. Rather, more than 80% is due to EQ, which includes the ability to live with contradictions, adapt to change, and be flexible enough to seek more than one answer to a question.

How does storytelling factor into this? Stories provide imaginative pictures of emotional intelligence in action. Stories are filled with challenging situations that require the protagonist to change, to take on a challenge, and to use his skills to communicate using emotional intelligence as he deals with problems. Additionally, stories stimulate the development of empathy towards others. The ability to live with contradictions is also demonstrated by the heroes of stories. By taking children on a journey in which these qualities are demonstrated in an imaginative and non-threatening setting, storytelling nurtures and develops the emotional intelligence of children and adolescents.

## Additional Benefits of Storytelling

Telling and working with stories with your children or students gives you insights into how they think about the world and their place in it.

- Stories help them build confidence in life. All is made right by the end of each story. We may be cynical and think that this is not how life truly is…yet, when we read biographies of people who have endured calamity and great suffering they invariably speak to us about profundity, compassion, and miraculous change being some of the fruits of their suffering.
- Discussing the stories with your children or students gives a platform for those who have more of a struggle reading and writing to participate in the learning environment in verbal ways. This puts them back on par with the rest of the class and also stimulates their interest in reading.
- It is in the presentation of archetypal imagery that has stood the test of time, that the story nourishes the soul, challenges the mind and awakens the spirit. Stories truly can help to heal the traumas of childhood and adolescence and inspire the child to take on new challenges with confidence and courage.
- Children from 3 to 7 years old can often remember the words of a story verbatim. The kind of memory the young child has is different than the kind of memory we adults have. Stories that are filled with beautiful words and imagery that seem to be beyond the understanding of the child can live in the child's psyche as a source of inspiration as the child grows and matures. The rich vocabulary of fairy tales and folk tales nurtures and develops the young child's ear for language. This sets the stage for a rich imaginative life and a strong vocabulary, and prepares the child for an active life of reading and playing with ideas.

That's *WHY* to tell stories to your children or students. Now let's take a look at *WHEN* you can weave them into your daily routine at home or your curriculum at school.

# CHAPTER 2

## When to Tell Stories
## to your Children or Students

### Make Storytelling Part of Your Daily Routine

Today, our busy schedules take us away from the home and each other. When we do come home, the television, computer, and other modern screen equipment await us, offering refuge and escape from the day's often hectic and exhausting activities. If we want quality time and interaction with each other away from the visual and auditory devices (cell phones, pads, pods, computers, mp3s, TVs, radios, etc.) it can come only through making conscious decisions to create it. We are a plugged-in culture that is losing the experience of face-to-face communication. We need to schedule together-time.

I understand that creating a rhythm and routine for children is more challenging today than ever before. However, when children are thrown into the world with little rhythm and routine in their lives, they do not know what to expect next. This unknowing can create anxiety. A routine offers the child comfort and ease. Children thrive on rhythm and routine because they can relax, knowing what is coming next.

Let's explore how to provide more structure, rhythm and routine that includes storytelling both at home and in the classroom.

### At Home: The Bedtime Routine, Your New Best Friend!

Children are often "wound up" at the end of the day and have trouble settling down for bed. Parents lead busy lives and need some down time

29

of their own. They are tired at day's end, too. A regular bedtime routine can help parents and children end the day together on an up note, especially if you incorporate storytelling.

However you design it to fit your family and circumstances, the routine must be easily managed so that it can be followed faithfully. **Once it is in place,** it will become a source of relaxation, pleasure, and connection for the whole family. The routine itself becomes the disciplinarian. Your children will remind you, and tell each other to "get with it." Once of the best gifts you can give yourself and your family is the creation of a consistent evening routine.

Here are some ideas for you to consider. Begin after dinner with a kitchen "clean up" event followed by a game together as a family (board games, card games, guessing games, hide-and-go-seek... whatever's appropriate for your child's age). Homework time can be added, depending on the age of the children, or homework might be better accomplished before dinner. A bath time routine could follow with story time just before bed. Lighting a candle, and saying a poem or verse before bed, sets the mood for a story. Tell the tale and follow that with a few shared thoughts about the story, then say goodnight and lights out! Blowing out the candle together after saying a simple phrase like, "Night, night, sleep tight, see you in the morning light" is a way of drawing the bedtime routine to a close.

Some parents tell the story with the whole family on the couch. Some tell the story in the bedroom with children already in bed. Find the right space and time for *you* then stick with it faithfully.

Don't hesitate to tell stories multiple times. Children love to hear the same tales over and over as they sink in more deeply. After a while, they will *help* you tell it, and gladly inform you when you've left something out. Thank them for their help with a smile and steady on.

As they get familiar with a tale, perhaps you'll want to play with it. You can draw or act out scenes from the story. Use colorful strips of cloth, or use hats and other simple items to "dress up" and play the parts. You can borrow many other ideas from the next section in the guide for Teachers.

# In the Classroom: Storytelling and Your Curriculum

The inspiration to write this book arose out of my teaching experience. As a Steiner/Waldorf teacher, I had the great opportunity of teaching the same group of children from first through eighth grade. I told or worked with a story in class almost every day.

My usual routine was to tell a new story on Monday. For the rest of the week we would work with the story together. Here are some ideas to get you started:

1. <u>Tell the story on the first day</u> of the week, perhaps at the end of the lesson just before recess. Retell the story the next time you are with the children. This is especially good for children in Kindergarten and grades 1-3. In retelling the story in Kindergarten, use puppets or dolls or animals to help you. You may want to add some new details or be more dramatic in your telling the second time around.

2. <u>By mid-week</u>, they've now heard you tell the story twice and are ready to tell *you* the story. Begin the story then ask what happened next. The hands will shoot up. Be sure to tell the children that if someone leaves out an important detail, it is okay. Someone else can add it back in. Just raise your hand. Encourage them to use a phrase like, "And also this happened before that happened…" Rather than "Alice forgot to mention that…" That way, Alice does not need to be mentioned and is not embarrassed. Another approach is to choose one child to begin and then go around the room row by row having each child add something in. Tell them that if something is left out, the next person can add it back in. Remind them before you begin that there are no mistakes.

3. <u>Also by mid-week</u>, for children in grades 1-3, have them help you create a few sentences about the story that they can write into a personal storybook. Then have them draw a picture from the story. You may want to begin such a picture on the board to help those who have trouble getting started and to give them all a little lesson in drawing. The children then finish their own pictures. In grades 3 and up, review the story by highlighting the key events of the story and perhaps writing them on the board. Have them tell you their favorite part of the story. In grades 4 and up, have them write about what they liked best about the story. Create "story" books by 3-hole punching plain paper and tying it together with yarn. They can then draw a picture and write about the

story in the same book. Blank books can also be purchased from stationary stores online. Children can then draw a picture and write about the story in the same book.

4. Towards the end of the week, play a guessing game using gestures. In this activity, have one child come up and make a gesture from a moment in the story. Children are very clever doing this. They "freeze" in the pose of the gesture for a minute or so. Then the others raise their hands and when called upon by the child who made the gesture, guess what moment in the story the child is showing the class through the gesture. The person who guesses correctly comes up next to do the next silent gesture from the story. Great fun. It is really amazing what they come up with and remarkable how the others can find the precise moment in the story that is being acted out by their classmate.

5. Act out a scene from the story. Have a basket of colorful scarves or hats in the classroom. Or make capes from squares of brightly colored cloth by running a hem along one edge of the square and putting a piece of string through it–or ribbon–or whatever you have handy. Divide the children into groups of 3 or 4 to work together to create a scene from the story and offer it to the class. The groups could be spread out around the room while they practice their scene. Then the scenes are shown to the class and the class guesses where in the story they occur. The scenes can include dialogue or simply be a pantomime.

6. At some point during the week, include a writing exercise. In the younger grades this could be a sentence or two that you compose in class together and you write it on the board and they copy into their story "books." Creating a storybook is a great project. Using blank paper gives room for pictures and for sentences about the story to be added as well. In older grades, you could, of course, have them write something more.

7. In grades 4 and up, the discussions become more of an exploration into the story itself. What questions do you have about the story? A child could ask the question and another child could answer it. Or the whole class could have the opportunity to answer it, by writing in a story notebook. In the process of discussing their questions, interesting interpretations of the story come forth. Writing about such interpretations could be another follow-up activity. By asking the story questions, you bring the story into the center of the children's attention and focus, and you allow the story to work into the children's thought life more deeply.

Avoid "right answers." Every story is a world unto itself and offers a plethora of possibilities to nourish the self. Work towards multiple meanings with the children. Express your delight and surprise at the creativity the story arouses in the children and adolescents.

**Note:** Once storytelling has found its way into your curriculum, you will discover that you have a powerful tool to motivate your students, change behavior, and enrich your curriculum.

**English**. Stories expose your class to more challenging vocabulary, and the essence of plots as they work to improve their own writing skills. Introducing a novel? Give your students a feel for one of the characters the author created. Tell a tale from the author's life or the main character's life.

**History**. Storytelling adds color and interest and helps the children make the inner journey back in time to a different century, a different country. Telling a short biography of one of the characters who populate the halls of history invites the children into the lesson and gives them the opportunity to identify with the characters you are presenting. Having students give oral presentations about historical figures or events is enlivened by asking them to include a few vignettes from the lives of the persons involved and to begin their presentation with those stories. Dressing up in the time period you are presenting and walking into the classroom, as a character from history is great fun for teens aged 13-18. They love seeing you take on a different persona. They enjoy your willingness to be playful and expose yourself and your vulnerability.

**Geography** Enrich lessons by creating a character who visits the region, encounters the landscape, the flora and fauna, and some of the locals who live there. Locals reflect the geography in their way of meeting the world.

**Science**. Biographies of scientists or just a vignette from the life of a scientist bring science alive especially when spiced with a bit of humor. Discoveries made by scientists often took years to accomplish. Telling that story of struggle and fortitude inspires students and gives them a healthy picture of self-sacrifice to an idea.

**Different kinds of learners**. As you are undoubtedly aware, your classroom is filled with different types of learners. Storytelling serves all of them. Visual learners will appreciate diagrams and drawings of the story on the board, auditory learners love the rhythms of the language and varied voices as the story unfolds, and kinesthetic learners revel in the gestures and the teacher's striving to make the story come alive in the space.

OK. Now that we've considered *WHY* you should tell stories to your children or students, and *WHEN* to weave them into your schedule or curriculum, let's tell a story!

# CHAPTER 3

## Let's Tell a Story

### Relax! We are all storytellers!

We tell tales of our vacations, our latest great "reads," our relationships, our loves, our successes, and our failures.... all day long. We gossip stories, we sing songs, we lament losses, and we celebrate our victories and commiserate about our shortcomings. In each case, we rely on our audience for feedback...we check in through our senses...is the story making sense? Do I need more humor? More detail? Is something missing? We do this automatically as we "read" the response of our listener in their eyes, smile, and body language. It happens effortlessly. It's just the same when telling a story to your child or student except that the content is often a story you must learn. Using the techniques in this book, you will soon be able to learn and tell stories in your own voice without any need for memorization.

If you don't get all the details right when you tell a story the first time, no worries. You will want to tell the same story multiple times, especially to younger children to allow the stories to sink in. If you forget a detail the first time around, add it back in the next time. Your children or students will often ask questions that help you fill in the gaps, and you can count on them to remind you if you forgot something you told the last time. They will relish their participation in recalling the story during the second or third telling.

The day will come when you will muster the confidence to make up your own stories out of yourself! You will be amazed at the attention this arouses in your children or students. They seem to know intuitively that you are making it up, and they are thrilled to see your imagination at work! In the meantime, as you tell traditional tales, your children or students will connect with you in a deep way like no other.

To help you discover the most comfortable way *for you* to learn a traditional story like a fairy tale or fable that you have read in a book, here are several suggestions. First: read the story a few times. The first time through, get the story line clearly in mind and make a list of the major events of the story in the order they occur. My storyteller friends call this list the bare bones. Next, jot down the locations in the story as it progresses. Some stories have all the action in one place. Others have several locations. The second time you read it, pay more attention to your imagination of the settings—see the pictures in your mind's eye. Jot down the highlights of the story for you. Note where you were most engaged in the story. Note any places in the story that were not clear to you or that raised questions. Read the story again. Take a few more notes. Then try telling the story to a friend as if it were gossip! Exaggerate. Use gossipy words and phrases like, "*You won't believe what happened; Cinderella, that mouse of a girl who sat in the ashes all day long, remember her? Well, she just married the prince! Go figure! How could that have happened, you ask? Well, let me tell you. First...*" and so on. This is a quick and fun way to get the flow of the story clearly in your own mind and get the nitty gritty structure of the story down in order. It's relaxing and helps us let go of the idea of "perfection." We don't need to be professional storytellers to tell a good tale. We just need to relax and enjoy the gift that stories bring to us and to our students and children. In the story world we are truly free to make mistakes. You forget a detail? You can weave it back in later. Or, maybe it wasn't so important anyway. And next time you tell that story, well, there it is just where it's supposed to be! Take the story for a walk. Alone or with a friend, walk and tell the story out loud as a gossip. Walking and telling gets the story into your body. It's relaxing and stimulating at the same time.

Another tool for learning a story is to draw a simple sketch of the buildings and places where the story happens. Draw a semi-circle in a rainbow arc across the page. Put an "X" at the bottom in the middle of the arc. (See the next page for an example.) Now draw simple stick images of the major locations in the story. Don't include the people or too many things, just the places. Then put your "map" on the floor in front of you and use it as a guide to show yourself those locations around you in space. You are standing on the "X". So whenever you want to point out Cinderella's house and hearth it's right there on your left. And the castle is over there on the right. Having a story map helps you ground the story in your own imagination and helps your listener "picture the story" along with you. This is a wonderful memory tool. When you use gestures as you tell the story, you show your listeners where the story events are taking place. It's as if they're sitting in the middle of the story and it's happening all around them. Experiencing the story like this stimulates your children's or students' imaginations and allows them to "see" the details more clearly. This manner of telling a story is particularly useful for children who tend to be visual, spatial, or kinesthetic learners. It helps them to understand the story and experience it more deeply.

You are now ready to add in some details that the story has left out. The story mentions a meadow, a forest or a wise old woman. Use your imagination to describe them. What was the color of the dress the wise old woman wore? What did the wind in the trees sound like? Was there a harp playing or the sound of paper rustling? The more often you tell a story, the more your imagination will engage, invent and create images to share with your listeners as you lift the story off the page and into their hearts and minds. The next time you tell the story, it will change a bit. You will have learned more about the story and will naturally embellish it. Your children may surprise you by insisting you tell it the same way as before! Don't be dismayed. Smile and ask them to help you remember how that part went!

Enjoy it when your children or students correct you or remind you of something you left out. The warmth of connection that develops between you during this process will inspire you. The relationship that develops through storytelling is rewarding to both parent and child, teacher and student. As your children or students observe you exercising your imagination, it stimulates theirs, and your connections to one another expand and deepen. You open a door to your own creativity and discover parts of yourself that were waiting for a chance to emerge!

To illustrate this process of learning to tell a story, let's look together at "Sweet Porridge," a charming Wonder Tale from the Brothers Grimm collection. Remember that, while there are multiple levels of interpretation in each of these tales, part of the fun and enjoyment is found in the moments of wonder themselves, where we suspend our disbelief as we enter the realm of the extraordinary, the world of imagination.

## Sweet Porridge

Once upon a time, there was a poor but kind little girl who lived with her mother in a tiny cottage at the edge of a great forest. Now it happened that one day they no longer had anything to eat. The little girl went into the great forest looking for something to eat. She knew of places in the forest where berries grew. As she wandered amongst the tall trees she met an aged woman who was aware of her sorrow and her need. The wise woman presented her with a little pot. Then she taught her how to use it. When she spoke the words, "Cook little pot cook," the little pot would cook good, sweet porridge, and when she said, "Stop, little pot, stop," it ceased to cook. The girl took the pot home to her mother, and now they were freed from their poverty and hunger. They ate sweet porridge as often as they chose.

Once when the girl had gone out her mother was hungry and she said, "Cook little pot, cook." And it did cook and she ate till she was satisfied, and then she wanted the little pot to stop cooking, but did not know the right words. So, it went on cooking and the porridge rose over the edge, and still it cooked on until the kitchen was full of porridge and it kept on cooking until the house was full of porridge, and it kept on cooking and the next house was full, and the whole street, and it kept on cooking. It seemed as if the little pot wanted to satisfy the hunger of the whole wide world. Now, there was great distress in the village, but no one knew how to stop it. At last when only one house remained, the child came home and just said, "Stop, little pot, stop." And the little pot stopped and gave up cooking, and whosoever wished to return to the town had to eat his way home.

## The Story Map

Now let's make a list of all the places in the story and put them on a map of the story. You, as the storyteller, are standing on the **X** facing your audience.

In your mind's eye, locate the little girl's cottage, the wood where she meets a wise woman, the local village, and the village the little girl traveled to on an errand. These are the places where the story journeys.

Your map could look something like this:

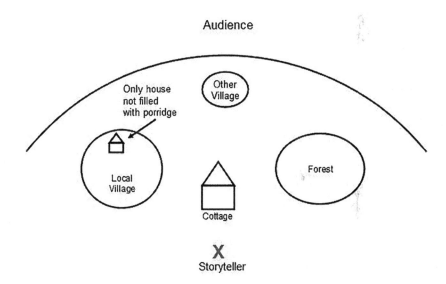

## Bare Bones Outline of the Story

On the same page as the story map, let's make a list of the events that occur in the story: the bones of the story.

### Sweet Porridge "Bare Bones" example:

*Mother, child–hut on edge of village*
*No food*
*Girl goes to forest*
*Wise woman gives her pot*
*Girl knows words to start and stop pot*
*Pot cooks porridge*
*No more hunger*
*Child goes to next village on errand*
*Mother tells pot to cook*
*Mother forgets words to make pot stop*
*Pot keeps cooking*
*Fills village homes with porridge*
*One house is left empty*
*Girl returns and stops pot*
*Everyone in village had to eat their way home*

Take the bones and trim it down even further to two or three words per action. Now you are ready to gossip the story. It is a great help to have a storytelling partner to practice with and to trade stories back and forth. If this isn't possible, no worries; find a quiet space to practice and gossip the story out loud to your pretend audience. I've done this many times.

Next, place the map on the floor in front of you and make a gesture to indicate each location in the story in the space around you. Speak out loud and show yourself where everything is…i.e. "The village is there to the left, the forest is there to the right, the other village is on the right beyond the forest," and so forth. Once you know where the places of the story are in space, practice making a few gestures in front of a mirror. That will help you experience the importance of making your gestures **large.** As you get used to making simple gestures that use your whole arm you will find that it also helps you to imagine the story unfolding in the space in front of you and to the left and the right of you.

## Gossip the Story Line

Now, gossip the story again using gestures as you move through the story. Drawing a map, listing the events of the story, and gossiping the story are traditional ways of learning a story by heart. Find a friend and tell the story. Or if time is a constraint, tell the story out loud three times using the same gestures to show where the action occurs as the story progresses. Now you are ready to tell the story. Remember, children are thrilled to see your imagination at work. They are also very forgiving. If you forget something the first time, you can add it back in the second time.

**Gossip Example:** Note: having a friend to gossip with makes the gossip experience more powerful. But, in a pinch, just gossip out loud to yourself!

> *"You remember that little girl who lives with her mother on the edge of the forest? Well, you won't believe it but they ran out of food. The little girl was so hungry, she went into the woods looking for something to eat, but, of course, she found nothing. But, then she ran into this old woman who was so tuned in that she already knew the girl's problem without even talking to her, if you can believe that! The old woman gave her a pot, you know an ordinary cooking pot only she said this pot was anything but that; in fact, it was a pot that would cook porridge, sweet porridge mind you, whenever you told it to; can you believe that? The wise woman gave the girl the right words and sent her home. When she got there, she set the pot down and immediately said, cook, little pot, cook…and would you believe it, that pot did, it filled itself up with porridge in no time at all and just as it was about to overflow, the girl said stop little pot, stop. Well, they were never hungry after that. But, one day, the girl left to get something in the next village. The mother got hungry and started the pot cooking, but couldn't remember just the right words to stop it, sooooo…. you guessed it: the pot kept on cooking! That porridge, it overflowed the pot, filled up the house and then flowed out the door, down the street and filled up every house along the road! And if that wasn't enough, it kept right on cooking filling up every house in the town. By the time the little girl came home and said, "Stop, little pot, stop!" There was only one house left that wasn't filled with porridge. The girl said the right words, and the little pot stopped. Anyone who wanted to get home had to eat his way home!"*

**Shorter Version:**

*"You will not believe this, but you know that little girl who lives with her mother on the edge of town, well, one day she was so hungry she went into the woods looking for berries and she met this wise woman who already knew her sorrow and gave her a pot that cooks porridge all by itself, if you can believe that! So she cooked whenever they were hungry and all was well until one day she trotted off to the next village on an errand and her mother got hungry, and started the pot cooking, but, as luck would have it, when the pot was full she couldn't remember the right words to make it stop! Go figure. So the pot kept on cooking, filled up the house, flowed out the door, filled up the street and every house in the town except one. When the girl returned and said, "Stop, little pot, stop," it stopped. Everyone had to eat their way home."*

This is just an example of a gossipy version of the story. Try your own version right now, before reading any further. Exaggerate, speak loudly, and if you forget a bit of it, add it back in right away as soon as you recall it. Just say "Oops" or "by the way" or "I forgot to mention that…"

Children ages 3 to 6 love the role reversal in this story and enjoy the humor of a town full of porridge. The 3-year-old is just discovering the power of language and of using the right word at the right time, especially the power of the word NO! So for the 3 -year-old, "Sweet Porridge" is just the right story.

## Setting the Mood

When you prepare to tell a story to your children or students, it's important to set the mood so they'll be ready to settle down and shift their attention to the tale. Here are some suggestions.

*At Home:* Dim the lights and light a candle. Change your location and sit down so you are at eye level with your child. Lower your voice and make eye contact with your child or children. Begin with a song, a verse, and one of the "Invocations" below.

*In the Classroom:* Changing the classroom mood can be accomplished by turning off the lights, playing an instrument, making a gesture, and using one of the "Invocations" below. For younger children in Kindergarten to 3<sup>rd</sup> grade, try singing a song or saying the same verse or poem together before telling the story. Sitting in a circle on the floor is fun if you have the space. In grades 2 and 3, it may be simpler to have the children stay put at their desks. For children from 4<sup>th</sup> grade to 6<sup>th</sup> grade, a more complicated verse is in order. You can speak it, have everyone say it together, or have one child recite it alone.

## Beginnings and Endings

*Beginning a Story:* An invocation to a story lets the listeners know that we are now leaving the world of the every day and entering the world of wonder, adventure and surprise.

Finding an invocation that suits you or making up your own is part of the fun of becoming a storyteller. The invocation helps you to relax for a moment. As you gaze around at your children or students, the invocation connects and prepares everyone to enter the world of story. In that silent moment following the invocation the teller and listeners take a deep breath together.

Here are some for you to try.

> *Once upon a time…*
> *Once upon a time, where did it happen? Where did it not happen? When did it happen? When did it not happen?*
> *A long time ago when I was very young…*
> *Once upon a time when pigs spoke rhyme…*
> *'Twas not in my time, 'twas not in your time, but it was in somebody's time…*
> *This was in a time gone by, and I'm goin' to tell you a story 'bout it…*
> *There was once in old times, in old times there was…*
> *So long ago that no one can quite say when… (Scandinavian)*
> *Once upon a time, in a time and place beyond measure…*
> *Once upon a time, so long ago, nobody but the storytellers remember…*
> *Once upon a time, when the grass grew greener, the trees grew taller, and the sun shone more brightly than it does today, there was a …*
> *Now here's a story I heard tell…*
> *Long years ago, in the early ages of the world… (Hungarian)*

*Long before you and I were born, there lived... (Tartar)*
*In a place, neither near nor far, and a time, neither now nor then...*
*A story, a story, let it come, let it go... (Traditional West African)*
*In the days when music was sweeter and fire was hotter and ice was colder than now, there was...*

**Ending a Story:** Story endings are equally important. They let everyone know you are finished and you are preparing to move on to the next activity (or sleep, as the case may be). There is no ambiguity. They end the story, but can also set a tone that suggests that the story is still happening today.

Give these a try:

*Snip, snap, snout, this story's told out!*
*...and they lived happily ever after.*
*...and if they have not died, they are living there still.*
*A mouse did run; my story's now is done. And so it was, and so it is.*
*I go 'round the bend, I see a fence to mend, on it is hung my story's end.*
*If my story is not true, may the soles of my shoes turn to buttermilk. (Ireland)*
*In that town there was a well and in that well there was a bell. And that is all I have to tell. (Russia)*
*My story is done. But this story will go on, as long as grass grows and rivers run. (Native American)*
*So the bridge was mended and my story's ended.*
*They grew to be very old, and lived happily all the days of their life.*
*Three apples fell from heaven: one for the teller, one for the listener, and one for whoever takes it to heart. (Armenian)*
*That is my story. I heard it when I was a child. And now you've heard it too!*

## Exercises to Warm Up your Voice

We parents and teachers use our voices often and in many varied tones and volumes. Doing a few speech warm-ups prepares your voice for the day and helps protect it from becoming strained. Here are some voice warm-ups, tongue twisters, and exercises to try.

You WILL notice a difference in your voice's power and projection. And not only YOU. Teach them to your children or students. They're fun and will improve their articulation.

**Around the rough and rugged rock
the ragged rascal ran.**

Repeat this warm-up several times, going a bit faster each time. This is an especially effective activity for grades 1 – 3. Have a child run in a circle around the perimeter of the classroom while the class says the verse. Or move the desks, make a circle of children in the space and have a child run around the outside of the circle back to his place. The child tries to get back to his space before the verse is finished. Emphasize the "r" sounds.

**Speak the speech, I pray you,
As I pronounced it to you,
Trippingly on the tongue.
*Shakespeare, "As You Like It"***

This lively exercise is for older students in grades 4 and up. Be sure to have students breathe at the end of each line. Work on making the verse rhythmical by honoring the commas with a slight pause and a quick breath and flying through the last line enunciating each syllable clearly.

**Clip**
**Clip plop**
**Clip plop plick**
**Clip plop, plick glick**
**Clinked, clapper, quickly**
**Knocking the trappings, rapidly tripled.**
*Rudolf Steiner, found in <u>Creative Speech</u>, by Marie Steiner*

This seemingly simple exercise gets the entire mouth and jaw warmed up. Moving from one syllable, to two, to three, and so on, exercises the muscles of the mouth and palate. Exaggerate the consonants and be sure the vowels are well formed. The exercise also trains the breath. Each line should use one full breath of air. Can be used with students from age 12.

Tongue twisters are a wonderful way to playfully engage children in grade three and up while improving articulation and developing a sense of rhythm simultaneously.

**She sells seashells by the seashore.**
**The shells she sells**
**Are seashells, I'm sure.**

**A tutor who tooted the flute**
**Tried to tutor two tooters to toot.**
**Said the two to the tutor,**
**"Is it harder to toot**
**Or to tutor two tooters to toot?"**

**Peter Piper picked a peck of pickled peppers.**
**A peck of pickled peppers Peter Piper picked.**
**If Peter Piper picked a peck of pickled peppers,**
**Where's the peck of pickled peppers Peter Piper picked?**

All right. We've limbered up our voices, and found out how to learn and tell a story. But not all stories are created equal. How do you know what's the best story to tell your children or students? How do you know what they need and what they're ready to hear? Let's explore that next.

# CHAPTER 4

## Choosing the Right Story at the Right Time

Now that we've learned a bit about why, when and how to tell stories to your children or students, how do you go about picking the ones that will help them the most along their journey through childhood?

I've given a lot of thought to this over the years, and the stories provided in this book are grouped by stages of child development to give you a head start on this process. Here you will find story genres that are most appropriate and effective for specific stages of childhood.

Challenges children face may be of an inner or outer nature. Inner shifts in their consciousness occur as they mature and their perspectives broaden and deepen. Some examples of outer shifts include a change in school, moving into a new house, or loss of a relative, friend, or pet. The right story told at the right time can be a comfort and an inner guide through difficult life circumstances, as well as a support to the child through normal shifts in his or her developing awareness.

Stories are rich in meaning. To give your children the best chance of internalizing these wonderful tales, you would do well to repeat them several times over as many days. It gives the message a chance to sink into the children's subconscious and nourish the imagination on a deep level. With each new telling, add a few more details. As the children learn the story, invite them to help retell it. As you play with the story along with your own children or your class, together you will uncover new meanings and significant moments in the story that you had previously overlooked.

As your own relationship to the story deepens, your ability to share the story becomes more natural and filled with meaning. The energy with which you tell the story builds as your confidence and understanding develop. You begin to allow the story to speak through you, and, at the same time, you make the story your own.

It may be hard to believe that telling a story can truly change a child's behavior. The imagination is a powerful teacher. A story shows us how to imagine ourselves in a new light. We see our dilemma reflected back to us by the story. We see the hero change ever so slightly and yet profoundly as a self-discovery is made and integrated into the character's being. After all, behaviors do become habits, and, over time, it seems they have always been part of us. Then along comes a story in which a hero appears who has our difficulty clothed in metaphor and this hero conquers his fears and overcomes his behaviors and moves forward to accomplish his mission in life. She or he becomes a great leader, a sympathetic wise helper, who knows what it is like to be in need. The child sees himself or herself reflected in the tale and can come to believe that they, too, can overcome. They imagine a way forward. Seeing your own behaviors portrayed outside yourself opens the door to change.

# Part 2:

# Storytelling and Stages of Child Development

# CHAPTER 5

## Child Development Overview

The journey from childhood to adulthood traditionally encompasses twenty-one years. Unlike our animal friends who stand up on all fours within minutes of their birth, we humans take two to three years to learn to walk. The newborn child moves through the infant stage of sleeping and eating. Then, one day, the parent walks into the child's room to check on the infant and does a double take. "Didn't I leave her on her tummy, yet, here she is on her back!" "Oh my, she's rolled over!"

Rolling over from front-to-back is soon followed by rolling over from back-to-front. Scooting along the floor forwards and sideways follows. Cooing sounds begin to change, becoming more rhythmical. Then one day, the infant is found sitting up! Scooting develops into crawling. With practice, the infant gets faster and faster until he/she has discovered every room in the house, and begins surprising you in the kitchen fixing dinner by crawling circles around you as you chop veggies!

To get a feel for the hard work the little ones do to accomplish these steps, lie on your tummy on the floor and slowly push yourself over onto your back. Notice all the subtle shifts needed for your body to get you there. Then roll back over onto your stomach. Notice the differences between the two experiences and jot down some observations.

Next try scooting on your tummy pulling yourself along by wiggling your arms and legs. When you are exhausted, sit up and look around. Grab a pad and pen and jot down a few notes about the difference in perspectives that you have just experienced. Then crawl over to a chair or couch and pull yourself up to standing, still holding on.

Look around and notice the new perspective. Write a few more notes. How does it feel to be upright as opposed to horizontal? Next, hold onto a chair or a couch and take a few steps. Take your time. Move around the room holding onto things. Write about your experience of the difference between standing and crawling and walking upright.

How does the young child learn to roll over, scoot, crawl, stand, walk, and talk? Young children are continually watching, listening, tasting, feeling, and smelling their world. They learn through observation and imitation. Through their senses, they learn to mirror or imitate what they experience in the world around them. They interact with the world by doing. The world around them seems alive and exciting.

We can think of the path from childhood to adulthood as a journey from dependence to independence, from a world of external sensory experiences to the landscape of the interior world of the mind and soul, from a life dominated by things and physical experiences to one of our own creation within the mind. Let's look at an overview of this journey.

One of the most helpful concepts for me as a teacher and parent was learning about the developmental stages of childhood as presented in the Waldorf/Steiner School Curriculum. Often, a picture is worth a thousand words, so I have included a graphic representation of the three 7-year cycles that define the journey through childhood on the next page as a framework on which to hang our exploration of child development as presented in this book.

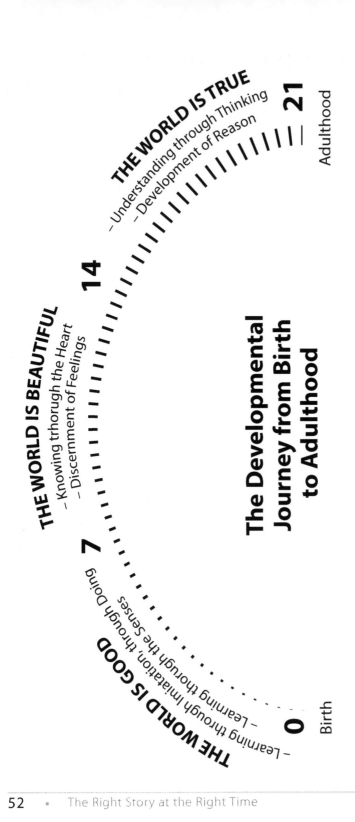

**THE WORLD IS TRUE**
– Understanding through Thinking
– Development of Reason

**21** Adulthood

**14**

**THE WORLD IS BEAUTIFUL**
– Knowing trhorugh the Heart
– Discernment of Feelings

**7**

**THE WORLD IS GOOD**
– Learning through Imitation, through Doing
– Learning thorugh the Senses

**0** Birth

**The Developmental Journey from Birth to Adulthood**

# The Three 7-Year Cycles of Child Development

There are three primary periods of development from birth to twenty-one. The first stage is birth to age 7. During this time, children learn primarily through imitation and doing. They are physically very active, learning how to crawl and walk and speak. They explore the world through the senses: taste, touch, smell, sight, and hearing. Ideally, we hope that children of this age experience the world around them as a place permeated by goodness.

In the next stage of development from age 7 to 14, children are no longer learning primarily through the senses. They are exploring the world of feelings. They "feel" what is right and what is just. They begin to consciously appreciate the beauty of the world and understand some of the challenges facing that beauty today. They become passionate about causes. For example: saving the whales, creating a nature park, or raising money to support environmental projects. Their budding awareness of the larger world around them piques their curiosity and arouses their feelings of compassion and concern for those less fortunate and for creatures that need our protection.

From 14 to 21, adolescents are exploring the realm of truth. They are seeking challenge. They are keen to develop their power of reason, to explore science, math, and expository writing. Playing or singing music, travel, and helping those less fortunate, are some of the important tasks that serve adolescents through these years. Challenge is a key image for this age group. They need many kinds of challenges in order to test their mettle, their bodies, their feelings, and find their passion and goals for life.

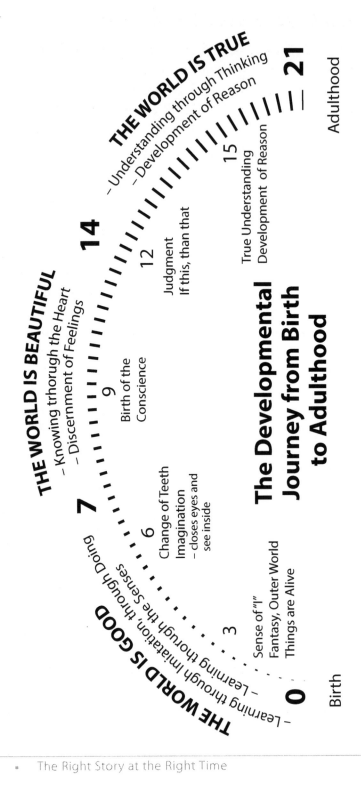

**THE WORLD IS TRUE**
– Understanding through Thinking
– Development of Reason

**21**

Adulthood

True Understanding
Development of Reason

15

**THE WORLD IS BEAUTIFUL**
– Knowing trhorugh the Heart
– Discernment of Feelings

**14**

12

Judgment
If this, than that

9

Birth of the
Conscience

**The Developmental
Journey from Birth
to Adulthood**

**7**

Change of Teeth
Imagination
– closes eyes and
see inside

6

**THE WORLD IS GOOD**
– Learning through Imitation, thorugh the Senses
– Learning through Doing

3

Sense of "I"
Fantasy, Outer World
Things are Alive

**0**

Birth

# The 3-Year Cycles of Child Development

There are several 3-year cycles of child development embedded within the 7-year cycles discussed on the previous page. This second graphic representation inserts the three-year milestones. Rather than periods of time, think of these as moments within the developmental cycle.

The first three years of life are a time of learning through the senses and through movement. During this stage, young children perceive themselves as connected to the world in a way we have forgotten. They use the self-referential word, *me,* when referring to the self. "Me want to go outside." "Me want a cookie." This curious phenomenon happens in every language. About the age of 3, they take another step in self-awareness, and begin to use the self-referential word, *I.* "Me" disappears. Again, this seems to be a universal experience in all languages and cultures. They will continue to learn primarily through imitation up to the age of 6 or 7, depending on the child.

At age six, the child's baby teeth begin to fall out, announcing the arrival of the permanent teeth. The change of teeth heralds the end to this first stage of childhood and the birth of a new inner capacity—imagination.

A bit later, somewhere between 9 and 10, the child develops a sense of responsibility, a conscience. Children at this age can also begin having nightmares, they might question whether they are adopted, and they become much more self-aware.

By the age of 12, their powers of thinking take another step in development, and they are now able to stand back from the world as an observer. They are beginning to understand cause and effect, and can use their own powers of judgment in their day-to-day life to make decisions and choices.

By the age of 15, there is a growing sense of one's uniqueness and independence, which is often accompanied by a new awareness of one's aloneness. The ability to discern and make judgments through thinking matures from here to twenty-one when adulthood is reached.

Keep this overview in mind as you read the following chapters that will explore the developmental milestones I have just mentioned accompanied by stories and activities appropriate and effective for each stage of development.

# CHAPTER 6

## Birth to 2 Years Old

*Rock-a-bye baby in the treetop*
*When the wind blows, the cradle will rock*
*When the bough breaks the cradle will fall*
*And down will come baby, cradle and all.*

## Characteristics of the Child at this Age

A child is born! In that mysterious moment before the child's first breath, before its first cry, a hush falls over those present. The stillness is palpable. Time stops. The resounding first cry of consciousness is heard! That raw cry uttered as the breath enters the lungs and is expelled into the world, announcing the arrival of a unique individual!

Unlike our animal friends that, in the case of the colt or lamb, immediately stand up, are licked clean by the mother and find their way under their own power to her teats, the human child is completely dependent upon others for its nourishment and survival.

Vital to the growing health of the infant is the gentle stimulation of each of the senses. Particularly important are the senses of touch, hearing, rhythm, and movement. Research on the development of orphans who lack regular stimulation of these senses indicates significant impacts on the child's ability to bond with others and develop higher levels of communication and cognition as they mature. (See for instance, Univ. of Wisconsin, Madison, *Eastern European Orphanage Experience Alters Brain Development.* Feb. 2003.)

The earliest stories the infant hears are the cooing sounds and simple melodies spoken and sung by the parents or the caregivers to the child.

The baby is an amazing collection of sense organs, completely open and undeveloped. It is no accident that every culture has its unique Nursery Rhymes that gently stimulate the infant through rhythm and rhyme, setting the stage for a warm and comfortable relationship to language, music and poetry. They carry deep wisdom in their tender rhythms, engaging rhythms, and subtle messages that speak a language that nourishes the infant and young child. If a gentle rocking motion accompanies the rhythmical sounds and melodies of the rhymes the child is soothed and stimulated simultaneously.

The meaning of the rhymes takes us back to a time when life was simpler and more in tune with the rhythms of nature. The rhymes and rhythms suggest the movement of the wind, the tides and the swaying treetops. These rocking movements and rhythmic sounds remind the child of the swaying motion of being carried inside the womb as the mother moved through her day. The rhythmic quality of the Nursery Rhymes gives the little child a healthy experience of the beauty and comfort of the native tongue.

Nursery Rhymes are our oldest stories and are often complex in their messages. They hearken back to a time when all stories and rhymes were passed along from generation to generation orally.

The Nursery Rhyme at the beginning of this chapter, "Rock-a-Bye Baby", is a metaphor of the birth of a baby. This familiar Nursery Rhyme is found in similar versions in many languages. Explore the Nursery Rhymes in your culture and softly sing them as you rock your baby. If you're worried about singing off-key, sing anyway! It's the sound of your voice and the gentle rocking rhythm that will comfort and stimulate your little one, just as it has done for thousands of years.

The first year and a half of life is critical for the healthy development of the child. Children need to be held, massaged gently, sung to, spoken to, and experience being welcomed into the world by the loving adults in their lives. Rhythm in the daily life of the child arranges itself around the feeding times. Day by day, the children spend more time awake, exploring the world around them with their whole body. Making up your own rhymes and rhythms can enliven your experience with your child. Young children seem to awaken new powers of imagination and playfulness in adults, so take advantage of these early years and reconnect with your own playful inner child.

When your child begins to smile, coo, roll over and stand up, it is time to start making up tiny stories about the world around you. Why not whisper a story about the bees as you lay together outside under the trees? Or sing a song about the butterflies? At bedtime, create a tiny story that describes your child's day, and work in gentle praise of new accomplishments. It is a fitting way to end the day.

There's lots of story material to be found in the garden. Make up tiny stories about the creatures and the flowers that live in your yard. When the dandelions turn yellow, tell a story about it. When they turn to fluff, tell a story and blow the fluff into the air. When you see a bird or an ant or clouds in the sky, tell a little tale about them. Just make it up on the spot. The more you do, the easier it will become. Your imagination will awaken and surprise you with your own creativity. Your child will ask you to tell the story again the next time you are in the garden. You can add details or just keep it simple.

Inside the house, tell a story about the dust bunnies. And offer your little one a soft cloth to catch them on the tabletop. Gaze out the window together and tell a story about what you see. Build a village in a corner of the room, and tell a story about the people and animals who live there. Tell the story of a day in the life of a bird or a flower or a cat or a dog or whatever strikes your fancy.

# The Human Voice and Storytelling

Storytelling offers the opportunity to use the voice your children love as you take them on a journey to other lands and other times. As you tell a story, your children's understanding of the world develops and expands. In the midst of the daily details that fill our lives, a quiet story at day's end or before naptime can carry you and your child together into a rich world of meaning and shared delight as it refreshes your connection to one another.

Strange as it may seem, the soothing voice of the storytelling parent reminds children of their own babyhood, their younger childhood, and allows them to deeply relax in a way that only young children and babies know. It gives you an opportunity to let go of the day's tasks and journey with your child into a world that is inhabited by just the two of you. It is intimate. It offers connection and shared feelings of joy, surprise, sorrow, and wonder. It is a gift you offer your child; and your child's loving attention and gentle wonder is his or her gift to you.

# NURSERY RHYMES (Ages Birth to 6)

*The Grand Old Duke of York*
*He had ten thousand men*
*He marched them up the hill*
*And marched them down again.*
*And when they were up,*
*They were up.*
*And when they were down*
*They were down.*
*And when they were only*
*Half way up they were*
*Neither up nor down*

*Hey Diddle Diddle,*
*The cat and the fiddle*
*The cow jumped over the moon*
*The little dog laughed to see such sport*
*And the dish ran away with the spoon.*

*Diddle, diddle, dumpling, my son John*
*Went to bed with his trousers on;*
*One shoe off, and one shoe on,*
*Diddle, diddle, dumpling, my son John!*

*A wise old owl sat in an oak*
*The more he heard, the less he spoke*
*The less he spoke, the more he heard,*
*Why can't we all be like that wise old bird!*

*Baa baa black sheep, have you any wool?*
*Yes sir, yes sir, three bags full!*
*One for the master, one for the dame,*
*And one for the little boy*
*    who lives down the lane.*

*Pease Porridge hot, pease Porridge cold*
*Pease Porridge in the pot, nine days old.*
*Some like it hot, some like it cold,*
*Some like it in the pot nine days old.*
*Jack Sprat could eat no fat.*
*His wife could eat no lean.*
*'Twixt them both they cleared the cloth*
*And lick'd the platter clean*

*Jack Sprat could eat no fat,*
*His wife could eat no lean.*
*So 'twixt the two,*
*They licked the platter clean.*

*Little Boy Blue*
*Come blow your horn*
*The sheep's in the meadow,*
*The cow's in the corn.*
*Where's the little boy who looks*
*after the sheep?*
*Under the haystack fast asleep.*

*One two buckle my shoe*
*Three, four, shut the door*
*Five, six, pick up sticks.*
*Seven, eight, lay them straight.*
*Nine, ten, a big fat hen*
*Eleven twelve, dig and delve.*
*Thirteen, fourteen, maids a courting,*
*Fifteen, Sixteen, maids in the kitchen*
*Seventeen, eighteen, maids in waiting*
*Nineteen, twenty, my plate's empty.*

# CHAPTER 7

## The 3-Year Change

*Round and round the garden hops the little hare…*
*One hop, two hops, tickle you under there!*

## The Terrible 2's and the 3-Year Change

Sally is almost 3 years old. She has been a delightful baby. She's always been calm and relaxed and has never cried very much. Even as a baby, she slept soundly at night and had a predictable sleep pattern. She is a good eater, a child who eats slowly and enjoys her food. She loves snuggling and being wrapped up in a blanket. Suddenly, overnight, she's changed. She is stubborn about what she will eat and what she will do. Foods that she liked before, she now refuses. She resists her parents at every turn. She is more stubborn than a mule. She is not loud or demanding, rather, she is quietly stubborn. And if and when she does throw a fit, watch out! She can yell like a banshee!

What has happened to our delightful, well-adjusted child? Sally's parents wonder. Every three years in the life of a child a significant developmental step is achieved. Each of these 3-year cycles can be likened to a mini-birth, for each developmental stage brings new capacities and a heightened sense of self. These transitions are exciting for both parents and children. As parents, we are thrilled to see our child maturing and becoming more capable. Yet, we are sometimes surprised to find that the new stage of awareness, the next developmental step, *is preceded by emotional outbursts and challenging behavior.* This is a common pattern in child development, the essence of which is echoed in every child's biography.

While the pattern of change is archetypal, each child's journey is unique, fresh, and unpredictable in its manifestation. It is a common experience for a step forward in inner awareness to be preceded by a crisis. The child becomes moody, restless, has trouble falling asleep, and generally does not seem like him/herself. While some children seem to sail through developmental thresholds, others have more of a struggle. Each child takes a journey that is uniquely his/her own.

Children before the age of 3 are mastering a remarkable set of skills: rolling over, scooting, crawling, standing, walking, and talking! Until the age of 3, children use the self-referential word "me." This phenomenon occurs in every language.

Children at this age feel at one with their surroundings, with parents, family and friends. They do not yet perceive themselves as a separate being in the way we do as adults. As physical skills are mastered, their self-awareness grows and matures.

Most adults don't remember much before the age of 3. The ability to recall that far back usually requires a significant event such as an accident or other trauma to have occurred during that time. If you do remember that time in your life, consider yourself blessed and take some time to reflect and write about it. You may be surprised by the vividness of that experience and the impact is has had on your life. I recall a moment when I was riding my first tricycle. I was 3 years old. I was in front of my mother who was pushing my younger sister in the baby buggy. Suddenly, a boy appeared out of nowhere on a bicycle, and, as he passed by he hit my tricycle. I flew off and hit my head as I landed. My next memory was of waking up on the couch in our living room with the face of a policeman smiling down at me. I remember thinking that he must be an angel. He had been directing traffic on the corner of the street and had seen the accident, run over and picked me up, and carried me into the house. I have never forgotten the kindness in his eyes. He was the first "stranger" I had ever known. From reflecting on that experience, I recognize that it gave me a sense of trust "that help always comes." I have had the courage to reach out to others, including strangers my whole life. Spend a few minutes thinking back over your childhood. Was there a memory that stands out for you at about age three? Next, think about your children and what experiences happened to them at about age three. Jot down some notes.

Sometime around the age of 3, children's self-awareness matures to the next stage of self-development. Their sense of deep connection to the world gradually changes as they begin to experience themselves as separate, independent beings. Inwardly, they sense for the first time that "I am independent of my parents, of nature, of family." At the same time, the child leaves behind the self-referential word "me" and now refers to him/herself as "I." This new self-referential expression tells us that the inner life of the child has reached a new stage. It is the first conscious step towards the inner integration of one's own independent existence.

Usually, this is a gradual process, but it *can* happen in the blink of an eye and quite dramatically. One of my dearest friends had a wonderful experience of this moment with her granddaughter. One morning in the kitchen in the presence of both her mother and her grandmother, the child suddenly exclaimed, "Mummy, I'm an I!" "I'm an I, Mummy!" They both reported that the child beamed broadly looking at first the Mother and then the Grandmother expressing her wonder and joy at her realization!

This is the only example of a child recognizing this change in this way that I have ever heard about. It is a wonderful picture for us to contemplate. Usually, a day arrives and without much fanfare at all, the child simply begins to call him/herself "I." In studying biographies of persons in various cultures, it is common that children experience an outer event in their lives just at the time the inner shift occurs. These events include moving house, birth of a sibling, death of a pet, an accident or injury, or a myriad of other eventful experiences.

As you can imagine, this change can bring some discomfort to the child. Nothing seems to be right. Their connection to the world around them is shifting. Little by little, they begin to see themselves as separate persons. Birthing a sense of self and a feeling of separation from others and the world is uncomfortable and can be accompanied by outbursts of challenging behavior followed by tears for no obvious reason. Children who were easy going and relaxed suddenly begin to test their parents at every turn. Tears flow, feet stomp, and shrieks can be heard. By anticipating this stage and recognizing it as an essential step that leads the child to a new level of self-awareness, parents can relax a bit, trusting that they will come through!

At the age of 3, children are also becoming more aware of the power of language. They recognize that certain words carry more power than others and begin to experiment and "play" with words. A "testing of the parents" occurs. What happens if I say "no?" Do they mean what they say? The power of the word *no* is a revelation and children use it loudly and often! What a discovery! That words have power is a new and exciting experience for the young child. Children enjoy the reaction certain words illicit and the power that specific words wield. The testing and exploration of the word "no" is one of the cornerstones of the child's developing sense of self at this age. Pitting themselves against their parents and other authority, with such a simple and powerful word is not only exciting but also compelling for the child. Don't worry; this too shall pass.

# Stories for Children Age 3 and Up

## Fairy/Wonder Tales

The child of 3 is ready to hear fairy tales or wonder tales of the simplest kind. The inner world of imagination develops around this age, and children are now able to focus on a story for longer periods of time, and to hear stories that are more metaphorical.

For instance, this is an ideal age at which to tell your child the Wonder Tale, "Sweet Porridge" (see Chapter 3). The young child of 3-4 is fascinated by the power of words. This story satisfies a need in the heart of the child to understand more deeply the power of language.

Here's another Wonder Tale that is appropriate to this age group.

# The Golden Goose (ages 3-6)

A humorous tale that children in this age range love.
*(Honesty, dishonesty, straightforwardness, steadfastness, persistence)*

Once upon a time, where did it happen? When did it happen? There was a man who had three sons, the youngest of whom was called Simpleton. He was despised, mocked, and sneered at on every occasion.

It happened that the eldest son wanted to go into the forest to cut wood. His mother gave him a beautiful sweet cake and a bottle of wine in order that he might not suffer from hunger or thirst.

When he entered the forest he met a little grey-haired old man who bade him good day, and said: 'Do give me a piece of cake out of your pocket, and let me have a draught of your wine; I am so hungry and thirsty.' But the clever son answered: 'If I give you my cake and wine, I shall have none for myself; be off with you,' and he left the little man standing and went on.

But when he began to hew down a tree, it was not long before he made a false stroke, and the axe cut him in the arm, so that he had to go home and have it bound up.

After this the second son went into the forest to cut wood. His mother gave him, like the eldest, a cake and a bottle of wine. The little old grey man met him, and asked him for a piece of cake and a drink of wine. But the second son, too, said sensibly enough: 'What I give you will be taken away from myself; be off!' and he left the little man standing and went on. His punishment, however, was not delayed; when he had made a few blows at the tree he struck himself in the leg, so that he had to be carried home.

Then Simpleton said: 'Father, do let me go and cut wood.' The father answered: 'Your brothers have hurt themselves with it, leave it alone, you do not understand anything about it.' But Simpleton begged so long that at last his father said: 'Just go then, you will get wiser by hurting yourself.' His mother gave him a cake made with water and baked in the cinders, and with it a bottle of sour beer.

When he came to the forest the little old grey man met him and said: "Give me a piece of your cake and a drink out of your bottle; I am so hungry and thirsty." Simpleton answered: "I have only cinder-cake and sour beer. If that pleases you, we will sit down and eat." So they sat down, and when Simpleton pulled out his cinder-cake, it was a fine sweet cake, and the sour beer had become good wine. So they ate and drank, and after that the little man said: "Since you have a good heart, and are willing to divide what you have, I will give you good luck. There stands an old tree, cut it down, and you will find something at the roots." Then the little man took leave of him.

Simpleton went and cut down the tree, and when it fell there was a goose sitting in the roots with feathers of pure gold. He lifted her up, and taking her with him, went to an inn where he thought he would stay the night. Now the host had three daughters, who saw the goose and were curious to know what such a wonderful bird might be, and would have liked to have one of its golden feathers.

The eldest thought: "I shall soon find an opportunity of pulling out a feather." As soon as Simpleton had gone out she seized the goose by the wing, but her finger and hand remained sticking fast to it.

The second came soon afterwards, thinking only of how she might get a feather for herself, but she had scarcely touched her sister then she was held fast.

At last the third also came with the same intent, and the others screamed at her: "Keep away; for goodness' sake keep away!" But she did not understand why she was to keep away. "The others are there," she thought, "I may as well be there too," and ran to them; but as soon as she had touched her sister, she remained sticking fast to her. So they had to spend the night with the goose.

The next morning Simpleton took the goose under his arm and set out, without troubling himself about the three girls who were hanging on to it. They were obliged to run after him continually, now left, now right, wherever his legs took him.

In the middle of the fields a parson met them, and when he saw the procession he said: "For shame, you good-for-nothing girls! Why are you running across the fields after this young man? Is that seemly?" Just then he took the youngest by the hand in order to pull her away, but as soon as he touched her he was stuck fast, and was obliged to run behind.

Before long the sexton came by and saw his master, the parson, running behind three girls. He was astonished at this and called out: "Hi! Your reverence, whither away so quickly? Do not forget that we have a christening today!" and running after him he took him by the sleeve, but was held fast to it.

While the five were trotting one behind the other, two laborers came with their hoes from the fields; the parson called out to them and begged that they would set him and the sexton free. But they had scarcely touched the sexton when they were held fast, and now there were seven of them running behind Simpleton and the goose.

Soon afterwards they came to a city, where a king ruled who had a daughter who was so serious that no one could make her laugh. So he had put forth a decree that whosoever should be able to make her laugh should marry her. When Simpleton heard this, he went with his goose and all her train before the king's daughter, and as soon as she saw the seven people running on and on, one behind the other, she began to laugh quite loudly, as if she would never stop. Simpleton asked to have her for his wife; but the king did not like the son-in- law, and made all manner of excuses. At last he said that Simpleton must find a man who could drink a cellar full of wine. Simpleton thought of the little grey man, who could certainly help him. He went into the forest, and in the same place where he had felled the tree, he saw a man sitting, who had a very sorrowful face. Simpleton asked him what he was taking to heart so sorely, and he answered: "I have such a great thirst and cannot quench it; cold water I cannot stand, a barrel of wine I have just emptied, but that to me is like a drop on a hot stone!"

"There, I can help you," said Simpleton, "just come with me and you shall be satisfied."

He led him into the king's cellar, and the man bent over the huge barrels, and drank and drank till his loins hurt, and before the day was out he had emptied all the barrels. Simpleton asked once more for his bride, but the king was vexed that such an ugly fellow, whom everyone called Simpleton, should take away his daughter, and he made a new condition; he must first find a man who could eat a whole mountain of bread. Simpleton did not think long, but went straight into the forest, where in the same place where he had found the first man another man sat who was making an awful face, and saying: "I have eaten a whole oven full of rolls, but what good is that when one has such a hunger as I? My stomach remains empty."

At this Simpleton was glad, and said: "Get up and come with me; you shall eat yourself full." He led him to the king's palace where all the flour in the whole Kingdom was collected, and from it he caused a huge mountain of bread to be baked. The man from the forest stood before it, began to eat, and by the end of one day the whole mountain had vanished. Then Simpleton for the third time asked for his bride; but the king again sought a way out, and ordered a ship that could sail on land and on water. "As soon as you come sailing back in it," said he, "you shall have my daughter for wife."

Simpleton went straight into the forest, and there sat the little grey man to whom he had given his cake. When he heard what Simpleton wanted, he said: "Since you have given me to eat and to drink, I will give you the ship; and I do all this because you once were kind to me." Then he gave him the ship that could sail on land and water, and when the king saw that, he could no longer prevent him from having his daughter. The wedding was celebrated, and after the king's death, Simpleton inherited his kingdom and lived for a long time contentedly with his wife.

There are, of course, many other Fairy/Wonder Tales appropriate for this age group. See the list of stories in Part IV of this book.

In addition to Fairy/Wonder Tales, there are many other types of stories you'll want to tell children in this age group. For instance, use the following delightful tales, "The Little Red House with the Star Inside," and "The Thick, Fat Pancake."

## The Little Red House with the Star Inside (ages 3-6)

*A gem of a folk tale addressing boredom and the wonder of nature (Have a red apple nearby with a knife to cut it open at the end of the story!)*

There was once upon a time a little boy who was tired of his toys and tired of his play.

"What shall I do?" he asked his mother. His mother thought a moment and said, "You shall go on a journey to find a little red house with no doors or windows, and with a star inside."

This really made the little boy wonder. "Which way shall I go?" he asked his mother. "I don't know where to find a little red house with no doors or windows."

"Go down the lane past the farmer's house and over the hill," said his mother, "and then hurry back as soon as you can and tell me all about your journey."

So the little boy put on his cap and his jacket and started out. He had not gone very far down the lane when he came to a merry little girl dancing in the sunshine. Her cheeks were like pink rose petals and she was singing like a robin.

"Do you know where I shall find a little red house with no doors and no windows and a star inside?" asked the little boy.

The little girl laughed. "Ask my father, the farmer," she said. "Perhaps he knows."

"Thank you," said the little boy. And the little boy went on until he came to the great brown barn where the farmer kept barrels of fat potatoes and baskets of yellow squashes and golden pumpkins. The farmer himself stood in the doorway looking out over the green pastures and yellow grain fields.

"Do you know where I shall find a little red house with no doors and no windows and a star inside?" asked the little boy.

The farmer laughed, too. "I have lived a great many years and I never saw one," he chuckled, "but ask Granny who lives at the foot of the hill. She knows how to make molasses taffy and popcorn balls, and red mittens. Perhaps she can direct you."

"Thank you," said the little boy and he went on until he came to Granny sitting in her garden of herbs and marigolds. She was as wrinkled as a walnut and as smiling as the sunshine.

"Please, Granny," said the little boy, "where shall I find a little red house with no doors and no windows with a star inside?"

Granny was knitting red mittens and when she heard the little boy's question she laughed so cheerily that the wool ball rolled off her lap and down the little pebbly path.

"I should like to find that little house myself," she chuckled. "I would be warm when the frosty night comes and the starlight would be prettier than a candle. But ask the wind who blows about so much and listens at the chimneys. Perhaps the wind can direct you."

So the little boy took off his cap politely to the Granny and went on up the hill rather sorrowfully. He wondered if his mother, who usually knew almost everything had perhaps made a mistake.

The wind was coming down the hill as the little boy climbed up. As they met, the wind turned about and went along singing beside the little boy. It whistled in his ear and pushed him and dropped a pretty leaf into his hand.

"I wonder," thought the little boy, after they had gone along together for a little while, "if the wind could help me find a little red house with no doors and no window and a star inside."

The wind cannot speak in our words, but it went singing ahead of the little boy until it came to an orchard. There it climbed up in the apple tree and shook the branches. When the little boy caught up, there at his feet lay a great rosy apple. The little boy picked up the apple. It was as much as his two hands could hold: it was red as the sun had been able to paint it, and the thick brown stem stood up as straight as a chimney, and it had no doors and no windows.

Was there a star inside? The little boy called to the wind. "Thank you," and the wind whistled back, "You're welcome."

Then the little boy gave the apple to his mother. His mother took a knife *(AT THIS POINT, START CUTTING AN APPLE CROSSWISE)* and cut the apple through the center.

And there, inside the apple, lay a star holding brown seeds!

"It is too wonderful to eat without looking at the star, isn't it?" the little boy said to his mother.

"Yes, indeed," answered his mother.

# The Thick, Fat Pancake (ages 3-6)

## A folktale from Germany
*(Sharing, selflessness, and compassion)*

Once upon a time there were three old women who wanted a pancake to eat. The first one brought an egg, the second one milk, and the third one, grease and flour. When the thick, fat pancake was done, it pulled itself up in the pan and ran away from the three old women. It ran and ran, steadfastly, steadfastly into the woods. There he came upon a little hare, who cried, "Thick, fat pancake, stop! I want to eat you!"

The pancake answered, "I have run away from three old women. Can I not run away from Hoppity Hare as well?" And it ran steadfastly, steadfastly into the woods.

Then a wolf came running toward him, and cried, "Thick, fat pancake, stop! I want to eat you!"

The pancake answered, "I have run away from three old women and Hoppity Hare. Can I not run away from Waddly Wolf as well?" And it ran steadfastly, steadfastly into the woods.

Then a goat came hopping by, and cried, "Thick, fat pancake, stop! I want to eat you!"

The pancake answered, "I have run away from three old women, Hoppity Hare, and Waddly Wolf. Can I not run away from Longbeard Goat as well?" And it ran steadfastly, steadfastly into the woods.

Then a horse came galloping by, and cried, "Thick, fat pancake, stop! I want to eat you!"

The pancake answered, "I have run away from three old women, Hoppity Hare, Waddly Wolf, and Longbeard Goat. Can I not run away from Flatfoot Horse as well?" And it ran steadfastly, steadfastly into the woods.

Then a sow came running up, and cried, "Thick, fat pancake, stop! I want to eat you!"

The pancake answered, "I have run away from three old women, Hoppity Hare, Waddly Wolf, Longbeard Goat, and Flatfoot Horse. Can I not run away from Oink-Oink Sow as well?" And it ran steadfastly, steadfastly into the woods.

> Then three children came by. They had neither father nor mother, and they said, "Dear pancake, please stop! We have had nothing to eat the entire day!" So the thick, fat pancake jumped into the children's basket and let them eat it up.

## The Cumulative Tale

The Cumulative Tale is one of the oldest of all tales. Today they are not well known. And yet, for young children, they are a great source of joy and self-empowerment. They contain numerous repetitive phrases that the children can join in and speak with the storyteller. The verbal repetitions include repetitive gestures that add to the fun. Young children enjoy the sounds, repetitions, and movements while learning new language skills at the same time. I include them here in hopes that they will find their way back into modern culture! Try writing one!

To create gestures, sit on a chair and imagine the actions of the story taking place in front of you in a semi-circle from left to right. Make a different gesture for each step of the story, and, as you tell that part, do the associated gesture.

## The Little Red Hen

Here are some gesture examples you can use as you tell the cumulative tale of The Little Red Hen. Use your map as a guide.

1. Make a gathering of wheat grains gesture to your far left.
2. Make a planting gesture next to the gathering gesture in front of you.
3. Make a watering gesture over the space where you planted the seeds.
4. Make a growing gesture over the same space.
5. Make a harvesting gesture.
6. Take the wheat to the miller to the right of center.
7. Make a grinding gesture in that same space.
8. Make a mixing, kneading gesture further to the right.
9. Bake the bread in the oven to the far right.
10. Slice the bread on an imaginary counter back at the center.

# The Little Red Hen (ages 3-7)

## A Cumulative Tale about cooperation and fairness
*re-written by my Storytelling students with a more inclusive ending.*

Once upon a time, a lamb, a cat, a pig, and a little red hen lived on an old farm on a flowery hill surrounded by fields of golden wheat. One day, the Little Red Hen found some grains of wheat scattered in the barnyard. "Look what I've found!" she said to the other animals. "Who will help me plant these grains of wheat?"

"Not I!" said the lamb.                "Not I!" said the cat.

"Not I!" said the pig.                "Not I!" said the goat.

"Then I'll do it myself," said the Little Red Hen. And so she did.

She knew that seeds need water to grow tall and strong. "Who will help me water these seeds?" asked the Little Red Hen.

"Not I!" said the lamb.                "Not I!" said the cat.

"Not I!" said the pig.                "Not I!" said the goat.

"Then I'll do it myself," said the Little Red Hen. And so she did.

The Little Red Hen watered the soil and waited patiently for the wheat to grow. When the wheat was tall and golden, she knew it was ready to be cut. "Who will help me harvest the wheat?" asked the Little Red Hen.

"Not I!" said the lamb.                "Not I!" said the cat.

"Not I!" said the pig.                "Not I!" said the goat.

"Then I'll do it myself," said the Little Red Hen. And so she did.

The Little Red Hen's basket was soon filled with wheat. "Who will help me take the wheat to the mill to be ground into flour?" asked the Little Red Hen.

"Not I!" said the lamb.                "Not I!" said the cat.

"Not I!" said the pig.                "Not I!" said the goat.

"Then I'll do it myself," said the Little Red Hen. And so she did. The kind miller ground the wheat into powdery, velvety flour, and the Little Red Hen carried it home in a rough brown sack. "Who will help me make this flour into bread?" asked the Little Red Hen.

"Not I!" said the lamb.          "Not I!" said the cat.

"Not I!" said the pig.           "Not I!" said the goat.

"Then I'll do it myself," said the Little Red Hen. And so she did. The Little Red Hen mixed the flour into sticky dough and kneaded it into a smooth loaf. "Who will help me put this bread into the oven to bake?" asked the Little Red Hen.

"Not I!" said the lamb.          "Not I!" said the cat.

"Not I!" said the pig.           "Not I!" said the goat.

"Then I'll do it myself," said the Little Red Hen. And so she did. The kitchen filled with the delicious scent of baking bread, and the other animals came to see what was happening. The Little Red Hen took the warm, crusty loaf out of the oven, and set it on the table.

"Who will help me eat this fresh, tasty bread?" asked the Little Red Hen.

"I will!" said the lamb.          "I will!" said the cat.

"I will!" said the pig.           "I will!" said the goat.

"No, you will not," said the Little Red Hen. "You didn't help me plant it, or water it, or harvest it, or mill it, or bake it. I shall eat it myself!" And so she did.

The next time the Little Red Hen found some grains of wheat, the lamb planted it in the rich, brown soil; the cat watered it carefully every day; the pig harvested the wheat when it had grown tall and strong; and the goat carried it to the miller to be ground into flour. The Little Red Hen mixed the flour into sticky dough and kneaded it into a smooth loaf. Then she baked it in the oven. When the loaf was baked, the animals made hot chocolate and they ate the fresh, warm bread together. It was delicious!

# The Rooster and the Bean (ages 3-7)

## A Cumulative Tale

*Make up your own gestures. Create a map and use it as a guide to making meaningful gestures as the story moves to each place in the map. This story is about cooperation, kindness, and determination.*

Once there was a rooster and a hen who were pecking up bits of corn and beans in the farmyard. The rooster put a nice fat bean in his beak and swallowed it, but the bean got stuck in his throat.

"Hen, Hen, please fetch me some water from the river, for a bean is stuck in my throat."

"That will I gladly do," cried the hen and she ran to the river.

"River, river, please give me some water, that I may take it to the rooster, for the rooster has a bean stuck in his throat."

"That will I gladly do," said the river, "but first please bring me a leaf from the lime tree."

So, what did the hen do? She ran to the lime tree. "Lime tree, lime tree, please give me a leaf that I may take it to the river, so the river will give me water, that I make take to the rooster, for the rooster has a bean stuck in his throat."

"That will I gladly do," said the lime tree, but first, please bring me a thread from the peasant's daughter."

So, what did the hen do? She ran to the peasant's daughter. "Peasant's daughter, peasant's daughter, please give me a thread, that I may take it to the lime tree so the lime tree will give me a leaf that I may take it to the river, so the river will give me water that I may take to the rooster, for the rooster has a bean stuck in his throat.

"That will I gladly do said the peasant's daughter, but first, please bring me some buns from the baker."

So, what did the hen do? She ran to the baker. "Baker, baker, please give me some buns that I may take to the peasant's daughter, that the peasant's daughter will give me a thread that I may take to the lime tree, that the lime tree will give me a leaf, that I may take to the river, that the river will give me water that I may take to the rooster for the rooster has a bean stuck in his throat."

"That will I gladly to, say the baker, but first please bring some wood from the wood cutter."

So, what did the hen do? She ran to the woodcutter. "Woodcutter, woodcutter, please give me some wood that I may take it to the baker, that the baker will give some buns that I may take to the peasant's daughter, that the peasant's daughter will give me a thread that I may take to the lime tree, that the lime tree will give me a leaf that I may take to the river, that the river will give me water that I may take to the rooster, for the rooster has a bean stuck in his throat."

And the woodcutter gave the hen some wood. "Thank you," said the hen. And she ran to the baker and gave the baker the wood.

"Thank you," said the baker. And the baker gave the hen some buns. "Thank you," said the hen. And she ran to the peasant's daughter and gave her the buns.

"Thank you," said the peasant's daughter, and she gave the hen a thread. "Thank you," said the hen and she ran to the lime tree and gave it the thread.

"Thank you," said the lime tree. And the lime tree gave the hen a leaf. "Thank you," said the hen and she ran to the river and gave the river the leaf.

"Thank you," said the river and the river gave the hen some water. "Thank you," said the hen and she ran to the rooster and gave the water to the rooster.

The rooster swallowed the water and the bean went down.

"Cock-a-doodle-doooooo," cried the rooster!

# Developmental Movement Activities for Ages 3–6

One of the most interesting and potentially valuable studies being conducted today is the relationship between physical movement and mental development. Children who are physically active and who are challenged to develop their sense of balance, coordination and physical stamina, experience improvements in focus and concentration in mental activities, too. Today, there is an active movement afoot to bring exercise into the daily life of children at every age and stage of childhood. Specific games and activities that stimulate the inner ear, improve hand-eye coordination, develop a rhythmical sense through running and other repetitive movements, are helping children and adolescents to not only move more gracefully and confidently, but also to think more clearly. Nursery rhymes, speech rhythms, and poetry train the ear and stimulate higher levels of thinking. Developmental movement activities replace the games that children used to learn on the playground fifty years ago. And some of those games are coming back, too. Today, the evidence has become a groundswell, and most neuroscientists agree that movement and cognition are powerfully connected. (Source: *Teaching with the Brain in Mind, 2nd Edition*, by Eric Jensen. Additional sources can be found on the web.)

Here are some activities and games that work on hand-eye coordination, rhythm in speaking and movement, focus and concentration, and are just plain fun. These games are another form of storytelling where the child gets to act out the "story" of the game. Introducing a game with a tiny story is recommended to enkindle the imagination of the child and give meaning to the game or movement activity.

Finger games, jumping games, repetitive circle games have been helping children with finger dexterity, language development, and hand-eye coordination for hundreds of years. They stimulate brain activity, develop a sense of rhythm and rhyme in the body and the ear, and prepare the child for using the rhythm of language in learning how to read. Let's get them back in the classroom, on the playground, in the park, and in the backyard! Here are a few to get you started.

Before you introduce one to your child or group of children, make up a little story about the characters you will be using in the finger play. For example: *Once there was a bunny who loved to hop, hop, hop! In fact, you could say she never wanted to stop, stop, stop. She went over the hill, down into the valley, round the tree and back home as quick as could be!*

For this verse, explain that *hare* is another word for rabbit and of course a bunny is a baby hare or a baby rabbit!

# Finger Play for ages 3–4

## The Bunny Hop

Make your hand into a bunny with your first and second fingers straight up for the ears and your thumb holding the third and fourth finger down (the "peace" sign) and hop on your young child's arm or leg or tummy while repeating…

*Round and round the garden hops the little hare…*
*One hop, two hops, tickle you under there!*

Tickle her under the chin or arm or whatever suits your fancy and repeat.

## Eye, Eye, Winkie

Touch the corner of an eye and say… *Eye, eye, winkie*
Touch your nose and say… *Nose, nose, nebbie*
Touch your cheek and say… *Cheek, cheek, cherrie*
Touch your ear and say… *Ear, ear, earie*
Touch your mouth and say… *Mow (like wow), mow, merry*
Tickle your child's chin and say… *Chin chopper, chin chopper, chin, chin, chin*

Your young child will imitate your gestures. You can also touch your child's eye, nose, cheek, ear, and mouth when you speak the verse.

## The Little Birds (ages 3 and up)

| Rhythmically Chant... | While making these gestures... |
|---|---|
| Way up in the sky, the little birds fly. | Flap hands like birds over your head. |
| While down in the nest, the little birds rest. | Make a nest with your palms up and hands cupped. |
| With a wing on the left, | Put left hand under left armpit. |
| And a wing on the right, | Put right hand under right armpit. |
| The little birds sleep, all thru the night. | Put hands together against right ear and tilt head to the right. Close eyes. |
| Shhhhh! They're sleeping! | Put your finger on your lips. |
| The bright sun comes up! | Clap hands together above head. |
| The dew drops away. | Both hands face down. In rhythm with words, move hands up and down as if banging on a piano. |
| "Good morning, good morning," the little birds say. | Repeat same gesture as in first line. |

## Farmer Giles

Tell a little story about visiting a farm and seeing the rooster (also called a cock-a-doodle a long time ago), the hens, and the chicks. Then do this action game with your child. Your child will imitate your movements. Or do the movements on your child's face the second time after you have shown him on your own face.

*Here sits Farmer Giles* (put your finger on your forehead).
*Here sit his two men* (put a finger from each hand on each of your eyes).
*Here sits the cock-a-doodle* (put a finger on your nose).
*Here sits the hen* (put a finger on your chin).
*Here sit the little chicks* (put three fingers on your chin).
**Here they run in** (tap your fingers into your mouth).
**Chin chopper, chin chopper, chin, chin, chin!** (tickle child under chin).

## The Way the Ladies Ride...

Sit with your legs crossed and seat your child on your foot (or on your knee with your legs uncrossed) hold your child's hands in your hands and pretend your child is riding a horse. You are the horse!

As you speak the verse, move your foot up and down in rhythm to the sound of the following words.

*This is the way the ladies ride, the ladies ride, the ladies ride.*
*This is the way the ladies ride, so early in the morning.*

Now speed up the movement of your leg to challenge your child to hold on!

*This is the way the gentlemen ride, the gentlemen ride, the gentlemen ride.*
*This is the way the gentlemen ride, so early in the morning.*

Now move your leg up and down as fast as you can!

*This is the way the roughnecks ride, the roughnecks ride, the roughnecks ride.*
*This is the way the roughnecks ride, so early in the morning!*

You and you child should be out of breath right now and laughing heartily together!

## Slinky Malinky, the Rascally Cat

A delightful stretching game from my friend Kathleen Neuwirth, retired Kindergarten teacher.

Gather the children in a circle sitting on the floor. Tell a tiny story about a cat named Slinky Malinky. Have the children tell what they know about cats. Then demonstrate the movements accompanied by the words. Have everyone join in.

**Slinky Malinky, the rascally cat** *(walk like a cat)*
**Stretched in the sunshine and sat** *(stretch and sit)*
**He looked this way and that way,** *(move head side to side)*
**and up and down,** *(move head up & down)*
**Smiled big...and frowned.** *(make a big smile and then frown)*

# Circle Games

Circle games offer the young child an experience of wholeness. Everyone is included in the circle. A feeling of connectedness is experienced. The games encourage cooperation and collaboration. They involve teamwork while giving the young child an experience of belonging to the whole group.

## "Good Morning to You" Circle Greeting (ages 3-6)

Start slowly and repeat the entire verse three times, getting faster each time. Make a large circle with the whole group of children. Then gesture while you speak as follows:

| Chant in a rhythmical way with emphasis on the word "you"... | While making these gestures... |
| --- | --- |
| "Good morning to you." | Gesture with right hand to those on your right. Have the children do it with you. |
| "Good morning to you." | Make a big gesture to the left with the children. |
| "And to you, and to you." | Gesture across the circle including everyone. Again have the children join in. |
| "My feet are quite chilly, but I'll soon warm them through." | Arms are down at your sides, and you stamp your feet left and right in rhythm with the words. |
| "I clap with my hands." | Clap hands in rhythm with the words "clap with my hands." |
| "And stamp with my feet." | Stamp feet left and right in rhythm with the words "stamp with my feet." |
| "And now I am ready, the new day to greet." | Stand still; make large greeting gesture encompassing everyone. Repeat the entire verse with gestures three times, getting faster each time. |

# The House of Snail

Before beginning this activity, engage the children with a conversation about snails. Then explain that the snail's shell protects him because it is hard. Now ask the children if they know what a knight is and talk about the coat of mail that the knights wear to protect themselves in battle. Gather children in a circle. Join hands. Teacher drops hand with child on the left and begins to lead the children to her right inside the circle and in front of the children to her left. The circle follows her and gradually turns round and round until the teacher is in the middle with three or four circles of children spiraling around her. Then she turns and spirals back the way she came and unwinds the spiral. The surprise is that everyone is now facing out of the circle rather than facing into the circle as they had been facing at the beginning.

This is the verse that is spoken while you slowly walk the spiral in and out.

> *Let us go and pay a visit to the curly house of snail*
> *In we go and there we'll find him hidden in his coat of mail.*

At this point, keep going inward in silence until you can go no further—it's quite tight, just as it might be if you were inside a snail shell! —then the leader turns around and begins to walk in the opposite direction still in a circle…and says…

> *Then we turn and go back homeward, still unwinding all the way,*
> *'til we come out of the darkness into radiant light of day!*

The first time you do this with a particular group of children, stop when you have the circle and all are facing out. Enjoy the moment of surprise and wonder!

# CHAPTER 8

## 4–5 Years Old

*The eensy weensy spider went up the waterspout,*
*Down came the rain and washed the spider out*
*Out came the sun and dried up all the rain*
*And the eensy weensy spider went up the spout again!*

## Characteristics of the Child at 4 and 5 Years Old

Andy is 5 years old. Stocky and strong, he walks with his eyes straight ahead, his heels planted firmly on the ground. You can hear his footsteps coming and going. He has bright red hair, freckles, and a mischievous twinkle in his eye. He loves to play in the sand box building roads for his trucks to travel upon and mountains for his jeeps to climb up. Adding water to the sand box is one of his favorite activities. Building with sand and mud, he creates bridges over rivers and moats around castles. He enjoys playing with his friends and always has strong opinions about which game to play. His voice carries over the hum of the kindergarten classroom as he expresses his ideas with enthusiasm and eagerness. He can be impatient and impetuous and can lose his temper when he doesn't get his own way. He loves animals and his dog Max. He is fascinated by spiders and bugs and knows where to find them. He has a big heart and a strong physical presence.

Lately, things have changed. Suddenly, he stops in his tracks. He sits down and doesn't know what to do. This has never happened before. He's always played with abandon. But now, he's a bit out of sorts. There's nothing to do. He wants to go to the park, but some days, even the park is boring. He's done everything there. Even the Kindergarten class is boring. What's happening?

Boredom appears in the life of every child around the age of 5. It is important that parents and teachers meet this challenge with humor, creativity and gentle firmness. Smile at him/her and say something like, "Oh, I see you are bored. It looks like you need more to do." Sometimes, just saying those words aloud is enough to send him/her off on a new adventure. It's a reassuring experience to be seen by someone who verbally validates one's inner experience. It sets us free to make a shift. Other times, doing a project together can be just the ticket.

Suggest some activities and chores that need doing around the house and do them together. This phase of boredom is the harbinger of the next change in inner development that occurs around the age of six.

This is a good time to put your child to work to help dig the garden, shovel the snow, and trim the bushes. Side-by-side with Mom and Dad, they will appreciate the opportunity to do something "real," something challenging that is part of the life of the family. Practical activities with family members give them a feeling of satisfaction and accomplishment, camaraderie with family, and recognition of their developing skills and abilities. They feel seen, challenged, and appreciated.

If you have a task that needs doing at the same time every day, challenge your children not only to do it, but also to remember *when* to do it on their own, and praise them for remembering. Such responsibilities honor their growing capabilities. Present the idea to them by reminding them that they are maturing; they are old enough to help do the dishes after dinner with Mommy or Daddy or big sister or brother. They can sweep kitchen floors, gather up toys and put them away, or help in the garden. But if they have already been doing these tasks for some time, this is when they need more to do. If they ask to do something that they are too young to do like mow the lawn, tell them that you appreciate the offer and that soon they will be old enough to take on such a task, but not quite yet. Their sense of time is developing, and they will appreciate your clarity.

Children are very capable at 4 and 5 and appreciate being told so! They can make many things. They can paint and draw beautiful pictures; they can create amazing worlds in the sand box. They can build dams after the rain in the mud or sand and create stories about the people who live there. They can make their bed, set the table, clean up their toys, sweep the floor, empty the trash and will do it all with pride and satisfaction. Getting a few child-size tools like a small broom and dust pan, a small rake, and their own rags for cleaning is a simple way to get them more involved around the house, too.

Your inner attitude is critical in order to have clear communication with your young child. If you are really interested in having them help you, then they will know it intuitively. But if you are simply too busy or in too much of a rush to sort things out for them to be able to help you, then leave these ideas to another day when you truly have time to be present with your child. Young children are very perceptive and know when we are being present with them and when we are distracted. If you don't have time, just say so. And offer a time soon when you will be available. "In fifteen minutes, I will come and read with you." Then be sure you do it. This kind of clear communication and follow-through builds trust between you and your child.

Eventually, they will conquer the boredom on their own. They will set forth on the next step of the growing up journey, more aware of their inner ability to create things to do out of their own imagination.

## Stories Can Help with Boredom, too!

Simple stories about heroes and heroines who overcome difficulties inspire children to take on the challenge of boredom and overcome it with their own creativity. Meeting this challenge is a developmental milestone that sets the stage for a life of meaning and achievement. It may be challenging for us to watch them journey through it, but it is essential that they master it at this age and become "the heroes of their own lives," as Horst Kornberger so aptly says in his excellent storytelling book, *The Power of Stories, Nurturing Children's Imagination and Consciousness.* For children who are 9 or older, The Phantom Toll Booth is a great story about a boy who is bored.

Here's an idea to get you started on creating your own stories to address problems like this as your child encounters them. You can easily do it, using something like this:

## The Bored Little Child

A long time ago, there was a little (girl or boy to match your child) who smiled and played happily all day long. She/he made up games to play with toys and ran races with friends in the neighborhood. One day, she/he woke up and felt strange. He/she didn't know what to do. He/she walked around the house feeling cross and uncomfortable. He/she went outside to play in the sand box, but it was boring. He/she went to school and was bored there, too. The boys and girls he/she enjoyed playing with were also bored. They began to sit around on the grass outside or the floor inside and complain about how bored they were. After some months, they began to lose interest in complaining and went back outside to play ball and tag and other games they created. Whenever someone said they were bored, someone else piped up and said, "Let's do something new." And they would figure it out together.

Another option is to put the story you make up in the animal kingdom. Create a bored lizard, or a bored lion cub, or a bored penguin. Start the story as above. Describe the habitat in detail and the life of a young animal. Then create the moment of boredom followed by a moment of rising to the challenge and overcoming the stagnation of "boredom."

Here's an animal example:

## Dolly Duck

Dolly duck was plucky and busy. She loved to gather the other ducklings and organize games and races across the pond. One day there was no wind and the sun was hot. Dolly felt lazy and bored. She told her mother who shrugged her shoulders. She told her father who told her to go fishing. She told her friends. They were all bored just like Dolly. Dolly hung her head. Her friends hung their heads. The air was still. The ducks were hot and then hotter. Then Dolly fluttered her wings and flew across the pond. The others followed her. They began making circles in the sky and then figure eights. They swooped down to the surface of the pond and swished back up again. They played tag in the sky. They laughed and they quacked and soon they were off on an adventure to a nearby pond that they had forgotten. They took turns thinking up what to do next and their boredom vanished like the wind.

# Chore Tips in a Nutshell!

The 4/5-year-olds develop a remarkable set of skills as they move through this two-year growth period. It is important that they be given REAL tasks to accomplish around the house, garden and the outside play areas. They find doing essential skills rewarding and engaging. Through doing regular chores and tasks, children feel more of an essential part of the family.

Organizing their daily schedule so that these tasks are accomplished at about the same time each day will develop the child's memory "body." This is more than just a metaphor. The young child actually remembers through the physical body, through action, movement and other physical activities. Begin the task with the child at a specific time each day. Do the physical action with them with as few words as possible. This will get them started. Then let them do more and more of it on their own.

Gradually, you will find the children can accomplish the tasks completely on their own while you tackle some of your chores at the same time. It is important that you give them the opportunity to accomplish the chores on their own. They will feel you have confidence in them and that you trust them to do the job well.

Praise them simply: "Well done!" "Nice work!" "Thanks!" If it's not well done, then say, "Let's start over and do it together."

# Recommended Activities Box

*For Use at Home and in the Classroom*

This kind of an Activities Box can be used with children of most any age, but it's particularly apropos for children at this age. Having a basket of large pieces of cloth (4' x 4' work well) of various shapes, colors and textures offers children hours of playtime fun. When children of 4, 5, & 6 cover up their clothes with a "cape" of red or green or blue, it gives the imagination wings!

They can take on the role of various people they encounter in their life or discover in the stories you tell them. As they imitate real-life roles, they learn. They are exploring the adult world in a safe and imaginative way, using the skills they have learned so far. Their imaginative play becomes more complex, especially if they hear stories and have other children to play with a few times a week.

Wood blocks of various sizes and shapes, old pots and pans, silverware and dishes, random bits of wood or logs, offer opportunities for role playing that stimulate the imagination and the use of complex language.

Children love to act out the roles they see adults take on in the world. Doctors, lawyers, cooks, teachers, writers, wallpaper hangers, policemen, dentists, clowns, street sweepers, tree-trimmers, all these characters are hiding inside their minds and just waiting for the chance to emerge and play.

## Stories for 4/5 Year-Olds

"The House That Jack Built" is a wonderful, repetitive story that children of this age enjoy. It challenges them to repeat each phrase in the story in order and add a new phrase at the beginning or end of the next repetition. It includes lively imagery that is humorous and delightful. Repetitive stories strengthen the memory, challenge and encourage language development, and build a sense of rhythm in language. The child's "ear" for language is developed through such stories. A developed "ear" for language helps with learning to spell, to read, and to sound out words that aren't familiar or known to the child. Work on this story with your child or your class of children over several weeks. Make up simple gestures and place the things of the story around you in space, and have the children do the same. Draw a picture of each character in the story, too.

**Note**: For this and subsequent stories, I've included key words to alert you to the meanings and use of the story. Do NOT share these with your listeners. It is important that they work out meanings for themselves. It's part of the internal work they must do to allow the stories to work into them.

### This is The House that Jack Built (ages 4-7)

Mother Goose
*(Cooperation)*

This is the house that Jack built.
This is the malt that lay in the house that Jack built.
This is the rat that ate the malt that lay in the house that Jack built.
This is the cat that killed the rat that ate the malt that lay in the house that Jack built.
This is the dog, that worried the cat, that killed the rat, that ate the malt,
    that lay in the house that Jack built.
This is the cow with the crumpled horn, that tossed the dog,
    that worried the cat,
    that killed the rat, that ate the malt,
    that lay in the house that Jack built.
This is the maiden all forlorn, that milked the cow with the crumpled horn,
    that tossed the dog, that worried the cat,
    that killed the rat, that ate the malt,
    that lay in the house that Jack built.

This is the man all tattered and torn, that kissed the maiden all forlorn,
    that milked the cow with the crumpled horn,
    that tossed the dog, that worried the cat,
    that killed the rat, that ate the malt,
    that lay in the house that Jack built.
This is the priest all shaven and shorn, that married the man all tattered
    and torn,
    that kissed the maiden all forlorn,
    that milked the cow with the crumpled horn,
    that tossed the dog, that worried the cat,
    that killed the rat, That ate the malt,
    that lay in the house that Jack built.
This is the cock that crowed ay morn, that waked the priest all shaven and
    shorn,
    that married the man all tattered and torn,
    that kissed the maiden all forlorn,
    that milked the cow with the crumpled horn,
    that tossed the dog, that worried the cat,
    that killed the rat that ate the malt
    that lay in the house that Jack built.
This is the farmer sowing his corn, that kept the cock that crowed in the
    morn,
    that waked the priest all shaven and shorn,
    that married the man all tattered and torn,
    that kissed the maiden all forlorn,
    that milked the cow with the crumpled horn,
    that tossed the dog, that worried the cat,
    that killed the rat, that ate the malt,
    that lay in the house that Jack built.

I used "The House That Jack Built" as a reader in first grade. Each student created his or her own book. First, we learned it by heart, and then we drew pictures of each phrase on blank paper and wrote the words under the pictures, one sentence for each page. Then we created movements to do while we recited the entire poem.

# Fairy (U.S.) or Wonder (Europe) Tales –
# An Introduction

Fairy Tales and Wonder Tales are two different terms for the same story genre. Generally, in the United States, these stories are called Fairy Tales; while in European cultures, they are called Wonder Tales. The stories in this genre are characterized by an element of transformation that occurs (i.e., something or someone is transformed into something else or someone else). There is a suspended sense of the everyday, hence the word "wonder." This story genre includes stories with elemental beings also known as fairies, dwarves, and elves.

Fairy or Wonder Tales sprang up all over the world in all cultures at the same time. No one knows where they came from. In each culture, they were handed down for centuries through word of mouth before they were ever written down. Every story in this genre describes the inner transformation of an individual human being who has taken a journey, made a sacrifice, and become a different person. These tales are metaphors of the life of the human soul on its journey to wholeness.

I am often asked about the traditional gender roles depicted in the classic Fairy Tale or Wonder Tale. This is a critical question that every parent and teacher or teller of these tales to children must resolve before telling these stories. **The intent of the teller will come through the tale to the young child on a subconscious level.** Very few of these stories have fairies in them, but they always have a moment of transformation, of wonder, where something is changed into something else. The servant girl becomes a queen; the frog becomes a prince, and so forth. The Fairy or Wonder Tale most often concludes with a marriage. A dear friend of mine, who had told stories to children since before I was born, explained to me that the marriage is a metaphor of the individual having grown up and integrated the various aspects of her/his self and then, of course, was able to set his/her own course in life and thereby become the king or queen of her/his own life. Having told many wonder/fairy tales for over 40 years, I have found other interpretations, but this one rings truest for me. You can contemplate the many other characters that appear in these stories as challenges you must face in life, whether they represent inner challenges to the self or whether they come towards you from the world. The ability to overcome such challenges comes from within and without. If the fairy or wonder tale is told objectively with little emotion or emphasis, girls *will* identify with the male characters, as well as the female ones, and boys *will* identify with the female characters, as well as the male characters.

Today, we often speak of life as a two-fold journey: an inner journey to wholeness and an outer journey to fulfill our dreams. Life today, as in the past, is fraught with challenge and difficulty. Overcoming selfishness and self-centeredness is a lifelong task. To realize our dreams takes courage, forthrightness, determination, a willingness to change, and a sensitivity to help others. The wise leaders of the past believed that the power of the imagination was an essential human quality that needed to be nourished and developed in order that the human being live a fulfilling life. Imagination was considered critical to the successful navigation of the trials and tribulations that each human being would encounter on his or her unique journey. Therefore, stories that addressed the human challenge were told to the youngest of children.

Planted like seeds to ripen in their souls, these imaginative ancient tales told the stories of heroes and heroines who were often common folk: shepherds and serving maids, huntsmen and cooks. Through trials and adventures, they became princes and princesses, kings and queens. The heroes struggled against villains, such as witches and wizards, selfish sisters or brothers, and unkind stepparents, in order to find their true selves and their rightful place in the world. Invariably, they encountered wise helpers along the path. As they stood up for their inner ideals and faced their trials, they changed, developed, and realized their unique capacities. They began their journey as simple folk; some are even just called "simpleton" or "youngest brother" or "little sister" and ended their journey as queens and kings, the masters of their own destiny. When we dig deeper into the metaphor of the wonder tale or fairy tale, we begin to identify with the transformative quality of these remarkable tales.

In the Fairy Tale, the journey begins when the protagonist must leave home (the familiar place of birth and family) in order to seek help from the kingdom or the king and/or queen, or to find his or her way in the world. On this journey, the protagonist meets characters who pose a threat in some form or other. The protagonist is put to the test to see if he or she has a good heart. Is she compassionate and willing to help others before helping herself? Helpful characters always appear, but only the character who is kindhearted and generous is able to accept the help offered. Challenges appear that the openhearted character is able to surmount. The hubris of the other brothers or sisters is exposed, and they receive their just reward. In the end, the character with understanding and love from the "heart" restores the kingdom or conquers the villain and "marries the prince or princess."

These tales have different levels of meaning for different age groups. It may seem strange that we tell such complex and metaphorical stories to the youngest children. Yet, children from age 3 to 7 enjoy Wonder Tales and often remember them verbatim. It is best to tell them without drama or emphasis of any kind. When told simply, young children are left free to imagine a wolf in their own unique way without arousing unnecessary emotions or fears. They take whatever they need from the story and leave the rest for another time. The idea here is that these archetypal, ancient tales nurture young children when they are told in a simple voice without drama and emphasis. They build the imagination and offer wisdom about how best to live one's life. The fact that the good always wins out is something that young children love to hear again and again. Children enjoy the polarities portrayed by the characters. It is clear who is kind and who is not, who is sincere and who is not, who is selfless and who is selfish. Children recognize the clearly portrayed differences and carry the images into their play, taking turns being the selfish sister and the brave queen, or the jealous king and the kind huntsman.

## How to Tell a Fairy/Wonder Tale

A Fairy/Wonder Tale begins with an invocation. The invocation lets the child know that we are now on a journey into the imaginary world. The calm voice lets the child know the imaginary world is a safe world where the truth comes to light and victory is won by the honest kind-hearted hero or heroine. See Chapter 3 for a list of invocations or "story starters" and "story endings".

When we relax and tell the story in a calm and objective way, we leave ourselves open to discover something in it for us; some new nuance becomes clear each time we tell it. The mystery is that deep. The calm voice leaves children free to take what they need from the story. It eliminates the idea of a specific interpretation. When children ask you questions about the story, turn it around and reply, "Tell me what you think." Often the questions they are asking are not as literal as it first seems. Maybe they need a simple clarification. Or perhaps they misunderstood a part of the story. Finding out more about what their thoughts are before you answer the question allows you to give a more satisfying answer. This way of handling questions also offers the possibility for the adult to gain a deeper understanding of what the child is truly asking. As adults, we tend to superimpose our viewpoint when we hear a question and give an answer that is too sophisticated or complex. I am often surprised and delighted by the responses children offer to adults' questions. The child might also ask, "Is that story true?" This is very deep question, at the heart of which is the reason we are telling this story. There is a truth hidden in every story. If you have found the truth in the story for yourself, then you can answer simply by saying, "yes." This means you have to do your homework and uncover for yourself the relevance and meaning of the story.

How do we hold the attention of children when we tell a story simply without drama or unnecessary enthusiasm? Won't they lose interest? It's an important question that needs research on the part of the teller. Many children today are used to being the center of attention. A clear moment of eye contact can go a long way towards making a connection that inspires their interest and confidence. Feeling seen by the storyteller is usually enough. I always take a good look around and try to meet the gaze of each child for a second or so before I begin.

I have also found that if I love the story and am engaged in my imagination with the story, after a few moments, the children are with me in the telling. The imagery begins to expand and fill the room and the images come alive in the space between us. The children are free to use their own imagination to create images that work for them: images that are safe and instructive for their own unique needs and interests.

If there are children who are obviously older than most of the children present or if there are some hyper ones, I might reach into my pocket and take out the things I find there like keys or coins and ask one or two of them to hold them for me until I am finished telling the story or stories. They experience my trust and feel that I see them and notice that they are older. This often creates a bond that helps them to be more focused during the story, and their attention helps me with the audience. I also take a moment to expand myself into the whole room, and, if I am outdoors, at least to the edges of the audience. I thereby hold the space. I become bigger than I am. It is as if I am gathering them all together and then I can keep them in the story with me as I move from place to place along the story journey. It also helps me to extend my voice in order to fill the room or outside space without straining.

Sometimes, a child may never have heard a story told. He or she may have only heard stories read aloud from a book. The question may then come:

"Where are your books?"

"Oh, the stories are in my heart."

"You mean you're telling stories that are happening as you tell them?"

Such a wondrous question is an exquisite gift from a child. And yes, the stories are happening as they are being told. They are living pictures from long ago brought back to awaken the imagination and nourish the soul. Told without interpretation, stories nurture and instruct, give encouragement and courage, and offer guidance and perspective that will live on within the heart of the child.

*The Golden Key* is a classic Fairy Tale from the Grimm's Collection. It tells the tale of a young boy who goes out in the snow with his sled to fetch wood and finds a golden key! It is a story you can tell your child or class, and then, together, wonder and talk about what's inside the box that the golden key opens.

# The Golden Key (Ages 4–7)

*(Hard Work, Patience, Wonder, Imagination)*

Once upon a time, on a cold winter day when the snow was deep, a poor boy was sent forth with his sled to fetch wood. When he had gathered the wood together and stacked in on his sled in the way he wanted, he was so frozen with cold that he decided not to go home at once, but to light a fire and warm himself a little. So, he scraped away the snow.

And there where the ground was scraped away, he found a tiny, golden key. He thought to himself, where there is a key, a lock must be. And he dug in the ground and felt something hard. He dug further and found an iron chest. "If the key does but fit it!" he cried aloud. He thought to himself, there must be precious things in that little box. He searched, but no keyhole was there. At last he discovered one so small it was hardly visible. He put the key in the hole and thought, Ah, if the key does but fit!

And it fit exactly. Then he turned the key in the lock once around, and now we must wait until he has unlocked it and opened the lid, and then we shall learn what wonderful things were lying in that box.

# The Shining Loaf (Ages 5-7)

## A Wonder Tale

*(Love, Determination, Hope, Community)*

In a great kingdom there lived a king and his only daughter, the princess. One day the king became sick. All the doctors in the kingdom tried their best medicine, but none could make him well again. Desperate for help, the Princess set out to find the wise woman who lived amongst the people of the town. She found her beside her hearth in which a fire of wheat straw was burning with clear golden flames. The wise woman was kneading shining dough into a golden loaf of bread. The wise woman welcomed the princess and bade her speak.

"My father is very sick and no one can help him," cried the princess.

"Do you know what might make him well again?"

"Yes, said the wise woman, "Three crumbs from a shining oaf of bread that is a free gift from the people of his kingdom."

The princess was so happy that her father could get well that she declared, "I will bring the finest bakers in the world to make my father a shining loaf." But the wise woman told her that the shining loaf must be a gift freely given by the people of his own kingdom. The princess thanked the wise woman and went off to the town baker.

"Please, Baker, can you bake me a shining loaf?" she asked.

"If you can bring me some shining flour," the baker said.

So on to the mill went the princess where she asked, "Please Miller can you grind me some shining flour?"

"If you will bring me some shining grain," said the Miller.

So on to the threshing barn went the princess where she asked, "Please Thresher, will you thresh me some shining grain" If you will bring me a shining sheaf, the thresher told her.

So on to the field went the princess, where she found the reaper and asked, "Please reaper will you give me a shining sheaf?"

"If you will sow me some shining seed," said the Reaper. So on to the farm went the princess where she found the sower and asked, "Please, Sower, will you sow me some shining seed?"

The Sower was standing beside a branching oak tree listening to the sweet song of a bird. "Surely bird's song is a gift," said the sower. "Then let the sowing be a gift, too."

And as he sowed, he thought, "Why do I feel so happy?"

The young wheat sprang up, grew green and tall, and then turned golden and ready for harvest.

The princess went to the reaper and showed him the golden wheat. "It was a gift from the sower, she said.

"Then let the reaping be a gift, too", said the reaper, and as he reaped a shining sheaf, he thought, "Why do I feel so happy?"

"The princess took the shining sheaf to the thresher. "It was a gift from the reaper," she said.

"Then let the threshing be a gift, too." And as he threshed the shining grain he thought, "Why do I feel so happy?"

The princess took the shining grain to the miller. "It was a gift from the thresher," she said.

"Then let the milling be a gift, too." As he ground the shining flour he thought, "Why do I feel so happy?"

The princess took the shining flour to the baker. "It was a gift from the miller," she said.

"Then let the baking be a gift, too." And as he mixed it and kneaded it and shaped it and put it in to bake, he thought, "Why do I feel so happy?"

When the shining loaf came out of the oven, with its delicious smell filling the air, the princess went to the wise woman and together they took it to the king.

"Here, father, eat some of this golden bread. It is a gift form the people of your kingdom", said the princess. When the King had eaten but three crumbs, he was no longer sick, but well and strong. And remembering always the gift from the people of his kingdom he ruled wisely to the end of his days.

# The Elves and the Shoemaker (Ages 4-7)

## The Brothers Grimm
*(Steadfastness, Humility, Faith)*

There was once a shoemaker, who worked very hard and was very honest: but still he could not earn enough to live upon; and at last all he had in the world was gone, save just leather enough to make one pair of shoes.

Then he cut his leather out, all ready to make up the next day, meaning to rise early in the morning to his work. His conscience was clear and his heart light amidst all his troubles; so he went peaceably to bed, left all his cares to Heaven, and soon fell asleep. In the morning after he had said his prayers, he sat himself down to his work; when, to his great wonder, there stood the shoes all ready made, upon the table. The good man knew not what to say or think at such an odd thing happening. He looked at the workmanship; there was not one false stitch in the whole job; all was so neat and true, that it was quite a masterpiece.

The same day a customer came in, and the shoes suited him so well that he willingly paid a price higher than usual for them; and the poor shoemaker, with the money, bought leather enough to make two pairs more. In the evening he cut out the work, and went to bed early, that he might get up and begin betimes next day; but he was saved all the trouble, for when he got up in the morning the work was done ready to his hand. Soon in came buyers, who paid him handsomely for his goods, so that he bought leather enough for four pair more. He cut out the work again overnight and found it done in the morning, as before; and so it went on for some time: what was got ready in the evening was always done by daybreak, and the good man soon became thriving and well off again.

One evening, about Christmas-time, as he and his wife were sitting over the fire chatting together, he said to her, "I should like to sit up and watch tonight, that we may see who it is that comes and does my work for me." The wife liked the thought; so they left a light burning, and hid themselves in a corner of the room, behind a curtain that was hung up there, and watched what would happen.

As soon as it was midnight, there came in two little naked dwarfs; and they sat themselves upon the shoemaker's bench, took up all the work that was cut out, and began to ply with their little fingers, stitching and rapping and tapping away at such a rate, that the shoemaker was all wonder, and could not take his eyes off them. And on they went, till the job was quite done, and the shoes stood ready for use upon the table. This was long before daybreak, and then they bustled away as quick as lightning.

The next day the wife said to the shoemaker. "These little men have made us rich, and we ought to be thankful to them, and do them a good turn if we can. I am quite sorry to see them run about as they do; and indeed it is not very decent, for they have nothing upon their backs to keep off the cold. I'll tell you what, I will make each of them a shirt, and a coat and waistcoat, and a pair of pantaloons into the bargain; and do you make each of them a little pair of shoes."

The husband agreed and that evening when they had everything ready they laid out the presents on the table and hid themselves to see how the little men would behave.

At midnight they came skipping in and were about to set to work. But instead of the leather ready cut out, they found charming little clothes.

At first they were surprised, then delighted. With the greatest speed they put on and smoothed down the pretty clothes singing:

"Now we're boys so fine and neat, why cobble more for other's feet?" Then they hopped and danced about, and leapt over chairs and tables and out the door. Henceforward they came back no more, but the shoemaker and his wife fared well as long as they lived, and had good luck in all their undertakings.

# The Three Brothers (Ages 4-7)

## A Tale from the Brothers Grimm

*(Generosity, Kindness, Overcoming)*

Once upon a time, where did it happen? When did it happen? There was a man who had three sons, the youngest of whom was called Simpleton. He was despised, mocked, and sneered at on every occasion.

It happened that the eldest wanted to go into the forest to cut wood. His mother gave him a beautiful sweet cake and a bottle of wine in order that he might not suffer from hunger or thirst.

When he entered the forest he met a little grey-haired old man who bade him good day, and said: "Do give me a piece of cake out of your pocket, and let me have a draught of your wine; I am so hungry and thirsty." But the clever son answered: "If I give you my cake and wine, I shall have none for myself; be off with you," and he left the little man standing and went on.

But when he began to hew down a tree, it was not long before he made a false stroke, and the axe cut him in the arm, so that he had to go home and have it bound up.

After this the second son went into the forest to cut wood. His mother gave him, like the eldest, a cake and a bottle of wine. The little old grey man met him, and asked him for a piece of cake and a drink of wine. But the second son, too, said sensibly enough: "What I give you will be taken away from myself; be off!" and he left the little man standing and went on. His punishment, however, was not delayed; when he had made a few blows at the tree he struck himself in the leg, so that he had to be carried home.

Then Simpleton said: "Father, do let me go and cut wood." The father answered: "Your brothers have hurt themselves with it, leave it alone, you do not understand anything about it." But Simpleton begged so long that at last his father said: "Just go then, you will get wiser by hurting yourself." His mother gave him a cake made with water and baked in the cinders, and with it a bottle of sour beer.

When he came to the forest the little old grey man met him and said: "Give me a piece of your cake and a drink out of your bottle; I am so hungry and thirsty." Simpleton answered: "I have only cinder-cake and sour beer. If that pleases you, we will sit down and eat." So they sat down, and when Simpleton pulled out his cinder-cake, it was a fine sweet cake, and the sour beer had become good wine. So they ate and drank, and after that the little man said: "Since you have a good heart, and are willing to divide what you have, I will give you good luck. There stands an old tree, cut it down, and you will find something at the roots." Then the little man took leave of him.

Simpleton went and cut down the tree, and when it fell there was a goose sitting in the roots with feathers of pure gold. He lifted her up, and taking her with him, went to an inn where he thought he would stay the night. Now the host had three daughters, who saw the goose and were curious to know what such a wonderful bird might be, and would have liked to have one of its golden feathers.

The eldest thought: "I shall soon find an opportunity of pulling out a feather." As soon as Simpleton had gone out she seized the goose by the wing, but her finger and hand remained sticking fast to it.

The second came soon afterwards, thinking only of how she might get a feather for herself, but she had scarcely touched her sister then she was held fast.

At last the third also came with the same intent, and the others screamed at her: "Keep away; for goodness' sake keep away!" But she did not understand why she was to keep away. "The others are there," she thought, "I may as well be there too," and ran to them; but as soon as she had touched her sister, she remained sticking fast to her. So they had to spend the night with the goose.

The next morning Simpleton took the goose under his arm and set out, without troubling himself about the three girls who were hanging on to it. They were obliged to run after him continually, now left, now right, wherever his legs took him.

In the middle of the fields a parson met them, and when he saw the procession he said: "For shame, you good-for-nothing girls! Why are you running across the fields after this young man? Is that seemly?" Just then he took the youngest by the hand in order to pull her away, but as soon as he touched her he was stuck fast, and was obliged to run behind.

Before long the sexton came by and saw his master, the parson, running behind three girls. He was astonished at this and called out: "Hi! Your reverence, whither away so quickly? Do not forget that we have a christening today!" and running after him he took him by the sleeve, but was held fast to it.

While the five were trotting one behind the other, two laborers came with their hoes from the fields; the parson called out to them and begged that they would set him and the sexton free. But they had scarcely touched the sexton when they were held fast, and now there were seven of them running behind Simpleton and the goose.

Soon afterwards they came to a city, where a king ruled who had a daughter who was so serious that no one could make her laugh. So he had put forth a decree that whosoever should be able to make her laugh should marry her. When Simpleton heard this, he went with his goose and all her train before the king's daughter, and as soon as she saw the seven people running on and on, one behind the other, she began to laugh quite loudly, as if she would never stop. Simpleton asked to have her for his wife; but the king did not like the son-in-law, and made all manner of excuses.

At last he said that Simpleton must find a man who could drink a cellar full of wine. Simpleton thought of the little grey man, who could certainly help him. He went into the forest, and in the same place where he had felled the tree, he saw a man sitting, who had a very sorrowful face. Simpleton asked him what he was taking to heart so sorely, and he answered: "I have such a great thirst and cannot quench it; cold water I cannot stand, a barrel of wine I have just emptied, but that to me is like a drop on a hot stone!" "There, I can help you," said Simpleton, "just come with me and you shall be satisfied."

He led him into the king's cellar, and the man bent over the huge barrels, and drank and drank till his loins hurt, and before the day was out he had emptied all the barrels. Simpleton asked once more for his bride, but the king was vexed that such an ugly fellow, whom everyone called Simpleton, should take away his daughter, and he made a new condition; he must first find a man who could eat a whole mountain of bread. Simpleton did not think long, but went straight into the forest, where in the same place where he had found the first man another man sat who was making an awful face, and saying: "I have eaten a whole oven full of rolls, but what good is that when one has such a hunger as I? My stomach remains empty."

At this Simpleton was glad, and said: "Get up and come with me; you shall eat yourself full." He led him to the king's palace where all the flour in the whole Kingdom was collected, and from it he caused a huge mountain of bread to be baked. The man from the forest stood before it, began to eat, and by the end of one day the whole mountain had vanished. Then Simpleton for the third time asked for his bride; but the king again sought a way out, and ordered a ship that could sail on land and on water. "As soon as you come sailing back in it," said he, "you shall have my daughter for wife."

Simpleton went straight into the forest, and there sat the little grey man to whom he had given his cake. When he heard what Simpleton wanted, he said: "Since you have given me to eat and to drink, I will give you the ship; and I do all this because you once were kind to me." Then he gave him the ship that could sail on land and water, and when the king saw that, he could no longer prevent him from having his daughter. The wedding was celebrated, and after the king's death, Simpleton inherited his kingdom and lived for a long time contentedly with his wife.

# Fairy Tale Suggestions by Age

There are SO many other wonderful Fairy/Wonder Tales. Most of the ones on the list below can be found in *The Complete Grimm's Fairy Tales*, by Pantheon Press. I recommend this translation for its attention to artistic expression, clarity, and faithfulness to the original German collection. The stories are grouped by age-appropriateness. Any story in a section that is a younger age than the age of your children or students can also be told.

**Three-Year-Olds & Young Fours**
> Sweet Porridge (Grimm)
> Goldilocks and the Three Bears (Voland)
> Little Tuppens
> The Louse and the Flea (Grimm)
> The Turnip (Russian)
> The Mitten (Russian)
> Little Madam (Spindthrift)
> The Gingerbread Man
> The Runaway Pancake
> The Johnny Cake (English)
> The Hungry Cat (Norwegian)

**Four-Year-Olds & Young Fives**
> Mashenka & the Bear (Russian)
> Cat & Mouse in Partnership (Grimm)
> The Pancake Mill
> The Straw, the Coal, & the Bean (Grimm)
> The House That Jack Built
> Old Woman & Her Pig
> The Golden Key (Grimm)
> Mary Winecap
> The Elves & the Shoemaker (Grimm)
> The Donkey (Grimm)
> The Billy Goats Gruff (Norwegian)
> Wolf & the Seven Kids (Grimm)
> The Three Little Pigs (English)

**Five-Year-Olds & Young Sixes**

Star Money (Grimm)

The Man Who Tried to Keep House

Little Red Cap (Grimm)

The Poor Miller's Boy & the Cat (Grimm)

Bremen Town Musicians (Grimm)

Tom Tit Tot (English)

The Fisherman & His Wife (Grimm)

Hut in the Forest (Grimm)

King Thrushbeard (Grimm)

Queen Bee (Grimm)

Per, Paul & Espen Askelad (Norwegian)

Little Briar Rose (Grimm)

How Jack Went to Seek His Fortune

The Golden Goose

Cinderella (Grimm)

Cap 'O Rushes

Well of the World's End (English)

**Six- & Seven-Year-Olds**

Mary's Child (Grimm)

Thumbling (Grimm)

Water of Life (Grimm)

The Wishing Table (Grimm)

Jack and the Beanstalk (Grimm)

The Three Little Men in the Woods

Snow White & Rose Red (Grimm)

Little Snow White (Grimm)

Jorinda and Joringel (Grimm)

Hansel and Gretel (Grimm)

Rapunzel (Grimm)

The Golden Bird (Grimm)

The White Snake (Grimm)

The Two Brothers (Grimm)

The Six Swans (Grimm)

## Nature Stories (ages 5-7)

Nature stories take the child outside into the hidden places in the forest and meadow where animals live. These delightful stories were written by Jacob Streit and is now out of print and in the public domain. These tales capture the essence of each animal in its natural setting. Two animals meet and in their conversation, their unique characteristics are revealed. Here are three for you to enjoy. Why not make up your own using these stories as a model?

# The Fish and the Fresh Water Clam

Deep in the depths of a pond a fish swam about between the algae and water plants. Often it stayed in the same place for great lengths of time, its fins fanning gently. Nearby a clam pushed its way across the bottom. In the dim light, it looked as if a stone was moving. The fish glided near, looked at the hard-shelled clam from all sides, and couldn't understand how a stone could take a walk! It had not seen the clams little foot which reached out and groped about underneath the shell. With this foot the clam pushed itself forward. Then the fish saw a small opening on one side. He swam near to look in. The little crack closed!

"Aha!" thought the fish, "somebody lives there, and he is afraid of me; I will call to him!" He swam right up to the clam and said," Hey you in there, come out! I won't bite you!" From inside the shell came a soft mumbling.

"What shall I do out there? I like it better in here!" "Oh, come out," said the fish. "I want to see your beautiful tail fin!" "I don't have a tail fin," the clam mumbled. The fish was insistent. He wanted so badly to coax the strange creature out of his shell! "Oh, do come out! Then you may enjoy my glittering scales!" "I have no eyes," said the clam. This was hard to understand indeed. No eyes! Anxiously the fish swam about the clam. "Am I to believe that you have no tail, no scales, no eyes…you mean you have your two shells only filled with skin?"

"I have the waterdream," said the clam softly, "and I will not trade it for your scales or your tail." "Oh, tell me about it then," begged the fish. The clam replied, "I cannot tell about it. Each day I paint the dream upon my shell walls. I can let you glimpse them, but then leave me in peace!" Cautiously the clam opened his shell, and the fish saw strange and wonderful colours glimmering – red, green, blue, violet. It was a mysterious, brilliant glow. "Oh, like the rainbow in the waterfall," said the fish, but the gates were already closing as quietly as they had opened. The clam lay lightly upon his side and remained motionless. But very close by the fish could sense with its delicate fins how the water flowed in and out of the clam's waterdream. For a long time he stayed close to the shell, which on the outside was sandy-grey in colour, but inside hid the greatest wonder he had ever seen.

# The Squirrel and the Toad

Brown scales were falling through the branches of the fir tree. For a moment all was silent' then again more scales rained from above and a crunching sound could be heard. Finally a cone fell to the ground; but it was no longer a cone –it was only a stubble of what once had been one! That's all the squirrel ever leaves.

It was already late in the year; the beech and hickory nuts were ripe. The squirrel had already buried many in his cellars between the roots, but they were not enough yet for winter. Hardly had he cast the cone stubble to the ground, when he jumped from the spruce to a great beech, in a graceful, arched leap. So fast he went, that he seemed to fly from branch to branch, from limb to trunk! In the air he waved his tail like a flag, and all at once he was on the ground where the nuts were more abundant than stones. Quickly he sat up—looking, listening for hawk or fox, and then he was digging and scraping with his little forepaws amongst the leaves and roots, which were like snakes winding their way into the earth. Earth and leaves rustled and flew about as if caught in a whirlwind. With quick work of his paws and teeth, the nuts were packed in the cellars, and just as quickly the doors were closed.

At the edge of the woods stood an old, gnarled bush. It was a perfect place for hiding nuts, except that a big, brown toad lived in the hole under the largest root! He had not moved all day – not even blinked. He just sat there brooding and glowering with his round, glassy eyes, an ugly, frightful sight. The squirrel, with his furry tail flailing, darted up to the bush. Seeing the toad, he stopped and began to chatter and scold loudly. The toad only sat and stared. Finally he said, "This is my place; I won't move, except at night, when you're too frightened to leave your nest! Be on your way, you jittery, hairy tree-jumper!"

The squirrel, which meanwhile had sat up on his hind legs, laughed by wiggling his ears. He flicked his tail and said, "You don't have to guard my nuts for me, they're safe without you!" In three leaps and whisk of his tail he was on the top-most branch of the beech.

# The Lizard and the Snail

Over a heap of stones a snail crept at his usual pace. His "horns" stretched out to feel his way, and satisfied him that all was safe. All at once a lizard slipped out of a hole and in passing touched one of his feelers. Frightened, the snail quickly withdrew all four, saying to himself, "What kind of lightning was that?" Ssh…the lizard sat above him on a stone looking down upon him with glittering, glassy eyes. After a time, the snail sent out his feelers again. He saw his neighbor and said, "Were you the streak of lightning that struck my feeler? Can't you be more careful when snails are taking a leisurely crawl?" The lizard had sunned himself many a day on this rock, and saw the snail for the first time. He said: "Why do you creep about and besmirch my stones with slime?" "Where I am, there my house is?" answered the snail. "Look, on my back. I always carry it with me. I don't see *your* house! The stones here do not grow upon your back!"

The lizard was angry at the snail's words, and thought: "I will show this creeper what speed is!" Happily he spoke, "See snail, over there is my hole. I can crawl much faster than you! I can go in and out a hundred times before you even go once! Just look?" The lizard darted in and out so fast that the snail's eyes began to see spots. "Stop," cried the snail. "I'm dizzy!" The lizard's eyes flashed. After the snail had thought for a good long time, he said, "Listen, lizard, I can slip into your hole 100 times more slowly than you can. That is the greater art! Watch!"

Already his feelers began to shrink. In amazement the lizard watched how gradually the whole snail disappeared into his house. But he did not come out again! Instead, he remained where he was, glued to the stone. The lizard left him and crawled to the warmest spot on the stone and blinked into the sun, which burned upon the snail's roof. All at once the snail rolled into the shade below the rock pile. Toward evening, when a few raindrops fell, the lizard glided back into his hole. Then the snail finally came out again. As the rain fell on him, he mused, "It is good that the cloud mother shakes the clouds and lets the rain fall! Then all the nervous, hurried jumpers and wigglers disappear into their holes, and peaceful people may crawl about at a leisurely pace."

# Activities for Children Age 5 and up

## The Wild Horsey

Gallop around the house or the classroom in a rhythmical manner chanting this:

*Follow me; I'm the wild horsey,*
*Follow me; my mane is on fire*
*Follow me; I'm the wild horsey*
*Follow me; I'm a fleet-footed flyer, follow me!*

Repeat as often as you like. You can also chant this while skipping, but galloping is more fun, as it fits the image. Have one child lead, and then, take turns having others take the lead as the children gallop around the classroom or outside. Work on refining a rhythmical gallop in time with the song while the hands hold the reins, moving them forward and back at chest level in rhythm.

## The Little Tea Pot

Stand facing your child. As you sing the song, do the actions together.

| Sing... | Action... |
|---|---|
| "I'm a little teapot, short and stout." | Keep feet apart, hands at sides. |
| "Here is my handle" | Put right hand on right hip. |
| "Here is my spout." | Suggest a spout by making an "S" curve with your left arm on the left side of body. |
| "When I get all steamed up I do shout." ("Go ahead and have them shout!") | Hold position, bounce on the balls of your feet. |
| "Tip me over, pour me out!" | Bend over to the left and pour out tea. |

## Pitty Patty Polt

Tell a short story about a young colt who is old enough to have a pair of shoes! Horseshoes, that is. For example, "Once there were two friends who lived next door to one another. One day, they were invited to come to the farmhouse at the end of the lane to see the young colt that was ready for his first pair of shoes." Describe the event explaining why the colt needs "horse shoes." Once you have finished the story, then do the action and accompanying verse.

| Verse to chant... | Accompanying action... |
|---|---|
| "Pitty Patty Polt" | Lift your left leg in front of the right and strike the sole of the left foot with the right hand in rhythm three times, once on each word. |
| "Shoe the wild colt" | Switch sides; lift right leg in front of the left. Strike the right foot with the left hand again in rhythm to the words. |
| "Here a nail" | Lift your left leg BEHIND your right and strike the sole of the left foot with the right hand in rhythm with each word. |
| "There a nail" | Repeat the above with the right leg BEHIND your left. |
| "Pitty Patty Polt" | This time, bring the left foot in front of the right and slap the sole with your right hand once on the word "Pitty." Jump to the other foot, and bring the right foot in front of the left and slap the sole with your left hand on "Patty." Then jump back to the other foot and hit your left foot with your right hand in front of your right leg while saying "Polt." You have to jump fast from foot to foot to make this work. |

You can repeat it several times, attempting to go faster each time. This is a great developmental movement exercise! I am not an expert on developmental movement, but have studied it a bit, as I have observed that some children today are less facile in their movements. Crossing the body with hands or feet movements, and other dexterity building movements have been shown to stimulate the brain, in particular the interaction between the left and right sides of the brain. Working with balance is also important for the young child and this "movement game" does all of these things. Best of all, children love it.

## Rhythm Activity Game: Brave and True

Step and stomp to the rhythm of short, short, long in a circle or around the classroom on the perimeter speaking the words with emphasis on the "long" in the pattern "short, short, **long**"

Brave and **true** (two short steps on "Brave and" followed by a stomp on "true")

will I **be** (same stepping pattern on this and remaining lines as above)

Each kind **word**

sets me **free**

Each good **deed**

makes me **strong**

I will **fight**

for the **right**

I will **con-**

quer the **wrong**.

# The Story of My Sons' Day

When my two youngest sons were about the ages of 3 and 6, I would sometimes end the day by telling them the story of two brothers who were the same age as they were and lived in a similar house in a similar landscape. Of course they had different names. I would tell the boys the story of their day through the eyes of these two characters. Some of the little details were different, but I found that if I strayed off the path too far, my boys would correct me and tell me I had made a mistake and then explain what had really happened. They loved these stories, and it gave me a needed break from telling a classic tale.

Once, I thought I would prepare them for the next day by telling them the story of the other two boys and their adventure at the zoo. I wanted my boys to have an idea in story form of what the next day would hold for them. I began as usual, but as soon as I spoke about the trip to the zoo, my boys both exclaimed, "You can't tell us that story; they haven't done it yet!"

Then I recognized and understood more deeply the mystery we engaged in together each evening. The recalling of the day in such a story form nurtured each of us on a deep and profound level. They understood this so deeply that they could not allow the form to change. Of course, they were right; those two boys had not gone to the zoo yet so how could I tell that story! I laughed and told the right story then, which was the story of what they had just experienced THAT day! The memory of that time we shared together still warms my heart today.

# CHAPTER 9

## Communicating with Children

### Use Commands instead of Questions

What did you do today?

Nothing.

What did you learn in school today?

Nothing.

What would you like for dinner?

I don't know.

What clothes will you wear to school today?

I don't know.

Why is it so hard to engage children in conversation via questions? Aren't we just showing our loving interest in what they are doing or where they are going or how they are feeling?

Having been a parent who asked each of her four children at least 10 questions a day (do the math…that's 14,600 questions a year), I should know! Try counting the questions you ask per hour, per day, per week. You may be surprised like I was. No wonder they tune us out!

Let's look at what happens when a question is asked. When we ask a question it wakes the child up from his or her inner musing on life. It is a bit of a shock or a jolt. We've all experienced getting home from work or shopping and the questions come: "Where have you been? What have you been doing? How was the traffic? Who did you work with today? How's that project you've been working on going?" We want to share and communicate, but these questions are somehow jarring and just a bit annoying. They are too demanding in a moment that needs softness. It's no one's fault. It's just human nature.

How can we elicit more of a response from our children, from our students? How can we get a conversation or a discussion started? Try rephrasing the question as a command. A gentle command is less jarring. It allows the children to relax and gives space for any kind of response that comes to mind. It is non-specific. For example, instead of, "What did you do today?" or "How was your day?" try, "Tell me about your day." In the classroom, try using the command, too. Instead of saying, "Who can tell me about such-and-such?", try presenting it as, "Tell me what impressed you most about what we learned yesterday." It will lead you into a conversation that reveals what the students are most interested in or have understood or, perhaps, what they still need more information about. The command is open, shows we are interested and willing to hear whatever the child is willing to tell us. We have no expectations with a command. Therefore, it is less jarring. The children relax. They can say whatever they remember, whatever comes to mind. Anything goes. A listening space opens and can be spoken into more easily. "Tell me" lets each of us relax, the parent and the child, the father and the teenage, the teacher and the students. Children more easily begin to talk about things. Maybe not about what happened so much as what they felt. It leaves them much freer and helps both parties to create a calmer space together. Try it! You will be amazed at the difference in the level of communication.

It is hard to hold back the questions that will arise as the child speaks. Rather than ask a clarifying question, just insert another command. "Oh, tell me more about that." Or, "That's interesting, tell me more." Refrain from any negative or corrective comments. Practice deep listening. You will find yourself enjoying listening and you will hear things beneath the surface that will help you understand your children or your students. We parents and educators tend to jump to judgments quickly and ask too many questions. Judgments and questions make children and teens nervous and uncomfortable. The command eliminates the concept of a "right answer" and leads more deeply into an expression of the underlying ideas, thus expanding the points of view.

Try it on your partner and see how different a command feels than being asked a question. "How was your day?" may elicit a response of "OK." But if we say, "Tell me about your day," we may hear a door open slowly with a few creaks and groans that lead us into a conversation we have been longing to engage in with our spouse.

Questions put us all on the spot. They carry an innate tension. They elicit an inner conversation.

"Why is she asking me that?"
"Did the teacher call her?"
"Am I not doing well in school?"

Doubts flood the psyche.
" What is the answer they want to hear?"
"Am I in trouble?"

On the other hand, commands open the door to possibility.

Another tack is to tell your child something about YOUR day that you enjoyed or found challenging and worthwhile. When you have finished you may hear a question or two OR you may hear something about their day as a part of a casual conversation you are now having together. These are priceless moments not to be missed. Using commands and sharing your life a bit with your child or your students each day will create a habit of communication. This is especially helpful as it sets the stage for having more complex conversations as your children or students mature. Shared stories and communication then become a natural part of your shared lives.

By reducing the number of questions you ask your children about what they want to eat or do, or where they want to go, you help them to relax and trust your decision-making. You are their example, after all, of what it means to be human, so experiencing you being in charge is comforting and reassuring to your children. They want to know who's in charge. If you are not, then they *will* step up, and this is stressful for both of you.

Here's an idea about where to start this process. Spend a day paying attention to your normal conversations with your children or students. Take notes throughout the day about the questions, answers, and other remarks that pass between you. At the end of the day, read through your notes and notice where you could have used a command rather than a question. Jot down two or three commands that you could use to replace the questions next time around. Carry a little notebook around and look at it throughout the day to remind you to try a command before asking a question. Changing conversational habits is challenging, so start slowly. I predict that you'll enjoy the results.

## Just Say No!

Why is it so hard to say "no" to a child? I've asked myself this question many times. As a parent I, too, found it hard to just say NO. Yet, there it is, in its utter simplicity! A word that ends the conversation about acquisitions, bedtime arrangements, and countless other requests that issue forth from the mouths of babes! The arguments follow on…. Yet there is hope!

We would be shocked today if there were no fences around the school playground. The fence is a boundary. It encloses the space in which the children play. It creates a defined space. Everyone knows the boundary; there is no room for argument. It's physical. We can see it, feel it, and bump up against it. It eliminates the need for clear directions to the children about where to play. It's an agreement made without conflict or conversation.

The child can relax and create freely and safely within the boundary. The teacher can relax and allow the child the freedom to explore within the boundary. The parent at the park can allow the child freedom to play there in the fenced playground. The fenced backyard is another boundary. We accept and appreciate these boundaries for our children. How can we construct other kinds of boundaries for our children that will provide the same benefits of safety and freedom?

As children grow older, boundaries expand. This experience not only allows them more freedom, but also gives them more responsibility. Children want to be responsible, and they truly do (eventually) appreciate that privileges were withheld until they were ready to take on the new responsibilities. They actually feel safer when they know their parents are clear about boundaries. Naturally, they will test the boundaries! That's part of growing up! How boring to have nothing to bump up against and test your mettle upon! How wonderful to argue and even whine, and still the boundaries hold firmly!

Young children from birth to age seven are developing their will. Make no mistake, they WILL run the household unless the parents are prepared to tame that will with clear guidelines and a firm commitment. Taming the will means giving it direction through your firm and loving guidance.

The daily structure you create in the life of your child allows the child to relax, knowing what is coming next and trusting that the parent is in charge. The guidelines given by the parent are like the path a fence takes around the life of the child. The fence is the parent's commitment to creating a safe boundary for the child. Children whose wills have been put to good use in meaningful work around the house and garden will have a powerful tool at their disposal throughout life. Not only will they learn how to do many practical tasks, but, more importantly, they will have experienced the satisfaction of accomplishment and follow-through on a project. The will, once tamed, becomes a powerful tool for the child's entire life.

## The Power of a Child's Will

Advertisers know the power of the young child's will. They target their advertising at children, trusting the child will become so determined to have the "thing" that she *will* continue to exercise her powerful will until she has worn down the parent. Today, we see ads wherein the parents ask the child to choose the color of the new car. Advertisers count on the will of children to sell the parents everything from soup to nuts… squishy toys to high tech cars.

Advertisers also seem to want children to skip over as much of childhood as possible and become teenagers. Children's clothes today are modeled after teens clothing. The level of sophistication of clothing does impact the child. The child becomes self-conscious about how she looks at 4 years old! Isn't it enough to go through this stage at adolescence without creating a continuous culture of self-absorption from age 3 and 4 to age 16? It is not the child's fault. The child is innocent. Never before has there been such an assault on childhood. Storytelling has an additional role today. It is an antidote to the assault on childhood. It is a powerful medium that is focused on nurturing the individual at a specific age and stage of development and fulfills the child's need to make sense of the world using her/his individual imagination.

## My Parenting Experience – The Childhood Years

*Once upon a time…*

Where did it happen? Where did it not happen?

When did it happen? When did it not happen?

For many years, these words carried my children and me into a shared space of imaginative wonder. As I spoke these words, a feeling of calm enveloped us. My breathing slowed and deepened as I relaxed. Together, my children and I smiled at one another in expectation. Speaking this invocation aloud gave me a moment to relax, and to anticipate the shared world we were now entering. My body would soften as my heart opened. Together, we set forth on a journey into the world of story.

As I lit the candle on the table beside their twin beds, their eyes shone with anticipation. Their bodies relaxed in the ease and warmth of our shared connection. The sense of expectation was palpable. The journey into story opened a co-creative space between us. Their focused attention inspired my telling, and my telling aroused their questions and ideas making the telling richer. Over the years, this evening ritual served as an inspiration for us as a family. Through this active, subtle, and mutual engagement, we grew closer as we shared the familiar, yet, ever new, world of story.

In the early days of telling stories, I created this bedtime routine for them in order to make the bedtime more relaxed and less stressful for all of us. Then, I began to look forward to bedtime! Our nightly ritual nourished me, too. As they grew from little children into bigger children, and eye contact and physical contact became less frequent between us during the day, this evening ritual space offered a haven for us to reconnect. It was a place we knew well, a place where the world was held at bay for a while and we could become vulnerable again together. This time of sharing at days end served us well through all the years of childhood and into adolescence.

# CHAPTER 10

## The 6-Year Change

*A sailor went to sea, sea, sea,*
*To see what he could see, see, see,*
*But all that he could see, see, see,*
*Was the bottom of the deep blue sea, sea, sea!*

I learned the following action sequence to this classic children's verse from Jaimen MacMillan, at a Spatial Dynamics Training Course. It is printed here with the kind permission of Jaimen MacMillan.

| Words | Actions |
|---|---|
| A sailor went to sea, sea, sea | Slap your thighs on "a"; <br> Clap your hands on "sai-"; <br> Clap partner's right hand with your right hand on "-lor"; <br> Clap your hands on "went"; <br> Clap partner's left hand with your left hand on "to"; <br> Salute with right hand to forehead lightly 3 times on <br> "sea, sea, sea." |
| To see what he could see, see, see | Repeat above actions in same rhythm. |
| But all that he could see, see, see | Repeat above actions in same rhythm. |
| Was the bottom of the deep blue, sea, sea, sea | Repeat above actions in same rhythm. |

| Words | Actions |
|---|---|
| A sailor went to sea, clap, knee | Slap your thighs on "a"; Clap your hands on "sai-"; Clap partner's right hand with your right hand on "-lor"; Clap your hands on "went"; Clap partner's left hand with your left hand on "to"; Salute with right hand to forehead lightly on "sea"; Clap hands on "clap"; Slap your thighs on "knee" |
| To see what he could see, clap, knee | Repeat above actions in same rhythm. |
| But all that he could see, clap, knee | Repeat above actions in same rhythm. |
| Was the bottom of the deep blue sea, clap, knee | Repeat above actions in same rhythm. |

## Characteristics of the Child at 6 Years Old

"Mom, Dad, my tooth fell out! Look at the hole! Oh no, it's bleeding! Help! It hurts!!!" You walk into the bathroom and there is blood in the sink, on the floor, on his fingers, and he spits at you, spraying you with more blood! You try to calm him and explain that this is normal, even exciting. It means he's growing up. But, he is inconsolable. It really is painful and he doesn't want to go to school today. You get an ice pack and set him down with a pillow behind his head on the couch.

Kevin is a sensitive boy, tall for his age, and very thoughtful. When he speaks, he is focused and looks slightly downward. He has a tall, lanky body and walks with a bit of a shuffle. His favorite color is dark blue. In fact, he wears his favorite navy blue sweatshirt with the hood everyday to school. You have already noticed how observant he is, even though he is reticent to speak about his observations. He holds his tooth wistfully in the palm of his hand. He wants to stay home from school today. He doesn't want to be the center of attention.

At the ages of six and seven, children lose their "baby" teeth. Throughout first and second grade, the classroom is regularly disrupted by a tooth falling out! Everyone is interested. Sometimes it is painful; sometimes it is humorous. Always it is exciting. Sometimes they bleed. Sometimes they fall on the desk or the floor without any warning! I always had a count on the board of the total teeth lost over the course of the first grade year. It was an exciting moment for each child, a fascinating shared group experience.

Traditionally, the changing of the teeth heralded the moment when the child was ready to become more independent and head off to school. The coming of the permanent teeth was seen as an indication that the body had completed the first phase of the child's development. The inner forces that had been needed to complete this initial phase were now available to be used for the purpose of education. Children spend the first six years mastering the physical body. But now there are forces calling them to use what they've learned to develop other aspects of the self, including intellectual development.

The six-year change can be uncomfortable for some children. As the dreaminess of early childhood fades, they often feel a longing to return to an earlier phase of childhood. If the child has a younger sibling who is still not in school, the older child may feel jealous of the younger brother or sister. Like all transitions, this one has its ups and downs.

As the intellect develops, children are challenged to take on the tasks of learning to read, write, and practice arithmetic. Some may look back with a longing to return to the time before school when life was simpler and all they did was play! Usually, this is a short-lived experience. A good story can go a long way toward helping with the adjustment.

At this stage, children begin to notice their physical and behavioral differences. They become interested in the ways boys and girls are different. They often have questions about physical differences and can even become self-conscious about asking them. This period of self-consciousness is temporary. Children at six often want to know about where they came from. There can be an interest in the sexual organs. This is normal and should be treated objectively. One way to get to the bottom of their questions is to ask them to tell you more about what they mean. Use a simple command, for example. "Oh, I see; tell me more about what you mean." As adults, we tend to make too many assumptions about what they mean. When we offer the command, we give them permission to say whatever is on their mind. They are no longer searching for an answer to a specific question. In this gentler approach, we help them to get to the bottom of whatever is bothering them and what they are truly wondering.

Children at this age may realize that the tooth fairy and Santa are not "real," but they choose to believe. Before this change, a belief was not something conscious, now it is becoming more conscious. This stage can also bring moments that seem like a mini-adolescence. Temper tantrums and fits of crying are common. Prior to the six-year change, children live in a world of oneness; now, as they begin to feel more separate from the world, they are able to stand outside of their experience and look in on it. The child feels a need to be seen in a new way but doesn't yet know what that new way is. This change can be uncomfortable for a time until they move into a more relaxed and self-confident stage at the age of seven. In play, this age group will often act out family events.

They need more responsibilities around the house, and, if given the opportunity, will take on a surprising number of tasks. Projects inspire them and allow them to exercise their new awareness and abilities. Building projects, cooking projects, craft projects, learning to finger knit, learning to knit with knitting needles, and art projects offer opportunities for self-expression through the exploration of traditional handcrafts. Children feel more competent overall if they have the opportunity to learn to make practical items, to create works of art, and to cook.

While the 6-year change can have its ups and downs, it is an exciting time of exploration and dynamic change. Take a week to tell the same Wonder Tale or Fairy Tale every night or every day in the classroom. Have your child help retell the story along with you. In the classroom, use the suggestions in Chapter 2 for reviewing the story each day over the course of a week.

## Stories for the 6-Year-Old

Stories appropriate for the 6-Year Change include Fairy/Wonder Tales, Folk Tales, and Object Stories. Here are a few to get you started:

**The Frog and the Pail of Cream** is a Russian folk tale of courage and not giving up. It is pithy and humorous and beloved by all ages.

**NOTE:** before you tell this story be sure your child or your students know what a milkmaid is and what a pail of cream is. Create a pre-story about whatever is in the story that may not be familiar to your children or students. This is better than explaining it afterwards or having a hand shoot up with a question during the story that then breaks the mood and takes you out of the story and into a discussion.

Pre-story example for "*The Frog and the Pail of Cream*"

*"Once when I was your age, I visited my grandmother's farm in Ohio. I learned that the milk from the cow is thick and creamy. After the cows are milked, the milk is left to cool. As it cools, the cream rises to the top and becomes thick and sometimes sticky. When the cream is skimmed off the top of the milk and whipped with a spoon it congeals and becomes stiff. Today, we call it whipped cream or whipping cream. My grandmother also had a well that was near the house. It was a deep hole in the ground lined with stones and full of water that had risen up from the ground to fill the stone well. The water from the well was cool and delicious."*

Or you could begin by saying,

*"Who can tell me how you milk a cow? Who knows how to make cream? Who can tell me about what a well looks like and how you get water from it?"*

Have the children talk about these topics BEFORE telling the story. Hearing about things that are unfamiliar during the story can cause discomfort and lack of attention to the story. The children will enjoy and understand the story more if you do a little work with them first. Then tell the story and leave it alone until the next day. Let the children "sleep on it". The next day, come back and talk about it and discuss any questions that have come up overnight. This approach allows children to take the story in deeply and digest it before being asked to talk about it.

Remember, the notes under the story title that explain themes or what the story is about, are for you, the teller, only. Do not share these with your listeners as that robs them of the chance to exercise their imaginations and determine for themselves what the story means to them.

## The Frog and the Pail of Cream (Ages 6–9)

*(Courage, Steadfastness, Patience, Determination)*

One day a milkmaid was carrying a pail of cream. It was hot and she set the pail down on the ground to get a drink of water from the nearby well. A frog came hopping along and jumped right into the pail of cream! He swam round and round, kicking and splashing, trying to find a way out of the pail. Every so often he stopped for a rest. He wondered if he would ever find a way out of his predicament.

Then he started to sing as he swam. He found the singing made him stronger.

"I'm a little frog and if I stay strong, I'll find my way out before too long!" (Sing this three or four times making up a tune, get the child or children to join in…)

The frog refused to give up! He swam and swam, and sang and sang, until, without even realizing it, his little feet had churned the cream into thick rich butter!

Then he was able to climb up on the butter and hop out – just before the milkmaid came back for her pail.

## The Crystal Ball (Ages 6–7)

### Brothers Grimm Fairy/Wonder Tale
*(Honesty, Determination, Self-Sacrifice, Courage)*

There was once an enchantress, who had three sons who loved each other as brothers, but the old woman did not trust them, and thought they wanted to steal her power from her. Therefore, she changed the eldest into an eagle, which was forced to dwell in the rocky mountains. He was often seen flying in great circles in the sky. The second, she changed into a whale, which lived in the deep sea, and all that was seen of it was that it sometimes spouted up a great jet of water in the air. Each of them bore his human form for only two hours each day. The third son, who was afraid she might change him into a raging wild beast–a bear perhaps, or a wolf, went secretly away. He had heard that a king's daughter who was bewitched, was imprisoned in the castle of the golden sun, and was waiting to be set free. Those, however, who tried to free her, risked their lives. Three-and-twenty youths had already died a miserable death, and now only one other might make the attempt, after which no more must come. And as his heart was without fear, he made up his mind to seek out the castle of the golden sun.

He had already traveled about for a long time without being able to find it, when he came by chance into a great forest, and did not know the way out of it. All at once he saw in the distance two giants, who made a sign to him with their hands, and when he came to them they said, we are quarreling about a cap, and which of us it is to belong to, and as we are equally strong, neither of us can get the better of the other. The small men are cleverer than we are, so we will leave the decision to you.

"How can you dispute about an old cap," said the youth.

"You do not know what properties it has. It is a wishing-cap; whosoever puts it on, can wish himself to wherever he likes, and in an instant he will be there."

"Give me the cap, said the youth, I will go a short distance off, and when I call you, you must run a race, and the cap shall belong to the one who gets first to me."

He put it on and went away, and thought of the king's daughter, forgot the giants, and walked continually onward. At length he sighed from the very bottom of his heart, and cried, ah, if I were but at the castle of the golden sun. And hardly had the words passed his lips than he was standing on a high mountain before the gate of the castle.

He entered and went through all the rooms, until in the last he found the king's daughter. But how shocked he was when he saw her. She had an ashen-gray face full of wrinkles, bleary eyes, and red hair.

"Are you the king's daughter, whose beauty the whole world praises?" cried he.

"Ah," she answered, this is not my form, human eyes can only see me in this state of ugliness, but that you may know what I am like, look in the mirror–it does not let itself be misled–it will show you my image as it is in truth. She put the mirror in his hand, and he saw there the likeness of the most beautiful maiden on earth, and saw, too, how the tears were rolling down her cheeks with grief.

Said he, "How can you be set free? I fear no danger."

She said, "He who gets the crystal ball, and holds it before the enchanter, will destroy his power with it, and I shall resume my true shape. But so many have already gone to meet death for this, and you are so young, I grieve that you should encounter such great danger."

"Nothing can keep me from doing it," said he, "tell me what I must do."

"You shall know everything," said the king's daughter. "When you descend the mountain on which the castle stands, a wild bull will stand below by a spring, and you must fight with it, and if you have the luck to kill it, a fiery bird will spring out of it, which bears in its body a red-hot egg, and in the egg the crystal ball lies as its yolk. The bird will not let the egg fall until forced to do so, and if it falls on the ground, it will flame up and burn everything that is near, and even the egg itself will melt, and with it the crystal ball, and then your trouble will have been in vain."

The youth went down to the spring, where the bull snorted and bellowed at him. After a long struggle he plunged his sword in the animal's body, and it fell down. Instantly a fiery bird arose from it and was about to fly away, but the young man's brother, the eagle, who was passing between the clouds, swooped down, hunted it away to the sea, and struck it with his beak until, in its extremity, it let the egg fall. The egg, however, did not fall into the sea, but on a fisherman's hut, which stood on the shore, and the hut began at once to smoke and was about to break out in flames.

Then arose in the sea waves as high as a house, which streamed over the hut, and subdued the fire. The other brother, the whale, had come swimming to them, and had driven the water up on high. When the fire was extinguished, the youth sought for the egg and happily found it. It was not yet melted, but the shell was broken by being so suddenly cooled with the water, and he could take out the crystal ball unhurt.

When the youth went to the enchanter and held it before him, the enchanter said, "My power is destroyed, and from this time forth you are the king of the castle of the golden sun. You can give back to your brothers their human form." The youth set his brothers free of the enchantment.

Then the youth hastened to the king's daughter, and when he entered the room, she was standing there in the full splendor of her beauty, and joyfully they exchanged rings with each other. And if they have not died, they are living there still.

The Queen Bee presents a clear picture of **environmentalism**. The youngest brother protects the ants, the ducks and the bees from his older brothers who would harm them. The youngest brother later receives help from the ants, the ducks, and the bees in his efforts to free the castle from its enchantment.

## The Queen Bee (Ages 6–7)

*(Environmentalism, Protecting Nature, Honesty)*

Once upon a time two king's sons went out in search of adventure. By and by they fell into a wild, disorderly way of living, and they never came home again. The youngest son, who was called Simpleton, set out to find his brothers. After a long time he found them, but they mocked him for thinking that he in his simplicity could get along in the world any better than they who were so much cleverer than he.

Nevertheless, the three set off together and came to an anthill. The two older brothers wanted to destroy it and to watch the little ants scurrying about in terror trying to carry their eggs to safety. But Simpleton said: "Leave the creatures in peace; I will not allow you to disturb them."

They went onwards and came to a lake, on which many ducks were swimming. The two brothers wanted to catch a couple and roast them, but Simpleton would not permit it, and said: "Leave the creatures in peace, I will not allow you to kill them."

At length, they came to a bee's hive, high in a hollow of a tree. There was so much honey that it ran out of the hollow in the trunk of the tree. The two older brothers wanted to make a fire beneath the tree and suffocate the bees in order to take away the honey, but Simpleton again stopped them and said: 'Leave the creatures in peace, I will not allow you to burn them."

After some time, the three brothers arrived at a castle where stone horses were standing in the stables and no human being was to be seen. They went through all the halls until, quite at the end they came to a door in which there were three locks. In the middle of the door there was a little windowpane. They looked through the window and there they saw a little grey man with a long grey beard sitting at a table. They called to him, once, twice, but he did not hear them. They called him a third time and he got up and opened the three locks, and came out. He said nothing, however, he took them to a table that was spread with all manner of meats and vegetables and fruits. When they had eaten and drunk he took each of them to a bedroom.

The next morning the little grey man came to the eldest son and beckoned to him. He led him to a stone table on which were inscribed three tasks. Once these tasks were accomplished the castle would be freed from its enchantment. The first task was to find the one thousand pearls that belonged to the princess's. They were hidden in the forest beneath the moss. All of them must be picked up and if by sunset one single pearl were missing, he who had looked for them would be turned to stone. The eldest began to search for the pearls, he went hither and thither, and sought the whole day, but when it came to an end, he had only found one hundred, and what was written on the table came true, he was turned into stone. Next day, the second brother undertook the adventure; but it did not fare much better with him than with the eldest; He scurried about hither and thither beneath the tree but at the end of the day h e found only two hundred pearls, and was turned into stone. At last it was Simpleton's turn to seek in the moss; but it was so difficult for him to find the pearls, that he soon realized he would never succeed. He sat down upon a stone and wept. Suddenly, he heard a small voice calling up to him. He looked down, and there was the King of the ants. "You once saved us, and now we have come to help you in return" spoke the King. The King of the ants came with five thousand ants. They scurried hither and thither searching under cranny and crag, stone and leaf and at the end of the day, all the one thousand pearls were found. Simpleton thanked the King and all the ants.

The second task was to fetch the key of the King's daughter's bedchamber. It was at the bottom of the lake. Simpleton walked to the lake wondering how he would ever find a key at its bottom.

There he saw swimming towards him the ducks that he had saved. The ducks dived down into the water and the leader of the ducks swam to Simpleton with the key in his bill. Simpleton thanked the ducks.

The third task was the most difficult. Simpleton must chose between the three sleeping princesses, the one who was the youngest and dearest. They resembled each another exactly. The only difference between them was what each one had eaten before falling asleep. The eldest had eaten a sweet made of sugar, the second a sweet made of maple syrup and the youngest a sweet made of honey. Simpleton did not know how he would make his choice.

Suddenly, he heard a buzzing sound and in through the window flew the queen of the bees from the hive he had saved. She tasted the lips of each of the three sisters and stayed on lips of the one who had eaten the honey. Then Simpleton knew.

The enchantment was broken. Everyone who had been turned to stone woke up and became himself again. The horses began to neigh, the roosters began to crow, the cook began to stir the pot, and the King and Queen rejoiced. Simpleton married the youngest princess and after her Father's death he became King. His two brothers married the other two sisters. And if they have not died they are living there still.

**Author's Note:** The following story is particularly apropos for the 6-year change as it tells the story of a donkey who was a prince hidden in a donkey skin. Through his life experience, he learns to speak up for what he wants and to become his true self. He sheds his donkey skin, which is a great metaphor for the inner changes being experienced by the child of 6. It is also recommended for shy children, awkward children, or children who are not well integrated into the class you are teaching. It is a story of hope, perseverance, and also has a wonderful musical element to it. The donkey communicates through his instrument and hides in his donkey skin until he is seen for who he truly is. Then he sheds his donkey skin. Each of us longs to be seen for who we truly are.

## The Donkey (Ages 6–7)

### The Brothers Grimm
*( Hope, Perseverance, Overcoming one's limitations*
*The true measure of a person is within and often hidden)*

Once upon a time there lived a king and a queen, who were rich, and had everything they wanted, but no children. The queen lamented over this day and night, and said, I am like a field on which nothing grows. At last God granted her the wish, but when the child came into the world, it did not look like a human child, but was a little donkey. When the mother saw that, her lamentations and outcries began in real earnest. She said she would far rather have had no child at all than have a donkey, and that they were to throw it into the water that the fishes might devour it. But the king said, no, since God has sent him he shall be my son and heir, and after my death sit on the royal throne, and wear the kingly crown. The donkey, therefore, was brought up and grew bigger, and his ears grew up high and straight. And he was of a merry disposition, jumped about, played and took especial pleasure in music, so that he went to a celebrated musician and said, teach me your art, that I may play the lute as well as you do.

"Ah, dear little master," answered the musician, "that would come very hard to you, your fingers are not quite suited to it, and are far too big. I am afraid the strings would not last."

But no excuses were of any use. The donkey was determined to play the lute. And since he was persevering and industrious, he at last learnt to do it as well as the master himself. The young lord once went out walking full of thought and came to a well. He looked into it and in the mirror-clear water saw his donkey's form. He was so distressed about it that he went out into the wide world and only took with him one faithful companion. They traveled up and down, and at last they came into a kingdom where and old king reigned who had a single but wonderfully beautiful daughter. The donkey said, here we will stay, knocked at the gate, and cried, a guest is without. Open, that he may enter. When the gate was not opened, he sat down, took his lute and played it in the most delightful manner with his two forefeet. Then the doorkeeper opened his eyes, and gaped, and ran to the king and said, "Outside by the gate sits a young donkey which plays the lute as well as an experienced master."

"Then let the musician come to me," said the king. But when a donkey came in, everyone began to laugh at the lute-player. And when the donkey was asked to sit down and eat with the servants, he was unwilling, and said, "I am no common stable-donkey, I am a noble one." Then they said, "If that is what you are, seat yourself with the soldiers."

"No", said he, "I will sit by the king."

The king smiled, and said good-humoredly, "Yes, it shall be as you will, little donkey, come here to me." Then he asked, "Little donkey, how does my daughter please you?" The donkey turned his head towards her, looked at her, nodded and said, "I like her above measure, I have never yet seen anyone so beautiful as she is." "Well, then, you shall sit next her too", said the king. "That is exactly what I wish", said the donkey, and he placed himself by her side, ate and drank, and knew how to behave himself daintily and cleanly.

When the noble beast had stayed a long time at the king's court, he thought, what good does all this do me; I shall still have to go home again. He let his head hang sadly, and went to the king and asked for his dismissal. But the king had grown fond of him, and said, "Little donkey, what ails you? You look as sour as a jug of vinegar; I will give you what you want. Do you want gold?" "No", said the donkey, and shook his head. "Do you want jewels and rich dress?" "No." "Do you wish for half my kingdom?" "Indeed, no." Then said the king, "If I could but know what would make you content. Will you have my pretty daughter to wife?" "Ah, yes", said the donkey, "I should indeed like her", and all at once he became quite merry and full of happiness, for that was exactly what he was wishing for. So a great and splendid wedding was held. In the evening, when the bride and bridegroom were led into their bed-room, the king wanted to know if the donkey would behave well, and ordered a servant to hide himself there. When they were both within, the bridegroom bolted the door, looked around, and as he believed that they were quite alone, he suddenly threw off his donkey's skin, and stood there in the form of a handsome royal youth. "Now", said he, "you see who I am, and see also that I am not unworthy of you." Then the bride was glad, and kissed him, and loved him dearly. When morning came, he jumped up, put his animal's skin on again, and no one could have guessed what kind of a form was hidden beneath it.

Soon came the old king. "Ah," cried he, "So the little donkey is already up. But surely you are sad," said he to his daughter, "that you have not got a proper man for your husband."

"Oh, no, dear father, I love him as well as if he were the handsomest in the world, and I will keep him as long as I live."

The king was surprised, but the servant who had concealed himself came and revealed everything to him. The king said, "That cannot be true." "Then watch yourself the next night, and you will see it with your own eyes, and hark you, Lord King, if you were to take his skin away and throw it in the fire, he would be forced to show himself in his true shape." "Your advice is good", said the king, and at night when they were asleep, he stole in, and when he got to the bed he saw by the light of the moon a noble-looking youth lying there, and the skin lay stretched on the ground. So he took it away, and had a great fire lighted outside, and threw the skin into it, and remained by it himself until it was all burnt to ashes. But since he was anxious to know how the robbed man would behave himself, he stayed awake the whole night and watched. When the youth had slept his fill, he got up by the first light of morning, and wanted to put on the donkey's skin, but it was not to be found. At this he was alarmed, and, full of grief and anxiety, said, "Now I shall have to contrive to escape".

But when he went out, there stood the king, who said, "My son, whither away in such haste. What have you in mind? Stay here, you are such a handsome man, you shall not go away from me. I will now give you half my kingdom, and after my death you shall have the whole of it."

"Then I hope that what begins so well may end well, and I will stay with you", said the youth. And the old man gave him half the kingdom, and in a year's time, when he died, the youth had the whole, and after the death of his father he had another kingdom as well, and lived in all magnificence.

# Mother Holle (Ages 6–7)

## The Brothers Grimm
*(Laziness, Industriousness, Selflessness leads to fulfillment)*

There was once a widow who had two daughters–one of whom was pretty and industrious, whilst the other was ugly and idle. But she was much fonder of the ugly and idle one, because she was her own daughter; and the other, who was a stepdaughter, was obliged to do all the work, and be the Cinderella of the house. Every day the poor girl had to sit by a well and spin and spin till her fingers bled.

Now it happened that one day the shuttle was marked with her blood, so she dipped it in the well to wash the mark off; but it dropped out of her hand and fell to the bottom. She began to weep, and ran to her stepmother and told her of the mishap. But the step-mother scolded her sharply, and was so merciless as to say, "Since you have let the shuttle fall in, you must fetch it out again."

So the girl went back to the well, and did not know what to do: and in the sorrow of her heart she jumped into the well to get the shut-tle. She lost her senses. When she awoke and came to herself again, she was in a lovely meadow where the sun was shining and many thousands of flowers were growing.

Along this meadow she went, and at last came to a baker's oven full of bread, and the bread cried out, "Oh, take me out! Take me out or I shall burn; I have been baked a long time!" So she went up to it, and took out all the loaves one after another with the bread-shovel. After that she went on till she came to a tree covered with apples, which called out to her, "Oh, shake me! Shake me! We apples are all ripe!" So she shook the tree till the apples fell like rain, and went on shaking till they were all down, and when she had gathered them into a heap, she went on her way.

At last she came to a little house, out of which an old woman peeped; but she had such large teeth that the girl was frightened, and was about to run away.

But the old woman called out to her, "What are you afraid of, dear child? Stay with me; if you will do all the work in the house properly, you shall be the better for it. Only you must take care to make my bed well, and to shake it thoroughly till the feathers fly, for then there is snow on the earth. I am Mother Holle."

As the old woman spoke so kindly to her, the girl took courage and agreed to enter her service. She attended to everything to the satisfaction of her mistress, and always shook her bed so vigorously that the feathers flew about like snowflakes. So she had a pleasant life with her; never an angry word; and boiled or roast meat every day.

She stayed some time with Mother Holle, and then she became sad. At first she did not know what was the matter with her, but found at length that it was homesickness; although she was many thousand times better off here than at home, still she had a longing to be there. At last she said to the old woman, "I have a longing for home; and however well off I am down here, I cannot stay any longer; I must go up again to my own people." Mother Holle said, "I am pleased that you long for your home again, and as you have served me truly, I myself will take you up again." Thereupon she took her by the hand, and led her to a large door. The door was opened, and just as the maiden was standing beneath the doorway, a heavy shower of golden rain fell, and all the gold remained sticking to her, so that she was completely covered with it.

"You shall have that because you are so industrious," said Mother Holle; and at the same time she gave her back the shuttle which she had let fall into the well. Thereupon the door closed, and the maiden found herself up above upon the earth, not far from her mother's house.

And as she went into the yard the cock was standing by the well, and cried "Cock-a-doodle-doo! Your golden girl's come back to you!"

So she went in to her mother, and as she arrived thus covered with gold, she was well received, both by her and her sister. The girl told all that had happened to her; and as soon as the mother heard how she had come by so much wealth, she was very anxious to obtain the same good luck for the ugly and lazy daughter. She had to seat herself by the well and spin; and in order that her shuttle might be stained with blood, she stuck her hand into a thorn bush and pricked her finger. Then she threw her shuttle into the well, and jumped in after it. She came, like the other, to the beautiful meadow and walked along the very same path. When she got to the oven the bread again cried, "Oh, take me out! Take me out or I shall burn; I have been baked a long time!"

But the lazy thing answered, "As if I had any wish to make myself dirty?" and on she went on.

Soon she came to the apple-tree, which cried, "Oh, shake me! Shake me! We apples are all ripe!"

But she answered, "I like that! One of you might fall on my head," and so went on.

When she came to Mother Holle's house she was not afraid, for she had already heard of her big teeth, and she hired herself to her immediately.

The first day she forced herself to work diligently, and obeyed Mother Holle when she told her to do anything, for she was thinking of all the gold that she would give her. But on the second day she began to be lazy, and on the third day still more so, and then she would not get up in the morning at all.

Neither did she make Mother Holle's bed as she ought, and did not shake it so as to make the feathers fly up. Mother Holle was soon tired of this, and gave her notice to leave. The lazy girl was willing enough to go, and thought that now the golden rain would come. Mother Holle led her to the great door; but while she was standing beneath it, instead of the gold a big kettle of pitch was emptied over her.

"That is the reward of your service," said Mother Holle, and shut the door. So the lazy girl went home; but she was quite covered with pitch and the cock by the well side, as soon as he saw her, cried out "Cock-a-doodle-dooooo! Your pitchy girl's come back to you!" The pitch stuck fast to her, and could not be got off as long as she lived.

# Stone Soup (Ages 6–10)

## The original story from 1808
*(Community Building, Sharing, Overcoming Selfishness)*

A weary traveler arrived in a small village that lay to the north of Schauffhausen, on the road to Zurich in Switzerland.

A good woman sat spinning and singing at the door of her cottage. The traveler came up to her and talked first about the roughness of the roads and then about the prospect of a luxuriant vintage along the banks of the Rhine River. At last he asked her if she had any fire?

"To be sure, indeed I have a blazing fire!

"Well, then, said the Traveler, "as your pot is on, you can give me a little warm water."

"To be sure I can! But what do you want with warm water"

"If you lend me a small pot, I will show you," said the Traveler.

"Well, you shall have a pot. There! Now what do you want with it?"

"I want," said the Traveler, "to make a mess of stone soup!"

"Stone soup!" cried the woman. "I never heard of that before. Of what will you make it?"

"I will show you in an instant," said the man. So, untying his wallet, he produced a large, smooth pebble. "Here," he cried, "is the principal ingredient. Now toast me a large slice of bread, hard and brown. Well, now attend to me."

The stone was infused in warm water; the bread was toasted, and put into the pot with it. "Now," said the Traveler, "let me have a bit of bacon, a small quantity of sauerkraut, pepper and salt, onions, celery and thyme." In short, he demanded all the necessary ingredients.

The good woman had a store cupboard and a well cropped garden, so that these were procured in an instant, and the cookery proceeded with great success. When it was finished, the kind hostess, who had watched the operation with some anxiety, and from time to time longed to taste the soup, was indulged. She found it excellent. She had never before tasted any soup that was so delicious. She produced all the edibles that her cottage afforded; and spreading her table, she, with the Traveler, made a hearty meal, of which the stone soup formed a principal part.

When he took his leave, he told the good woman, who had carefully washed the stone, that as she had been so benevolent to him, he would, in return, make her a present of it.

"Where did you ever get it?" said she.

"Oh," he replied, "I have brought it a considerable way; and it is a stone of that nature, that if it be kept clean, its virtue will never be exhausted, but, with the same ingredients, it will always make as good a soup as that which we have this day eaten."

The poor woman could hardly set any bounds on her gratitude; and she and the Traveler parted highly satisfied with each other. Proud of this discovery, she, in general terms, mentioned it to her neighbors. By this means the recipe was promulgated; and it was in the course of many experiments at length found, that other pebbles would make as good soup as the one in her possession.

It then became fashionable throughout that land to make a stone soup with ones neighbors and friends frequently as the first course of the dinner on the peasant's table.

I have included The Three Billy Goat's Gruff because it is a wonderful tale for children that reminds them that they need to wait until the right age comes along for them to do and to have many things. Today, children are growing up ever faster and faster. This is a story that reminds us that it is best to wait until the right time to do the next step in life or to have the next fancy games, bikes or whatever. Waiting is a good experience. It is a wise choice. And in this case the wisdom of waiting is clear. Tell the story in a calm voice and see how your child responds. On the other hand, if you don't like this story, just skip it. This is a Norwegian Folk Tale. Norway is a beautiful country of fjords, pristine bays, wild mountains and colorful people. Trolls are the equivalent of wolves and witches that we find in European Wonder Tales.

## The Three Billy Goat's Gruff (Age 6 and Up)

### A Norwegian Folk Tale

Once upon a time there were three billy goats, who were to go up to the hillside to make themselves fat, and the name of all three was "Gruff".

On the way up was a bridge over a stream they had to cross; and under the bridge lived a great ugly Troll, with eyes as big as saucers, and a nose as long as a poker.

So, first of all came the youngest billy goat Gruff to cross the bridge.

"Trip, trap! Trip, trap!" went the bridge.

"WHO'S THAT tripping over my bridge?" roared the Troll.

"Oh, it is only I, the tiniest billy goat Gruff; and I'm going up to the hillside to make myself fat" said the billy goat, with such a small voice.

"Now, I'm coming to gobble you up," said the Troll.

"Oh, no! Pray don't take me. I'm too little," said the billy goat; "wait a bit 'til the second billy goat Gruff comes, he's much bigger."

"Well, be off with you," said the Troll.

A little while after came the second billy goat Gruff to cross the bridge…

"TRIP, TRAP! TRIP, TRAP! TRIP, TRAP! went the bridge.

"WHO'S THAT tripping over my bridge?" roared the Troll.

"Oh, no! Don't take me, wait a little till the big billy goat Gruff comes, he's much bigger.

"Very well, be off with you," said the Troll.

But just then up came the big billy goat Gruff

"TRIP, TRAP! TRIP, TRAP! TRIP, TRAP! went the bridge.

"WHO'S THAT tramping over my bridge?" roared the Troll.

"It's I THE BIG BILLY GOAT GRUFF," said the billy goat, who had an ugly, hoarse voice of his own.

"Now I'm coming to gobble you up," roared the Troll.

"Well, come along! I've got two spears,

and I'll poke your eyeballs out at your ears;

I've got beside two curling-stones,

and I'll crush you to bits, body and bones."

That was what the big billy goat said: and so he flew at the Troll, and poked his eyes out with his horns, and crushed him to bits, body and bones, and tossed him out into the stream, and after that he went up to the hillside. There the billy goats got so fat they scarce were able to walk home again; and if the fat hasn't fallen off them, why, they're still fat; and so …

**Snip, snap, snout, this tale's told out.**

# "Where Things Come From" or Object Stories
## Stories You Can Create for Children, Ages 6–8

Have you ever wondered how the first comb or hairbrush came into being? What did it look like? What was it made from? Why did someone think of it? What need did it satisfy? Why and how did scissors, crayons, paper, brushes, paint, colored pencils, cloth, and other things children use in their daily lives come into being? Children are curious and interested in the things of the world, particularly during the time of their development between the ages of 6 and 8. "Object Stories" satisfy that curiosity and, at the same time, develop reverence and appreciation for nature and her many gifts to human beings. Children have many things at their disposal today and often have no idea where they came from or how they were created. Object stories build a bridge between the things of the world and the kingdom of nature. Hearing such stories stimulates a sense of gratitude for the sacrifices nature makes so that we human beings can live creative lives on the earth. I thank Eugene Schwartz, a Waldorf Teacher and educator of teachers, who introduced me to object stories during my teacher training.

Object Stories tell the story of how a tool or other kind of object was created. They are fun to create and children enjoy them. Your children will help you create them once you have offered a few to get the ball rolling. The essential ingredients for the object story are: choose an object you use every day, describe a practical human need for the object, include a helpful person to provide guidance in creating the object, and describe the connection between the object and the world of nature. By describing the gift or sacrifice of nature that makes it possible for the object to be created and giving thanks to Nature and the creatures and helpful people who made it possible to create the object, we give the child a context for understanding and appreciating how the things of the world have been created. In a way, these stories are also ecology stories as they create an understanding of the symbiotic nature of the relationship between people and nature. Here's a sample story about how paper came into being.

In sum, the formula is as follows: **A need for the object, a journey, a wise helper, a gift from nature, an expression of gratitude for nature's**

**gift**, and **scientific accuracy**. When creating an object story, the most important thing to remember is to make the elements of the story ring true to nature. Here are two examples that I have written:

## How Paper Came to Be...

A long time ago, there was once a queen who had 12 children. She loved to paint and she wanted to paint with her children, too. In those days, people painted on sheepskins, but she was sad to use the skins and there were not enough for her and her children to use. She sent messengers far and wide throughout her kingdom to find something else to paint on. But no one was able to help her. Finally, she put on her cloak and left her castle. She journeyed into the forest looking for a wise old hermit who lived in a tiny cottage in the heart of the forest. She walked all day into the woods, and, just as the sun was setting, she came upon the tiny cottage. She knocked on the door. The door opened, and there stood an old man. He smiled at her and invited her to come in for some supper. She was tired and hungry and thanked the old man for the warmth of his fire. He brought her a bowl of vegetable soup. As they sat by the fire, she told him what she was seeking. Now, this old man was wise, and he knew many of the secrets of nature. He gave her a bed to sleep in and told her they would go out the next day together to search for the answer to her need.

The next morning, the little old man fixed her a big bowl of good sweet porridge for breakfast. Then they walked into the woods together. After a long time or a short time, they came to a wasp's nest that had been built in the crook of an old oak tree. They stood there a long time watching the wasps build that nest. It was made of plant fiber that had been chewed up by the wasps, spit out, and laid into thin gray layers to dry. The layers were lightweight and yet strong. The wise hermit and the queen studied the work of the wasps and decided to try to make the fibrous substance themselves using the inner core of some tree trunks that had fallen in a recent storm. It took them many days to mash the tree pulp and then lay it in fine layers in the sun to dry. Finally, the day came when they laid several wet layers on top of one another just as the wasps had done.

When the layers dried, they had become one layer that was strong enough to paint upon. They had learned to make the first paper ever seen in that part of the world. The queen thanked the wise man of the woods for his help and guidance. Some days later, she brought him a gift: the first painting that she created on the paper that she and he had made. They were friends for a long, long time. And that's the story of how the first paper was created.

## How the First Flute Came into the World

Once, there was a young prince who was very sad. No matter what anyone said to him, he did not smile or laugh. He walked with his head looking down on the ground and his feet shuffled softly. His parents were worried about him and brought doctors and wise women and men to see him. They all said the same thing. There was nothing to be done. The boy must cure himself. Finally, the King decided to take the matter in hand and he set off with his son on a journey to find the wild man of the woods.

Now this wild man was hard to find. No one had ever met him. Some few people had seen him from afar. *It was said that he himself had once been a king and had lost his only child in a great battle. His sorrow had driven him into the forest.* The wild man was said to have become wise over the years, and, sometimes, he would give advice if you could find him. The King and his son walked all day and at night came to a small cottage in the heart of the forest. The King knocked on the door and a little old man opened the door. The King bowed and asked if he and his son could have a place to sleep for the night. The little old man said not a word but motioned for them to enter.

The hut had one room with a fireplace and a window. The fire was blazing and the little old man offered the King his blanket to sit on the floor and warm himself by the fire. The little old man gave the King and his son some soup he had cooked over the fire. The soup was clear and seemed to be only broth but when they drank it, it tasted of meat and vegetables and warmed them from head to toe.

The King thanked the old man. Then the old man asked the King why he had come into the forest. "Ah," said the King. "I have heard of your wisdom and have brought my son to see you. He does not smile or laugh. Is there anything that can be done?"

The old man held the boy's hand and sat quietly. Then the old man went to the corner of the hut and took out a wooden box. With great care and gentleness, he unlatched the box and took off the lid. Inside the box, was a flute that was carved out of the wood of the elderberry tree. The man handed the flute to the boy and said, "I have waited for you for a long time and now you have come. Take this flute, for it belongs to you. You are a musician. Go forth into the forest and sit in the glade in the heart of the woods. There you will find the bird of believing. Listen to its song. Once you can play it on your flute, you will be ready to return home and take your rightful place beside your father, the King." The King was shocked. His son, who seemed unable to do anything, was a musician? He was about to protest, but the old man silenced him with a wave of his hand. "The world is waiting for the songs your son will sing and play on this flute. Be at peace."

In the morning, the King and his son thanked the old man and walked into the heart of the forest. A circle of trees stood like sentinels around the glade in the heart of the forest. The boy sat down as the old man had said in the center of the glade and waited. After a long time or a short time, he heard the most beautiful song he had ever heard. With all his heart he longed to play that song on his flute. He looked up to see where the song was coming from and could just barely discern the form of a magnificent bird sitting in the topmost branches of a tree. The bird sang and sang until the boy thought his heart would break with joy. The songs of the bird seemed to be the songs of each one of the people in his father's kingdom. Tears filled his eyes and joy began to swell in his heart. When he thought he could bear it no longer, the bird stopped singing.

The boy looked up, he looked around, but the bird had vanished. The boy was overcome with sorrow. What could he do? He wanted the songs to return. Then he remembered his flute. Tenderly he picked it up and began to play. At first, he was clumsy with his fingers and could hardly get a sound to come forth from his breath. But he kept on trying, and, soon, his fingers knew what to do and his breath streamed through the flute and the songs of his heart began to sing into the great forest.

No one can say how long the boy played. But after a long time or a short time, he paused, arose, and, without a word, he and his father walked home to the palace. The next day, the boy sat in the court-yard of the castle and played his flute. People were drawn by the sweet music and soon the courtyard was full of nobles and peas-ants, cooks and counts, princes and washerwomen. Everyday there-after, the boy played and the people gathered and the kingdom began to be known as a place of laughter and song.

And the boy became a minstrel and traveled far and wide bringing great joy to the kingdom. When his father died, he became King and ruled wisely and well. He played his flute throughout his long life, and it was said that his music healed the soul and inspired everyone who heard it. And ever since that time, flutes have been made and played around the world.

# Activities for Children Age 6 and Older

Physical activities that work with finger dexterity, left and right differentiation, and rhythm and rhyme, suit the young child and help to integrate the activities of the left and right brain.

## Wiggle and Waggle Action Activity

*With thanks to David Campbell, A Traditional Scottish Storyteller*

| Narrative | Activity |
|---|---|
| "I'd like you to meet two old friends, Wiggle and Waggle." | Hold up each hand in a fist with the thumb up and your arms spread about two feet apart in front of your chest. Wiggle your left thumb as you introduce "Wiggle", and waggle your right thumb as you introduce "Waggle". |
| "They live in the hills of Scotland (or wherever makes sense to you) and have been best friends since they were children. Every day they visit one another. Wiggle always has a riddle for Waggle, and Waggle always has a story for Wiggle." | Continue to hold your fists out with thumbs up. When you refer to "Wiggle," look at and wiggle your left thumb. When you mention "Waggle," look at and waggle your right thumb. After this, tuck your thumbs into your fists and pause a moment. Then continue. |
| "Along about tea-time they open their doors, pop out, and shut the doors – POP!" | When you say "open their doors", open the fingers on both hands to reveal the thumbs. When you say that they "pop out", pop your thumbs straight up in the air. When you say they "shut their doors–POP", close your fists again smartly on the word "POP" but leave the thumbs out. Both hands do this at the same time. |
| "They went up the hill, down the hill, up the hill, down the hill, up the hill, down the hill, and met each other under their favorite oak tree." | Move your hands up and down over imaginary hills in sync towards the center of your chest with the thumbs leading the way. They meet together when they get to your chest. |

| Narrative | Activity |
|---|---|
| "Wiggle, do you have a riddle for me?" | Look at and waggle your right thumb to represent Waggle speaking this line. |
| "Why yes, I do, Waggle" | Look at and wiggle your left thumb to represent Wiggle speaking this line. |
| Wiggle tells a RIDDLE | Continue to wiggle your left thumb and look back and forth between Wiggle and your audience as Wiggle tells the riddle. Then hold your left thumb still and look at the children to ask them if they know the answer to Wiggle's riddle. Give them hints as necessary and help them solve it. When they do, let Wiggle congratulate the children. |
| (Wiggle) "YES! You GOT it!" | Wiggle your left thumb as Wiggle speaks these words to the children. |
| "Waggle, will you tell us a story?" | Continue looking at and wiggling your left thumb while Wiggle says this. |
| "Why, yes, I will." | Look at and waggle your right thumb while Waggle says this. Then put your hands down for the story, or use them to make any gestures appropriate to the story. When it is done, put your hands back up to your chest with Wiggle on the left and Waggle on the right. |
| (Wiggle) "Thank you for that story, Waggle." | Look at and wiggle your left thumb to represent Wiggle talking to Waggle. |
| "You're welcome, Wiggle. Well, goodbye until tomorrow." | Look at and waggle your right thumb to represent Waggle talking to Wiggle. |
| "Goodbye until tomorrow, Waggle." | Look at and wiggle your left thumb to represent Wiggle talking to Waggle. |
| "And they went…up the hill, down the hill, up the hill, down the hill, up the hill, down the hill back home." | Move your hands up and down over imaginary hills in sync from the center of your chest to your original position with the thumbs leading the way. |

| Narrative | Activity |
|---|---|
| "They opened their doors, popped in, and shut the doors – POP!" | When you say, "opened their doors", open the fingers on both hands but with the thumbs still pointing up. When you say "popped in", pop your thumbs straight down into the palms of your hands. When you say they "shut the doors–POP", close your fists again smartly on the word "POP" and enclose the thumbs. |
| "One day, Wiggle couldn't wait until their regular meeting time, so he opened the door, popped out and shut the door – POP!" | You begin with the position where your arms are spread apart ending in fists with "Wiggle" on your left, "Waggle" on your right. Holding your right hand still, go through the motions to show Wiggle coming out of his house. When you say "opened the door", open the fingers on your left hand to reveal the thumb. When you say, "pop out", pop your left thumb straight up in the air. When you say, "shut the door–POP", close your left fist again smartly on the word "POP" but leave the thumb out. |
| "He went up the hill, down the hill, up the hill, down the hill, up the hill, down the hill, up the hill, down the hill, up the hill, down the hill, up the hill and down the hill to Waggle's." | As before, move your left hand up and down imaginary hills with the thumb leading the way. Since it was three hills to get to the oak tree in the middle, it has to be six hills to get all the way to Waggle's. Hold the right fist still and have Wiggle work his way all the way to Waggle's. |
| "He knocked on the door, tap, tap, tap. But nobody was home." | When Wiggle gets to Waggle's house, tap your left thumb on your right fist three times as you say "tap, tap, tap" to indicate the knocking. Look at the children and show a sad face when you say, "nobody was home." |

| Narrative | Activity |
|---|---|
| "So….he went back up the hill, down the hill, up the hill, down the hill, up the hill, down the hill, up the hill, down the hill, up the hill, down the hill, up the hill and down the hill to his house." | As before, move your left hand up and down imaginary hills six times until your left hand is back in the original position. |
| "He opened the door, popped in, and shut the door – POP!" | When you say, "opened the door", open the fingers on your left hand but with the thumb still pointing up.<br>When you say, "popped in", pop your thumb straight down into the palm of your hand.<br>When you say "shut the doors -POP", close your left fist again smartly on the word "POP" and enclose the thumb. |
| "Sometime later, Waggle had the same idea and he set off for Wiggle's house. He opened the door, popped out, and shut the door – POP!" | Holding your left hand still, go through the motions with your right hand to show Waggle coming out of his house.<br>When you say "opened the door", open the fingers on your right hand to reveal the thumb.<br>When you say, "popped out", pop your right thumb straight up in the air.<br>When you say, "shut the door–POP", close your right fist again smartly on the word "POP" but leave the thumb out. |
| "He went up the hill, down the hill, up the hill, down the hill, up the hill, down the hill, up the hill, down the hill, up the hill, down the hill, up the hill and down the hill to Wiggle's." | Repeat the up and down motions as before, this time moving your right hand (Waggle) over to the left hand (Wiggle's house). |
| "He knocked on the door, tap, tap, tap. But nobody was home." | When Waggle gets to Wiggle's house, tap your right thumb on your left fist three times as you say "tap, tap, tap" to indicate the knocking.<br>Look at the children and show a sad face when you say, "nobody was home." |

| Narrative | Activity |
|---|---|
| "So....he went back up the hill, down the hill, up the hill, down the hill, up the hill, down the hill, up the hill, down the hill, up the hill, down the hill, up the hill and down the hill to his house." | As before, move your right hand up and down imaginary hills six times until your right hand is back in the original position. |
| "He opened the door, popped in, and shut the door – POP!" | When you say, "opened the door", open the fingers on your right hand but with the thumb still pointing up. When you say, "popped in", pop your thumb straight down into the palm of your hand. When you say "shut the doors -POP", close your right fist again smartly on the word "POP" and enclose the thumb. |

I have found that children of all ages love this finger game, and it is a great way to open a story. It is also a useful developmental movement exercise as the children cross the midline barrier with both of their hands and arms repeatedly throughout the finger game.

## We Are All One Whole Class

Ages 6 and 7 (first grade)
*(Act out in a circle to the stepping rhythm of "short, short, long." Every "long" step is in bold print.)*

**(Single file)**
>We are **all** one whole **class.**
>One by **one** see us **pass**
>While our **feet** sing the **song,**
>Two short **steps** and one **long.**

**(Choose the person ahead for a partner)**
>Now we **walk** two by **two**
>In a **ring** round and **true**
>While our **feet** sing the **song,**
>Two short **steps** and one **long.**

**(Teacher chooses three children far apart in the circle, giving them the numbers: 1, 2 and 3)**
>In we **run,** merri**ly,**
>One to **Two,** Two to **Three**
>Three to **where,** One should **be**

**(All in a circle again)**
>While our **feet** sing the **song,**
>Two short **steps** and one **long.**

**Teacher chooses four children (in the same way as above) to run a square**
>Run a **square** and count **four** –
>One to **Two,** Two to **Three,**
>Three to **Four** And One **more**…
>While our **feet** sing the **song,**
>Two short **steps** and one **long.**
>**All stand in a circle with arms and legs out-stretched**
>We are **stars** full of **light**
>With five **rays** shining **bright**
>In the **dark** sky at **night**

**All join hands and move around the circle stepping sideways, hand in hand**
>While our **feet** sing the **song,**
>Two short **steps** and one **long.**

# Tall Trees in the Forest

| | |
|---|---|
| "Tall trees in the forest" | Jump up as if doing a jumping jack, and land with feet apart and arms spread wide over your head like the branches of a tree. |
| "Pine cones on the ground" | Give a little leap and land bending over, knees bent and hands on the ground in front of you. |
| Repeat above multiple times, then… | |
| "Tall trees in the forest" | Same as above |
| "Leaves all around" | Instead of squatting, stand with arms above you, sway back and forth fluttering your fingers like the leaves! |

Go faster and faster, and insert the "Leaves all around" at different points. The children will naturally be already squatting down anticipating that the line will be about "Pine cones on the ground" and will have to scramble to get back upright and do the fluttering leaves. Lots of fun; lots of laughter.

# CHAPTER 11

## Enhancing Your Storytelling
## Using the 5 Senses & the 4 Temperaments

## The Five Senses

Another way to enhance the story is to add a descriptive splash of the five senses: taste, touch, sight, smell, and hearing. Children especially enjoy hearing about how the food tastes, the tree bark feels, the burning wood crackles, the forest smells, and the pond near the fire looks. Adjectives awaken the experience of the senses and thereby make the story more familiar and real. Here is a short list to get you started:

**Taste:** sweet, sour, hot, cold, tart, yummy, refreshing, sticky, smooth, crunchy, syrupy, slimy, spicy, dull, unappealing, appetizing, delicious

**Touch:** soft, hard, smooth, rough, silky, moist, wet, soggy, slimy, prickly, windy

**Sight:** brilliant, sparkling, dull, sunny, overcast, hazy, dim, murky, dark

**Smell:** sweet, pungent, delicious, tantalizing, musty, dry, salty, repugnant, intense, disgusting, heavenly

**Hearing:** loud, soft, rumbling, ringing, crackling, splashing, rippling, beating, rhythmical, incessant, roaring, humming, sighing, whistling

## The Four Temperaments

As an elementary school teacher, I found that one of the most helpful tools for understanding young children from about age 6 to 12 was the concept of the Four Temperaments. The Ancient Greeks developed this way of looking at the world. They imagined the world as being composed of four elements: earth, air, fire and water. In their characterization of the world, naturally some of the most interesting phenomena were created when two of the elements met one another and interacted. For example, when earth met air, the wind was born; when fire met earth, deserts were created; and where water met air, swamps and humidity arose. Where water and fire met, lightning and thunderstorms were born.

The Ancient Greeks felt that these same elements were present in the human being and that human beings mirrored these four elements in the way they approached life. Human beings who tended to be more like fire in their approach to life, the Greeks called choleric. Those who tended to be more like water in their approach, the Greeks called phlegmatic. Those tending to be more like air, the Greeks called sanguine and human beings who tended to be more like earth in their approach to life the Greeks called melancholic. (Note: the use of the word melancholic in this context has nothing to do with being sad or depressed.)

Rudolf Steiner wrote about how to work with the temperaments with children in his booklet called, *The Temperaments*. As a teacher, I found that using these ideas in the classroom benefited the students. How can understanding the temperaments help us guide our children and students better? When we see and understand which temperaments a child tends toward, we are in a better position to help them recognize their strengths and overcome their weaknesses, and not get "stuck" in just one way of being and of approaching the world.

As we explore these four temperaments and relate them to the way children approach life, it's important to remember that the temperament is NOT the personality. Rather, it is a tendency in the way a person approaches life. Knowing a child's temperament can be very useful in helping her or him to come to terms with behavioral challenges and even overcome them. As children grow and mature, we want them to become inwardly flexible and able to develop compassion and understanding toward others and themselves. Working with the four temperaments in storytelling is a bit like holding up a mirror to the inner unconscious self of the child and showing the child a way to become more independent of her or his own inborn tendencies without the child feeling criticized or demeaned in any way. A child's innate temperament becomes most clear at about the age of seven. The temperament tendencies often shift and change between the ages of twelve and fourteen.

Let's first consider how the child's temperament may be reflected in the child's physical body and approach to life.

**Sanguine** or airy children can either be very lithe, thin and small-boned, or heavy-set and large-boned physically. They enjoy change, are almost always in motion, and, like the air, flit hither and thither in their feelings and interests. They walk on their toes, love to skip, and tend to gaze upward and all around them. They enjoy conversation and banter. Being focused on one subject for an extended period of time is often a challenge. They can also be forgetful and flighty. They are a delight to have around, as they are most always cheerful and full of fun. They can be trying at times if they forget to do what they promised. They are friends with everyone, but can hurt others without being aware of what they have done. They live in the present and are comfortable with it. The color the sanguine child is drawn towards is yellow.

**Phlegmatic** or watery children tend to be more heavy set, but can also be balanced physically especially if they have a sport or outdoor activity they enjoy. They ponder. They enjoy being invisible in a crowd or classroom. Like the water, they are reflective and can come to remarkable observations about the world around them. But they need to be drawn out. They won't offer their opinion too often. They are not in a hurry—ever. They often shuffle as they walk. They are good listeners but can also become so caught up in their own world that they need to be woken up a bit by a surprise. They prefer to have one or two good friends. They move easily from the present to the past and wonder about the future. The phlegmatic child is drawn to the color green.

**Choleric** children are fiery. They love being the center of attention. They often have loud voices and enjoy taking charge of the situation. They are often short and stocky and you can hear them coming. Their heels hit the ground solidly as they walk. They can seem insensitive as they think that everyone must approach the world the way they do and become impatient when things slow down. They enjoy being in charge and usually have lots of ideas about how to get things done. They can easily lose their temper, yet, in the next moment, can move on as if nothing had happened. They live more in the future than in the past. They are great planners and passionate about what they believe in. They can be difficult when they don't get their way. The choleric child is drawn to the color red.

**Melancholic** children tend to be lanky and thin. They're thoughtful and are often more introverted than extroverted. Their gaze is downward. They walk with a slight shuffle. They are often deep thinkers who ponder before they speak. They live more in the past than in the future. They take life seriously and are loyal and true to their friends. They can be hurt easily but try not to show it. They expect life to be difficult, and, in a certain way, they enjoy the difficulty. The color the melancholic child is drawn to is blue.

These characterizations are meant to be a general guide to help you determine the temperament of the children in your care.

Here are four poems describing the four elements and the their associated temperament, followed by a story of the temperaments in action.

# The Four Elements

## Poems for the four Temperaments

*Anonymous*

**Earth** (Melancholic)
We the stones on which you stand
Hold the waters and build the land.
In caves of darkest earth
Find we our crystal birth.
The sun with radiant light
Makes us sparkling bright
These are the gifts we hold for you
Of blood red, white and blue.

**Water** (Phlegmatic)
We are the waters cool and deep
That rush and run, or soundly sleep.
Down the mountain, through the lake
To the sea our path we make
Under moon and stars afloat
Across the waves we'll bear your boat,
We are the waters cool and deep
That rush and run, or soundly sleep

**Air** (Sanguine)
We are the winds that weep and wail
Blow a breeze and swell the sail
And wear a cloak of wonder rare
Of silver, gold and stars that stare.
And joy we spin in every fold
Our gift on earth for you to hold.
We are the winds that weep and wail
Blow a breeze and swell the sail.


**Fire** (Choleric)
We, the bright red fiery flames
Crackle and roar, that nothing tames.
Sparks like shooting stars they fly
Helpers we are of sun on high.
With golden sword the cold we slay,
Bring you warmth to cheer your stay.
We, the bright red fiery flames
Crackle and roar, that nothing tames.

## A Story of the Four Temperaments in Action

In the heart of a wood a huge tree had fallen across the path. It completely obstructed the way onward. A little girl came skipping along the path humming a tune when, suddenly, she discovered that her way was blocked by the tree! She laughed and wondered how this tree could have fallen. She began to look around and found some blue and yellow flowers and picked some for a bouquet. Then she noticed a squirrel scampering through the treetops. She began to climb up on the tree and pretend she was a squirrel and wonder where she might build her nest.

Sometime later, a little boy came walking along the path. He was looking down at the ground and thinking about what a grey day it was. He caught himself just as his foot struck the trunk of the tree. Ouch! He cried out loud. He sat down on the tree trunk and looked around. How had this happened? All he had wanted to do was to take a walk, but the fallen tree blocked his path. And now his foot hurt! Oh well, he thought. This is how life always is for me. I guess I will just give up this walk and go back home. And so he did.

Next, a little girl wandered down the same path first looking down at the ground and then up at the sky and all around at the tree-tops and then back down at the ground. She was hoping that there would be a cozy place for her to sit down and look at the flowers. And then she saw the tree trunk. Well, that looks like a good spot to sit down. So she sat on the trunk in a cozy spot under the leaves and gazed peacefully at the forest all around her.

Finally, a little boy came running through the woods. He was looking straight ahead and thinking about all the things he would do when he reached the other side of the forest. But, what's this? A tree has fallen across the road! Something must be done right now so people can walk on the path. Someone has to clear this away! So he hurried home to round up some of the men and boys in the neighborhood, and, before too long, the tree had been cut up and the path was clear again. Job well done, thought the boy.

Spend a few moments thinking about which of these characters you identify with. Often it will be two out of the four. Adults are more complex than children and often move between two of the temperaments. Think about how you were as a child in your tendencies and ways of dealing with situations.

## Using Temperaments in Storytelling

To add a touch of temperament to a story, use the four elements: earth for the melancholic child, air for the sanguine, water for phlegmatic, and fire for the choleric. Or add color by describing something blue for the melancholic, red for the choleric, yellow for the sanguine, and green for the phlegmatic.

Don't be too obvious in your portraits of the temperaments, but don't be afraid to add them to your story, because they act like a mirror for the child. Since they are woven into the story itself, there is no negativity associated with them. Make a list of temperament words using the four elements and the four primary colors (yes, well there are truly three, but we need green for the watery phlegmatic, and green is a combination of yellow and blue). When purchasing clothing for your child, notice the colors your child is drawn to...this will also give you a hint about their temperament. I had a student who loved navy blue, and was definitely melancholic. I had another student who loved bright colors, especially yellows and was definitely a sanguine. I had a student who loved pastels and subtle greens, a phlegmatic. And I had a student who liked bright orange, who was choleric in nature.

This diagram shows how temperaments can change during childhood and adolescence. When the temperament shifts, it tends to shift toward the temperament on either side. For example:

Sanguine **(S)** might shift either toward Choleric **(C)** or Phlegmatic **(P)**; Choleric **(C)** might shift toward Sanguine **(S)** or Melancholic **(M)**; Melancholic **(M)** might shift to either Phlegmatic **(P)** or Choleric **(C)**; Phlegmatic **(P)** might shift toward Sanguine **(S)** or Melancholic **(M)**.

In his wonderful stories of Winnie the Pooh, A. A. Milne used the temperaments very clearly. In the character of Pooh, we see the charming Phlegmatic. In the character of Piglet, we see the delightful Sanguine. In the character of Eeyore, we find the lovable Melancholic. And in the character of Tigger, we find the active Choleric.

Listening to music is another way for you to grasp the four temperaments. The 1812 Overture by Tchaikovsky or Beethoven's Symphony #5, the 4th movement or "My Way," by Frank Sinatra are great examples of choleric fire in music. For phlegmatics, Barber's Adagio for Strings, Moon River and Octopus' Garden by the Beatles are good examples. "Yesterday" by the Beatles, and "Blue Bayou" by Roy Orbison give us a feeling for the melancholic. And for the sanguine, "Yellow Submarine" by the Beatles and "Appalachian Spring" (variations on a Shaker Tune) by Aaron Copeland. (This piece has also been made into a song called, "Tis a Gift to be Simple").

As adults, we have settled into a temperament and can move to the one on either side when the mood or situation calls for it. We do this largely unconsciously. To explore your own tendencies, think about how you approach the world. How do you respond to a challenge? Do you get energized and excited? (choleric) Do you feel like life is always handing you a bit too much and withdraw? (melancholic) Do you decide it is best to think about it tomorrow? (phlegmatic) Do you start thinking of ways to cope with it from as many points of view as possible and thereby become a bit scattered (sanguine)? What colors are you drawn towards? What kinds of activities do you enjoy? How do you walk? Do you skip, shuffle, or step firmly with your heels? Remember, temperament is not personality, but it does give one insight about how we meet life, and it can be especially helpful for children who may be a bit stuck in their temperament to move forward.

In the life of each of us, there is a phase we live through that has a tone of each temperament, if you will. For example, a veil of sanguinity colors childhood from birth to about age 12-14. Adolescence and early adult life, age 14 -28, is colored by a choleric veil. Midlife, age 28-60, is colored by a melancholic veil, and old age, 60 and up, has a veil of phlegmatic wafting over it.

At the end of this chapter, there is a list of adjectives and nouns to get you started adding temperament "words" into your stories. As you recognize your child's natural tendency toward one or two temperaments, you can personalize the story to suit your child's temperament by using some of these words. As you enhance a description of the landscape or the house where the characters live with "temperament" words, you will gain confidence in your ability to use stories to help children overcome challenges and difficulties. Using words that enhance and strengthen temperament metaphors and imagery helps children become freer of their own temperament as their personality unfolds. Creating more clarity around a particular moment in the story by adding description gives your child or students more time to take in the story. You slow things down and open things up so that the story becomes more rich and available to your child or your students.

You can also work with the temperaments through the tone and energy of your voice. For parts of the story that slow down, slow yourself down and take more time by adding more description to the story. The phlegmatics will breathe easier. For parts of the story that are full of action, you can become more animated (without losing yourself in the story or dramatizing too much) to wake up the phlegmatics and make the cholerics feel seen. For parts of the story that are more contemplative or reflective, pause a bit and enjoy the moment with the melancholics. And for parts of the story where a surprise happens or suddenly bird song is heard…linger a bit so the sanguines can enjoy the moment.

Sometimes, children can become stuck in their temperament, and a good story can be just the ticket to helping things shift. For younger children, keeping the story in the animal kingdom is best. For teens, using biographical stories of persons who have overcome their own tendencies or challenges are helpful. For children who are extremely one-sided and seem to be suffering from their temperament, a "real-life" story can help them tremendously. You can also create your own story. See Part III Supplemental Information for ideas on story creating; and see Chapter 16 for an outline of a biographical story.

Here's a reminiscence from my childhood that illustrates the temperaments in action.

## When I Was a Child

When I was a child, I loved to skip. And to swing! I would throw my head back and let my hair stream on the ground as I flew up and down on the swing. I organized plays in our backyard and we hung a sheet over the clothesline for a curtain. We acted out many stories. I loved being Rapunzel and sitting on the wooden trellis that was attached to the playhouse wall. There was a window there and we could climb the trellis and jump through the window down onto a springy couch. Fun! I was a heavy-set child and yet I was quick on my feet.

I had a best friend who lived down at the corner who loved to be at home. She always wanted me to come to her house and play. She loved to eat and always had the best snacks! She preferred playing indoors rather than outdoors and liked to sit quietly as she rearranged the landscape we created for our dolls. When we grew older, I would spend the night at her house—a sleepover—but whenever she spent the night at my house, she would have trouble falling asleep, and I would wake up in the morning to discover that my mother had had to take her home. As a child, I never understood this, but as I look back today, I understand that part of the explanation may lie in her temperament, for she loved her routine at home.

I had another friend who lived across the street. He was tall and big boned and always took charge of the games we played. The children in the neighborhood would gather at the vacant lot to play tag, or softball, or hide and seek. He would round up anyone who was late. His eyes were bright and dancing. He would ask what we should play and then he would get it all organized and off we would go! I only remember him loosing his temper when someone was acting up and being too silly and slowing the organization of the activities down. His face would be bright red with enthusiasm or with frustration.

Around the corner lived one of my best friends. He was thin and tall and very pale. His soft green-brown eyes were watery. In third grade, we were boyfriend and girlfriend, and he would chase me home from school and kiss me when he caught me. I would laugh and run off again. He gazed downwards as he walked and loved to stand and stare at the river flowing below us on the bridge. It meandered through our town and the water made slow swirls as it flowed beneath the bridge. Sometimes, he would write poems about it. As he grew older, his gentle features grew more defined. He loved to read and spend time alone in the woods or in his room.

Match the temperaments to each of these characters. Then spend some time reflecting on your own childhood and your friends. Make some notes about them, and the concept of the temperaments will begin to make sense to you.

## Using Temperaments to Address Behavioral Challenges

Helping children see their own idiosyncrasies through a character in a story is a way to work subtly on behavioral challenges and to soften the effect of their natural temperament tendencies so they have more self-control. When children see another character outside themselves doing what they do, they begin to understand on an unconscious level what needs to change. Over time, their behavior shifts.

Adding temperament words to a story also ensures that each temperament is represented in each story. There is no judgment, blame, or negativity associated with this process. Working with the temperaments in storytelling in this subtle way allows the child to experience the effect of his or her actions objectively, and this inner experience can enable her or him to change behavior and have more confidence at the same time.

As adults, we too have one or, sometimes, two dominant temperaments. When we become aware of them then we can strive to bring them into balance consciously. Make some notes as you observe yourself over the next few days, and see if you can uncover your temperament as a child, and note how it has changed as you have matured into adulthood.

## The Temperaments as They Apply in the Classroom

In a classroom, the teacher can play with the temperaments in her presentations to the class by consciously moving between the temperaments during the lesson. Begin experimenting with this idea by using your voice to speed up, slow down, speak simply, speak dramatically and have a surprise in your back pocket. Gradually, you will become so adept at adding the temperaments into your presentations that it will no longer require conscious effort. You will be delighted by the changes you can perceive in your students when they are met in this way. For example, alternate between slow speech for the phlegmatic; quick, breathy speech for the sanguine; loud, dramatic speech for the choleric; and serious, contemplative speech for the melancholic. Sometimes, seating the same temperaments together helps students actually become weary of their temperament and adjust it a bit. In other words, two cholerics can temper each other, as can two melancholics, phlegmatics, or sanguines!

Bring in the outside world through your voice…talk about your morning ride into school and what you saw as you passed by the farms or high rises. What did you hear? Share a moment of each temperament out of your own experience. You will find you connect more deeply with your students and help them to arrive as you prepare them to dive into the lesson.

# Temperament Word Lists

Add a splash of each temperament to every story by adding descriptive words that reflect each of the four. Here are some word lists to get you started.

| Fire Words | Water Words | Earth Words | Air Words |
|---|---|---|---|
| passionate | calm | feeling blue | curious |
| energetic | fluid | depressed | curiosity |
| brave | meandering | melancholic | energetic |
| stubborn | splashy | sad | happy |
| assertive | bubbly | gazes down | eager |
| lively | icy | sadness | risk taker |
| impatient | snow | calm | impulsive |
| leader | hail | thoughtful | kinesthetic |
| pushy | rain | quiet | easily over stim- |
| bossy | liquid | solid | ulated |
| bully | tears | self-confident | music |
| bullish | iceberg | brown | clouds |
| mouthy | gulf | blue | movement |
| responsible | harbor | grass | imaginative |
| red | starfish | mountain | flighty |
| intolerant | oasis | valley | joyful |
| impulsive | reflective | silent | distractible |
| determined | well | reflective | unfocused |
| sunny | tap | observant | skipping |
| embers | aquifer | solid | hopping |
| flame | drops | reserved | swinging |
| frustrated | wash | intense | in motion |
| courageous | sweat | memory | laughter |
| fearless | icicles | sensitive | giggles |
| loud | reservoir | | forgetful |
| passionately | fountain | | |
| | spring | | |

# CHAPTER 12

## 7–8 Years Old

The Swing

By Robert Lewis Stevenson

*How do you like to go up in a swing,*
*Up in the air so blue?*
*Oh, I do think it the pleasantest thing*
*Ever a child can do!*
*Up in the air and over the wall,*
*Till I can see so wide,*
*River and trees and cattle and all*
*Over the countryside—*
*Till I look down on the garden green,*
*Down on the roof so brown—*
*Up in the air I go flying again,*
*Up in the air and down!*

## Characteristics of Children at Ages 7 and 8

Jamie is 7 years old. She loves to swing! Higher and higher she flies up, up, up! As she soars, she increases her momentum with each swing. Suddenly, she is upside down! Her hair streams along the grass. Laughing with abandon, she pumps her legs rhythmically and regains the heights. What would it be like to keep going up and up and over the top! She wonders. Down she flies, whooshing through the grass and swinging up high once more. Her back to the sky, she gazes down, down, down at the ground far below. The freedom from gravity exhilarates her. She leaves the swing energized.

Moments later, she is caught up in a game of tag. She runs in pursuit. She turns around. Where have her friends gone? A moment of panic consumes her. She feels lonely, confused. Alice comes over to her and the two girls walk quietly together. Seconds later they are racing to the swings, laughing and shouting.

This is the child of age 7/8! The swing is an apt metaphor for the ups and downs of this age group. Saints one minute and rascals the next. Swinging back and forth between states of wonder and worry in one moment, silliness and seriousness the next. Happy-sad, reverent-irreverent, buoyant-reserved, this age group tries on the plethora of feelings with fervor. The explorations in the realm of feelings by the child of 7/8 can be confusing and frustrating to parents and teachers alike. This *is* normal! This stage of exploration is a necessary step in becoming more conscious of the inner world of the self. Such mood swings are common and normal and we, as the adults, should welcome this change as it heralds a new awareness developing in the 7/8-year-old. The child's feelings must be honored and treated as real and true. Inwardly, they are experiencing an awakening to the differences between themselves and others. It is the beginning of the development of an awareness of the separation of "self" from the world that will mature around the age of 9/10.

Still very much children of the moment, this age group requires patience and understanding on the part of the parent and teacher. The feelings the child is dealing with are new and delicate, and the experiences that accompany them form the basis for the development of a healthy emotional life later in adolescence and adulthood. A calm and reflective attitude on the part of the parent and teacher will help the children understand their experiences and learn from them. At this stage, children are discovering social relationships and the concept of "best friend" appears. At the same time, they are becoming more individual in their likes and dislikes. Thus, we see they are working hard on both individual and social development.

Stories that inspire hope and trust that the world is good and true build confidence in life. At the same time, such stories help children to understand and recognize the subtleties of the myriad feelings they are experiencing. As the child becomes increasingly self-aware, feelings of jealousy and selfishness may arise. The power of these feelings can arouse guilt, confusion, and discomfort within. What are the stories to help the child through this exciting and challenging phase? There are three types of stories particularly suited to this age: stories of the lives of saints that inspire, fables full of humor and wisdom that point out human foibles, and animal folk tales that offer a picture of sacrifice for a higher purpose. Let's look at each of these story genres.

# Stories for Children Ages 7/8

## Stories of the Lives of Saints and Wise Women and Men

Stories of the saints of Ireland, India, Persia, France, and elsewhere speak to the soul of children at this age, offering rich food for their imaginations. An individual who has overcome selfishness and self-absorption and has dedicated his or her life to serving a higher purpose or serving others is intriguing to the 7/8-year-old. Such individuals have often had to overcome great challenges in their lives, and the children are drawn into these stories because it feels to them as if they, too, are experiencing trials and tribulations in their own lives. They are maturing, and part of that process is exploring what is right and wrong, fair and unfair, true and untrue. How do these stories help?

The story of the life of a saint or hero inspires the heroic longings and strivings of the child by suggesting ways that one can live one's life in a just and heroic manner. Why would someone give up a life of ease to help the less fortunate as St. Francis of Assisi did? Children find this question intriguing. Tales from the lives of modern-day saints and heroes such as Mother Theresa and Dr. Martin Luther King, Jr. offer inspiration and encouragement for life, as do the saints of old. What does it feel like to sacrifice one's personal needs so that others may be fed, clothed, healed, or helped? Stories of people who live a life of service to others in today's world speak to the heart and mind of the child in second grade. These stories should be told with warmth and humor and without drama. We don't want to share too much about the tragedies of our world with them. It is too soon.

Children of this age are also ripe for hearing stories of local heroes who have made a difference in their community. Firefighters, police officers, volunteers, teachers, doctors, and neighbors are all possible heroes of a good story. Again, we want to focus on the positive efforts of these local heroes. Today, children are exposed to a barrage of irreverence. One experience of reverence can make a profound difference in the life of a child. Taking a child to hear a concert, to the ballet, or to an art gallery can inspire a feeling of reverence that the child will remember many years later. Think back on your own childhood to about this age and recall a person who inspired you. These experiences usually involve a sense of awe at the human potential embodied by the person who was the source of inspiration. Telling stories of people who have overcome obstacles and dedicated themselves to higher causes will inspire and encourage this age group.

Hearing stories like these may inspire children of this age to want help others and to help more around the house. Helping others is a nurturing and fulfilling experience for this age group. Mowing a lawn for the old gentleman at the end of the street once a week, for example, gives the child seeking meaning and fairness an opportunity to be of service and make a new friend!

## St. Valentinus

Every year, all over the world, people celebrate Valentine's Day. We send flowers, share chocolates, and give gifts to those we love near and far. It is a wonderful tradition that offers us the opportunity to pause and reflect on the meaning of love itself as well as celebrate it in our lives. Most of the holidays we celebrate have a story or two behind them. I looked into the story of Valentine's Day and found its hero, Saint Valentine. Here is a little story from his life that explains where and how the first "valentine" came into being.

Before telling this story, talk about the day itself and have the children share some stories about their experiences of Valentine's Day. Then tell the story simply without much drama. In this way, you leave the children free to take in what they need from the story. When you are interested in the story, that interest is communicated through your voice to your child or students, and it will pique their interest. The child in this story is about the age of the children we have been talking about. I have always wondered where and how this holiday originated and hope you enjoy the story as much as I do.

## The Legend of Saint Valentine (Age 7 and up)

*(Love, Courage, Steadfastness in one's beliefs)*

A long time ago Valentinus was born in Rome. He was a kind man who became a follower of Christ. The Emperor of Rome at that time was Claudius II. He ordered all Romans to worship the twelve Roman gods. Valentinus was sent to prison because he did not do what Claudius asked.

While he was in prison the jailer asked him if he would teach his daughter Julia. She had been blind since her birth. Julia was a lovely young girl with a quick mind. She was about 7 or 8 years old. Valentinus read stories of Rome's history to her. He described the world of nature to her. He taught her arithmetic, and told her about God. She saw the world through his eyes, trusted his wisdom and found comfort in his quiet strength.

"Valentinus, does God really hear our prayers?" Julia said one day.

"Yes, my child. He hears each one," he replied.

"Do you know what I pray for every morning and every night? I pray that I might see. I want so much to see everything you've told me about!"

"God does what is best for us if we will only believe in Him," Valentinus said.

"Oh, Valentinus, I do believe," Julia said intensely. "I do." She knelt and grasped his hand.

They sat quietly together, praying.

Suddenly, there was a brilliant light in the prison cell. Radiant, Julia screamed. "Valentinus, I can see! I can see!"

"Praise be to God!" Valentinus exclaimed, and he knelt in prayer.

On the eve of his death, Valentinus wrote a last note to Julia, urging her to stay close to God, and he signed it "From Your Valentine." His sentence was carried out the next day, February 14, 270 A.D. near a gate that was later named PortaValentini in his memory. He was buried at what is now the Church of Praxedes in Rome. It is said that Julia herself planted a pink-blossomed almond tree near his grave. Today, the almond tree remains a symbol of abiding love and friendship. Every year on February 14, St. Valentine's Day is cele-brated around the world and messages of love and appreciation are exchanged between family and friends.

**Pre-story for The Rescue:** Throughout history, stories about wise women and men who heal and help others throughout their lives have been told. These remarkable people are found in every religious movement on the earth. This story comes from Ancient Persia where healers and teachers were given the title Hodja, which means "wise one." Ancient Persia was located in the area we know today as Turkey, Iraq and Iran.

## The Rescue (Age 7 and up)

*(Innocence and Humor)*

Nazrudin Hodja yawned. He stretched his arms in their gaily-striped sleeves. He stretched his long legs in their yellow pantaloons.

"Time for bed!" He rubbed his eyes. "But first a good cold drink of water."

Nazrudin Hodja reached for the earthen water jug. Empty!

"Fatima!" he called. "Fatima!" No answer! He must go to the well and fill the jug himself.

Drowsily he stumbled to his feet. He straightened his turban, which had fallen over one ear as he dozed. At the door he shoved his bare toes into his scruffily pointed shoes before he stepped out into the moonlit courtyard.

"Such an evening!" He breathed deeply of the cool night air. As he ambled across to the well, Nazrudeen Hodja was glad that Fatima had been asleep. It was worth the effort of coming out to the well just to see such a moon. He sniffed the fragrance of the almond blossoms, feathery soft in the silver light.

"I wonder if the water looks black or golden on a night like this," thought the Hodja. He leaned over to look down into the well. His drowsy eyes popped wide open. Instantly he gave a low scream. "What has happened?" he cried. He looked wildly about for someone to help him.

"Fatima!" he called. "Fatima! The moon has fallen into the well!"

No answer! There was no one to help. Something had happened

that would make the whole world a sadder, darker place. He, and only he, must make it right again. He would find a way. He would be a true hero.

Nazrudin Hodja fluttered about. He did not know exactly how to begin being a hero, but he did feel very brave and important.

"I have it!" he cried as he noticed the empty hook on the end of the rope he held in his hand. "If this hook can lift water jars in and out of the well, it surely can lift the moon out."

His hands trembling with excitement, he let the rope down deep into the well. The hook clattered on the rough stone sides as it went down. There was a muffled splash as it hit the water.

"Keep up your courage, good Moon!" The voice of the Hodja sounded hollow in the well. "I am here! All will soon be mended!"

He dangled the hook near the surface of the water, swinging it back and forth until he felt it catch on something solid. Giving never a thought to the jutting stones that lined the well, he was sure that it was the moon he had hooked.

He jerked and tugged, but the hook held fast.

"Jump when I pull, good Moon," he called. "Do not pull against me."

He braced his feet and put every bit of strength into one mighty yank. Up came the hook. Down on the cobblestones of the court-yard went Nasrudin Hodja. He lay on his back, blinking up at the sky.

Suddenly he forgot the pain of his fall. He rubbed his eyes and looked again. Yes, there above him shone the full round moon. That mighty pull of his had carried the moon out of the well and had shot it back to its rightful place as queen of the night sky.

"Oh, Moon," said the Hodja in triumph, "it was a hard fight, but I saved you. Now you can shine again for all the world."

Rubbing his bruised head, he scuffled back into the house. He was so content with his own heroism that he completely forgot the empty water jug at the edge of the well.

Fairness is a big issue at age 7 and 8. The following story let's us see the other side of Hodja Nazrudin and to understand why he was considered a wise teacher. A beloved story indeed.

## The Woodcutter and Hodja Nazrudin (Age 7 and up)

*(Fairness)*

High on a mountain trail, Nazrudin (pronounced Naz-roo-deen) Hodja pulled his donkey to a sudden stop. The ring of an axe, the sound of a man's voice, and the tinkling of donkey bells told him there was companionship in this lonely spot. And the Hodja did like people who would talk and listen. He turned his donkey into a tiny footpath that led toward the sounds.

Soon he came upon a group of six donkeys grazing on some cleared land. On all sides were piles of wood cut into stove lengths. Near by was a muscular man swinging an axe. The woodcutter stepped quickly back as a pine tree swayed, moaned, and toppled to the ground. On a stump in the cool shade sat a neatly dressed man who clapped and applauded as the tree fell.

"Bravo, my strong woodcutter!" cheered this second man who was not much more than half the size of the woodcutter. "That was a fine, big tree we cut. That will keep Siraj-ed-Din Bey warm many a winter day. Haidi bakalum! On to the next tree!"

Without looking at his comfortable companion, the woodcutter walked around an oak tree to decide where it should fall, took a firm grip on his axe handle, and started swinging just above the tree's roots.

Each time the woodcutter's axe bit into the tree, the little man on the stump would grunt. The Hodja sat on his donkey, watching this strange performance—the strong man swinging the axe without a sound passing his lips while the sitting man kept up a steady flow of grunts, groans, and cheers. It was too much for the Hodja's curiosity.

"Why do you make all the noise while the other man does all the work?" he asked the little man.

"Oh, I am helping him," chirruped the man. "He has agreed to cut thirty donkey loads of wood for Siraj-ed-Din Bey. Think what a job that would be for one man. I took pity on him and went into partnership with him. He swings the axe while I grunt and cheer to keep up his courage."

The Hodja watched the woodcutter who was saying nothing, but making the chips fly. "I think," mused the Hodja, "it is the woodcutter's strong arms that give him courage." The Hodja looked at the sun. It was growing late and he was not finding the two men very lively company. The Hodja gave the low throaty "Ughr-r-r," which started the donkey picking its careful way down the mountain trail toward home.

It was a fortnight later that the Hodja came upon the two men of the mountaintop again. He was loitering about the court, just in case the judge might need his advice about anything. It was amazing how often the Hodja's agile wit could pull the Judge's solemn wisdom out of a tangle. The two men of the mountaintop were disputing before the Judge. Their hands moved as fast as their tongues.

"I earned every ghurush of it myself," the big woodcutter was saying. "I did every stroke of the cutting of thirty donkey loads of wood for Siraj-ed-Din Bey. I loaded the wood onto the donkeys. I drove them to Siraj-ed-Din Bey's house, unloaded every stick of the wood alone, and went back to the mountain for more loads."

"He forgets!" the dapper little man of the stump interrupted. "He forgets how I cheered him at his work. I had a grunt for every swing of his axe, and a cheer for every falling tree. I earned a goodly portion of the money which Siraj-ed-Din Bey made the mistake of paying entirely to the woodcutter."

The Judge looked helpless. He had never met just such a case before. There was nothing in his law books about this kind of argument. He was relieved to see the familiar figure of Nazrudin Hodja elbowing its way through the crowd.

"I turn this case over to my able assistant, Nazrudin Hodja," said the Judge, sighing and leaning back, his troubles over. "Repeat your stories to the Hodja."

Both talking at once, the woodcutter and his self-appointed helper told their stories. The Hodja listened, nodding wisely, till both men had talked themselves silent. Then the Hodja beckoned a court attendant. "Bring me a money tray."

The tray was brought. The crowd pressed nearer to see what was going to happen. "Give me the money, good woodcutter, the money Siraj-ed-Din Bey paid you for the thirty donkey loads of wood."

"But it is my money," pleaded the woodcutter. "I sweated and toiled for every ghurush of it while this man just sat in the shade and made strange sounds."

"The money, please," repeated the Hodja, holding out his hand for the bag. Reluctantly, the woodcutter passed over the moneybag while the little man of the stump drew nearer, his eyes greedily aglitter.

One by one, the Hodja took the coins from the bag and rang them out on the money tray, talking to the man who was claiming a share.

"Do you hear that? Do you like the sound? Isn't that a cheery ring?

The little man nodded, drawing so close that his nose almost touched the ringing coins. His thumb and forefinger were rubbing together as they itched for the feel of the money.

The last ghurush had left the bag and had made its cheerful ring on the money tray. The big woodcutter writhed to see his hard-earned wages in danger. The little helper smirked to see so much money so near.

"You heard it all?" the Hodja asked the little man.

He nodded hungrily.

"Every ghurush of it?" asked the Hodja.

The little man continued to nod.

"Then you have had your wages." The Hodja began to sweep the money back into the bag. "The sound of the money is proper pay for the sound of working."

The Hodja handed the full moneybag to the smiling woodcutter, saying, "And the money is proper pay for the work."

# Fables

Stories of the lives of saints and holy people told alongside humorous and delightful animal fables give children the opportunity to observe human nature in story forms that satisfy both their desire for humor and their longing for truth and goodness.

Fables present the humorous side of life and are particularly appropriate stories for this age. They are delightful tales wherein animals take on the idiosyncratic behaviors of humans. They portray situations between animals that express a particular polarity of feeling clearly and with humor, as we shall see.

Let us begin with a word about how to present fables. The so-called "moral" of the fable should never be stated, as it oversimplifies the situation and takes away the joy of discovery for the child. Subtlety is lost. The opportunity of making the story their own, interpreting it in a way that connects it to their personal experience is ruined when the "point" of the story is reduced to a simple moralistic phrase.

Children are fascinated by the foibles and idiosyncrasies of people. Given the chance to determine what the fable is about on their own (with the guiding hand of the teacher or parent), they will create a rich and varied response through a lively discussion that is often humorous and always delightful. And they will arrive at a short description that is pithy, rich and engaging! In the process, they will have made conscious many of the issues, feelings, and situations that they experience and explored how to approach them more openly and with confidence.

Unlike other traditional stories, a fable is best told by beginning with a pre-story that leads the children into a conversation **before** they hear the tale. Let's take the Tortoise and the Hare as an example. You might begin like this: *"Have you ever known someone who, no matter how well you do something, they insist they can do it better or faster?"* Now you have their interest. Give an example from your own life. For example, "My younger sister is always trying to do everything I do only better! The other day, I told her that I was baking some brownies, and she immediately launched into an explanation of why her brownies are so much better than mine." Then ask the children to tell you examples from their own experience. The hands will go up, and you will hear all kinds of fascinating tiny tales from the children's personal lives about such situations. Listen to the comments without commenting yourself, for they will spark each other's memories, and eventually, everyone will have an example to share.

After a lively discussion, tell the children the fable and simply let it be. Don't talk about it again until the next day. After "sleeping on it," the children will then tell YOU what the story was all about. Working together with them, you can create a beautiful sentence or two that is more inclusive, succinct, and relevant to the meaning of the fable than any pre-written MORAL in a book. Creating a book of fable stories and pre-stories with drawings is a great project for second or third graders.

At home, you can use the same format. Children love to hear stories from their parents' childhoods. Tell a little tale from your own life that mirrors the story. Then ask them if they have been in a similar situation or have friends who have. After that conversation, tell the fable. Retelling it together the next evening and chatting about what the fable portrays will often lead to a level of conversation and understanding that allows you a peek into how your children are developing their thinking. Let the children take the lead and see if you can help by echoing or repeating back to them what they said *using different words.* For example, if your child says the hare deserved to lose because he was boasting about his quickness. You might offer: yes, the hare thought he was faster than anyone. This approach allows your child to reflect further and to continue to explore deeper levels of meaning on his or her own. This kind of mirroring back is a relaxing non-threatening way of encouraging children to express themselves more fully, as they articulate conclusions that are uniquely their own.

Here's the fable we have been discussing. Give it a try! Create your own pre-story that will lead into a conversation with your child, children or class. After a lively discussion, tell this story!

## The Hare and the Tortoise (Ages 7-9)

### From Aesop's Fables
*(Pride, Hubris and Steadfastness)*

The Hare was once boasting that he was the fastest of all the animals. "I have never been beaten," said he. Much to the Hare's surprise, the Tortoise quietly said, "I challenge you to a race."

"Very well," said the Hare, "I will dance rings around you all the way."

The Tortoise replied, "Shall we race?"

It was soon agreed that the Fox would set the course and be the judge. The race began and the Hare ran so fast that he quickly left the Tortoise far behind.

It was a warm sunny day. Once he reached the middle of the course, the Hare decided to take a nap. He stretched out on the soft grass and fell asleep.

While the Hare slept, the Tortoise plodded on and on straight toward the finish line.

By and by the Hare awoke from his nap. He looked all around. He looked back towards the starting point and the Tortoise was nowhere in sight. He looked ahead towards the finish line. There was the Tortoise! Racing to the finish line as fast as he could, the Hare was surprised to find the Tortoise with a smile on his face just crossing the finish line ahead of him.

This engaging story rings true in everyone's heart. We can relate to both of the animals and their salient characteristics. It is delightful to experience the subtle nuances involved in the actions of the tortoise that is perfectly content to just be himself and only races the hare to appease him, while the hare is always wondering about his prowess and is so self-absorbed that he cannot imagine what it is like to be a tortoise. The tortoise, being a more reflective character, has a good idea of what the hare is like. The hare becomes distracted by the heat of the sun, and, confident in his ability to outrun the tortoise, takes a nap.

The tortoise remains focused on the task at hand, and, in the end, passes the hare and wins the race–by a hair! The silly hare wakes up and realizes he cannot see the tortoise behind him, runs as fast as he can, and arrives at the finish line not relaxed and feeling in control, but panicked when he sees the tortoise crossing the finish line just ahead of him. Don't we see this story over and over again in our daily lives as we struggle to be conscious of our idiosyncrasies and overcome our own inner hare and tortoise? This is an image of common human characteristics played out in a seemingly simple story. Fables help children of 7 and 8 to understand the emotions that they experience and, thereby, to express their feelings more clearly.

## Using Pre-Stories with Fables

Here is another example of a pre-story that can be used to get children ready to listen to the fable of "The Fox and the Crow." *"I once had a neighbor who lived down the street. She loved to gossip about the other neighbors, for she seemed to think that she was better than they were. One day, she began to compliment me by saying, "Oh I wish I had that beautiful bracelet and necklace. You have such good taste! They must have cost a fortune! Have you had them a long time? I have the perfect outfit for them! Oh, and I need some jewelry. You always seem to have the best jewelry to match your clothes." I was so flattered that I offered to loan her my necklace. It was a long, long time before I finally got the necklace back. Has anyone ever tricked you out of something by flattering you?"* Following this discussion, tell the fable of "The Fox and the Crow."

## The Fox and the Crow (Ages 7-9)

### From Aesop's Fables
*(Flattery)*

A big black Crow was sitting on a branch of a tree with a piece of cheese in her beak, when she was seen by a hungry fox.

The fox walked under the branch, looked up at the Crow, and said," What a noble bird you are! Your beauty is without equal and the color of your feathers is exquisite. If your voice is as sweet as your looks, then I think you are the Queen of the Birds." The Crow was very flattered by the Fox's compliments and, just to show him that she could sing, she opened her mouth to caw. But as soon as she opened her mouth, the cheese fell to the ground, where it was snatched up the clever Fox.

After reviewing and retelling the story together the following day, have the children draw pictures of their favorite scenes from the story. This is another way to deepen the experience and to express their individuality creatively. If you have a basket of colored capes or material, or hats, have the children act out the story. Or choose one particular moment in the story that could be acted out by everyone who wants to try it. For example, one child could be the fox and call out to the other child who is the crow: "If your voice is as sweet as your looks, then I think you are the

Queen of the Birds." The "crow" then drops the cheese and the fox runs away with it. Reviewing stories imaginatively and using the whole body helps the child connect more deeply with the story. It also strengthens language skills, as children are encouraged to use more complex language than we often find today in every day conversation. Any follow-up activity you can create will make the story more alive and rich for the child.

Fables work deeply into the psyche of the 7/8-year-olds, helping them to understand the unique differences between one another, while encouraging them to have patience and understanding for others. Empathy is one of the most important qualities we can foster in children. Stories show examples of empathy, and fables are short, pithy tales that help clarify the differences between the many motives and feelings that children are exploring at this stage.

There are many wonderful collections of fables available for you to choose from. Two well-loved collections are *Aesop's Fables* and the Buddha's *Jataka Tales*.

**Pre-story for "The Lion and the Mouse."** Have you ever known someone who was strong and courageous and thought that he or she was better than anyone else? I once had a neighbor who was older than I was and she was always reminding me of how much more she knew than I did. I still played games with her after school but was always aware of her feeling of superiority even when I won!

## The Lion and the Mouse (Ages 7–9)

### From Aesop's Fables
*(Friendship, Courage)*

A mighty Lion was sleeping in his lair when he was awakened by a tiny Mouse running across his body. The Lion grabbed the frightened creature with his huge paw and opened his mouth to swallow him. "Please, O King," cried the Mouse, "spare me this time and I shall never forget your kindness Someday I may be able to repay you." The Lion was so amused by this idea that he let the poor creature go.

Sometime later the Lion was caught in a net laid by some clever hunters. Despite his great strength, the Lion could not break free. Soon, the forest echoed with angry roars.

The little Mouse heard the Lion and ran to see what was wrong. As soon as he saw the Lion, he began to gnaw away the ropes, and before long he set the Lion free. "There!" said the Mouse proudly, "You laughed at me when I promised to repay your kindness, but now you know that even a tiny Mouse can help a mighty Lion."

**Pre-story for "The Milkmaid and Her Pail."** Do you ever have daydreams? Do you imagine yourself being the pitcher who wins the World Series? Or becoming a great ballerina or singer and making records that everyone loves? Do you take music lessons, play sports, or have a favorite activity **in which you want to excel?** Have a discussion about this with your children or your students and then talk about what it takes to prepare to be a great pitcher or a singer or an actor or a nurse, etc. Then tell "The Milkmaid and Her Pail."

## The Milkmaid and Her Pail (Ages 7-9)

*(Focus, Distraction, "Staying focused on the task at hand")*

One afternoon a pretty Milkmaid finished milking the cows. She took the pail of fresh milk and put in on her head for that was the way that people carried milk in those days. As she walked along she began to think about what she would do with the money she would get for the pail of milk.

"I will sell this fine pail of milk at the market. With the money I will get for the milk, I will buy some freshly laid eggs. I will put the eggs under the old black hen and she will sit on them until they hatch!

"I will take good care of the chicks and by Easter time they will be big enough to sell at the market. I shall sell them for a good price. With the money from the chickens I shall buy an Easter hat for myself."

"There will be enough money for me to buy a new dress as well. I shall wear my new hat and my new dress on Easter Sunday. I shall look so pretty that all the young men will want to walk with me. But do you think that I shall let them?"

"No! I will just shake my head as much as to say..."

And the pretty Milkmaid did shake her head. What do you think happened to the pail of milk that she was carrying home on her head? The pail fell down and the milk went all over the ground. And all the pretty milkmaid's planning was useless.

From this story people have made an old saying...Do you know what it is? "Don't count your chickens before they hatch!"

## Animal Folktales

Animal folktales from around the world are another genre of stories ripe for this age group. The idea here is that the animal takes on the qualities of a human being and sacrifices itself to save a forest from fire or other animals from disaster. Animals risk their lives to help others, and, because of their great sacrifice, the animal receives a gift from a higher power. They have intriguing titles such as, "How the Bat Came to Be," "How Robin Got His Red Breast," and "Why Hares Have Long Ears." At this age, children are interested in how human beings interact with the animal kingdom. These stories offer insight into the nature of specific animals, and inspire children through the sacrifices the animals make for others.

## The Foolish, Timid Rabbit (Ages 7–9)

### A Jataka Tale from India

*[This story addresses irrational fears, gossip and exaggeration, and lack of forethought.]*

ONCE upon a time, a Rabbit was asleep under a palm-tree.

All at once he woke up, and thought: "What if the world should break up! What then would become of me?" At that moment, some Monkeys dropped a coconut. It fell down on the ground just back of the Rabbit.

Hearing the noise, the Rabbit said to himself: "The earth is all breaking up!" And he jumped up and ran just as fast as he could, without even looking back to see what made the noise.

Another Rabbit saw him running, and called after him, "What are you running so fast for?" Don't ask me!" he cried.

But the other Rabbit ran after him, begging to know what was the matter. Then the first Rabbit said: "Don't you know? The earth is all breaking up!"

The next Rabbit they met ran with them when he heard that the earth was all breaking up. One Rabbit after another joined them, until there were hundreds of Rabbits running as fast as they could go.

They passed a Deer, calling out to him that the earth was all break-

---

ing up. The Deer then ran with them. The Deer called to a Fox to come along because the earth was all breaking up.

On and on they ran, and an Elephant joined them. At last the Lion saw the animals running, and heard their cry that the earth was all breaking up.

He thought there must be some mistake, so he ran to the foot of a hill in front of them and roared three times. This stopped them, for they knew the voice of the King of Beasts, and they feared him.

"Why are you running so fast?" asked the Lion.

"Oh, King Lion," they answered him, "the earth is all breaking up!"

"Who saw it breaking up?" asked the Lion.

"I didn't," said the Elephant. "Ask the Fox—he told me about it."

"I didn't," said the Fox. "The Rabbits told me about it," said the Deer. One after another of the Rabbits said: "I did not see it, but another Rabbit told me about it."

At last the Lion came to the Rabbit who had first said the earth was all breaking up.

"Is it true that the earth is all breaking up?" the Lion asked.

"Yes, O Lion, it is," said the Rabbit. "I was asleep under a palm-tree. I woke up and thought, 'What would become of me if the earth should all break up?' At that very moment, I heard the sound of the earth breaking up, and I ran away."

"Then," said the Lion, "you and I will go back to the place where the earth began to break up, and see what is the matter."

So the Lion put the little Rabbit on his back, and away they went like the wind. The other animals waited for them at the foot of the hill. The Rabbit told the Lion when they were near the place where he slept, and the Lion saw just where the Rabbit had been sleeping. He saw, too, the coconut that had fallen to the ground near by.

Then the Lion said to the Rabbit, "It must have been the sound of the coconut falling to the ground that you heard. You foolish Rabbit!" And the Lion ran back to the other animals, and told them all about it. If it had not been for the wise King of Beasts, they might be running still.

## The Three Fishes (Ages 7–9)

### A Jataka Tale from India
*(Wisdom and Foolishness)*

Once upon a time three fishes lived in a far-away river. They were named Thoughtful, Very-Thoughtful, and Thoughtless.

One day they left the wild country where no men lived, and come down the river to live near a town.

Very-Thoughtful said to the other two: "There is danger all about us here. Fishermen come to the river here to catch fish with all sorts of nets and lines. Let us go back again to the wild country where we used to live."

But the other two Fishes were so lazy and greedy that they kept putting off their going day after day.

One day Thoughtful and Thoughtless went swimming on ahead of Very-Thoughtful. They did not see the fisherman's net and rushed into it. Very-Thoughtful saw them rush into the net.

"I must save them," said Very-Thoughtful.

So, swimming around the net, he splashed in the water in front of it, like a Fish that had broken through the net and gone up the river. Then he swam back of the net and splashed about there like a Fish that had broken through and gone down the river.

The fisherman saw the splashing water and thought the Fishes had broken through the net and that one had gone up the river, the other down the river. So he pulled in the net by one corner. That let the two Fishes out of the net and away they went to find Very-Thoughtful.

"You saved our lives, Very-Thoughtful," they said, "and now we are willing to go back to the wild country."

So back they all went to their old home where they lived safely ever after.

# The Cat Who Came Indoors (Age 7 and Up)

## An Animal Folk Tale from Africa

*(Determination to find one's place in the world, confidence, persistence.)*

Once there was a cat, a wild cat, who lived all by herself out in the bush. After a while she got tired of living alone and took herself a husband, another wild cat that she thought was the finest creature in all the jungle.

One day, as they strolled together along the path through the tall grass, swish, out of the grass jumped Leopard, and Cat's husband was bowled over, all fur and claws into the dust.

"O-oh!" said Cat. "I see my husband is covered in dust and is not the finest creature in all the jungle. It is Leopard." So cat went to live with Leopard. They lived together very happily until one day, as they were hunting in the bush, suddenly – whoosh – out of the shadows leapt Lion right onto Leopard's back and ate him all up.

"O-oh"! said Cat. "I see Leopard is not the finest creature in all the jungle. It is Lion." So Cat went to live with Lion. They lived together very happily until one day, as they were stalking through the forest, a large shape loomed overhead, and – *fu – chu* – Elephant put one foot on top of Lion and squashed him flat.

" O-o-o-o-oh!" said Cat. "I see Lion is not the finest creature in all the jungle. It is elephant." So Cat went to live with Elephant. She climbed up onto his back and sat purring on his neck, right between his two ears. They lived together very happily until one day, as they were moving through the tall reeds down by the river – *pa – wa!* – There was a loud bang, and Elephant sank down to the ground. Cat looked around and all she could see was a small man with a gun.

"O-o-o-o-oh!" said Cat. I see Elephant is not the finest creature in all the jungle. It is Man." So Cat walked after Man all the way to his home, and jumped up onto the thatch of his hut. "At last," said Cat, "I have found the finest creature in all the jungle." She lived up in the thatch of the hut very happily and began to catch the mice and rats that lived in that village. Until one day, as she sat on the roof warming herself in the sun, she heard a noise from inside the hut. The voices of Man and his wife grew louder and louder until – *wara-wara-wara…yo – we!* – out came Man, tumbling head over heels into the dust.

"Aha!" said Cat. "Now I *do* know who is truly the finest creature in all the jungle. It is Woman." She came down from the thatch, went inside the hut, and sat by the fire. And that is where she's been ever since.

Children of age 7/8 will enjoy the humor of this Animal Folk Tale. And who hasn't wondered how the cat came indoors? Use some of the techniques described earlier in the chapter to review the story over the next several days.

# The Flying Squirrel (Age 6 and up)

## An Animal Folk Tale

*(Adoption, persistence, friendship, self-confidence)*

*[Children at this age often daydream of flying. This story gives them an opportunity to live into that dream and find a home for it in their imaginations.]*

Once there was a young squirrel named Rosy who loved to play in the treetops. She was a bit careless now and then and her mother wondered what she could do to make Rosy stop taking so many risky flights from branch to branch. One day Rosy was flying through the treetops jumping wildly from branch to branch when suddenly the branch she landed upon broke. Rosy was flying down through the leafy branches trying desperately to grab onto a branch. Faster and faster she fell until suddenly she landed on a branch large enough to bring her to a stop. She landed on her tummy and the wind was knocked out of her. She was stunned and lay there on her tummy with her arms and legs dangling over both sides of the branch. She looked from side to side as she waited to get her breath. Whew! She was safe.

Finally her breathing became normal and she slowly lifted her head, her paws and then her feet up onto the branch. She crouched there for a long time looking down at the earth below. The longer she looked down the more afraid she became. Then, a beautiful red bird flew by and landed up above her. The bird flew so easily she was amazed by its grace and beauty. She thought how wonderful it would be if squirrels could fly. After that day, she dreamed of flying when she was awake and when she was asleep.

Not long afterwards a squirrel came into the forest that no one had ever seen before. She was a little larger than the other squirrels and when she spread her arms there was a web of skin that stretched between her arms and her body that worked just like wings! She was a flying squirrel! The young squirrel ran up the branches of the tree as fast as she could to meet the flying squirrel.

"Hello!" she called out. "Oh how do you fly? I want to fly, too! Can you show me how?"

The flying squirrel talked kindly to the young squirrel.

"Raise up your arms and show me your wings," she said.

"But I don't have any," replied the young squirrel.

"Show me!" commanded the flying squirrel.

The young squirrel raised up her arms and the flying squirrel carefully examined her.

"Yes you do. You just have to wait until you get bigger and you will be able to fly just as I do."

"Really?" asked the little squirrel.

"I am sure of it," replied the older squirrel. "Take me to your mother."

So the squirrel took the flying squirrel to her mother.

The flying squirrel smiled at the young squirrel's mother and asked, "Are you a flying squirrel and is this your child?"

The mother loved the young squirrel very much. She understood that it was time to tell her child about her parents. Gently the mother gathered the young squirrel in her arms and told her how she had found her when she was just a baby. She knew she was a flying squirrel but had decided to raise her as her own child when she learned that the flying squirrel's mother and father had died.

"So, you see, my dear squirrel, I am not your first mother, rather, I am your second mother. I was not sure you would be able to fly like your mother since you had no one to show you how to fly. But now that you have met this flying squirrel perhaps you are old enough to learn to fly and she can show you how!"

After that the flying squirrel visited the young squirrel every day. The flying squirrel showed her how to catch the wind with her wings as she jumped from one branch to another. Together they practiced jumping from branch to branch until the day came when the young squirrel opened her wings and flew! Her mother was proud of her! The flying squirrel was proud of her! The young squirrel was happy doing what she in her heart had always known she could do!

# The Legend of the Big Dipper (Ages 7–9)

*(Focus/concentration to accomplish a difficult task, wisdom of childhood, sacrifice for others, and the mystery of how the stars came to be.)*

Once upon a time, a little girl lived with her mother in a small village at the edge of a mountain. There came a time when no rain fell, and the land grew dry. The streams dried up and the crops did not grow well. Many people were hungry and grew weak, including the little girl's mother. One day the mother was too weak to rise from her bed and the little girl set off to find water for her mother. She took her mother's old tin cup with the long handle and walked away from her village up the hill towards the mountains. As she walked she thought about how much she wanted to help her mother to feel strong again.

Among the rocks on the mountainside she heard the sound of water trickling! She discovered a small spring bubbling up from under the cool rocks and dropping down into a streambed. The little girl sat down and held her cup beneath the dripping water. Slowly the cup filled with water. When the cup was full she stood up carefully and began to walk slowly down the mountain so she would not spill a drop.

As she neared the village, she heard a whimpering sound. There under a tree lay a little dog. He was too weak to move. "Poor little dog," said the girl. "I will give you some of my water. It is meant for my mother, but she would want you to have some, too." She poured some water into her hands and let the dog lap it up. The dog was so grateful that it got up and wagged its tail. The little girl was so busy smiling at the dog that she did not notice that her tin cup had turned to silver, and was full again!

Holding her cup carefully, the little girl entered her village. She saw an old man leaning against a stick, trying to find something to eat in his garden. She could see that he was barely strong enough to stand. "Here, old man," she said. "Have a drink from my cup. It will give you strength." The old man drank from the cup and then sighed a big sigh. "You are very kind," he said. "I feel so much better now. Thank you, my child." The little girl was so happy for the old man that she did not notice that the long-handled cup had turned gold, and was full again. She carefully made her way home.

There was her mother lying in the bed, weak and pale with her eyes closed. "Mother," she called, "I have brought you some water. Let me help you to drink. I had to give some away, but I think there is enough to help you a bit." She helped her mother to sit up and watched as she began to drink from the cup. At last, her mother looked at her and smiled, "I feel so much better, dear," she said, "and I have saved the last little bit for you." But just before the little girl could drink, there came a knock at the door.

The little girl went to the door to see a woman she had never met before, looking very weak and covered in dust from the road. "Would you have a bit of water of a tired traveler?" she asked through parched lips. The little girl stepped outside. "Of course, ma'am. " She handed the woman the cup. But the woman did not drink from the cup. She lifted it high up into the air. Suddenly the little girls saw that her long-handled cup was now made of beautiful sparkling crystals. The woman turned it upside down and the last drops spilled onto the ground. Where they landed a spring burst forth. The woman then turned and hurled the long-handled cup high into the air – so high that it never came down That night as the townspeople gathered to wonder at the new spring, they looked up overhead and saw the girl's long-handled crystal cup shimmering in the sky. It is there to this day, and we call it the Big Dipper.

# Telling Family Stories

Families have their own unique stories. I remember listening to the stories my grandmother told about her childhood growing up on a farm in southern Indiana. My sisters and I were fascinated by her stories of raising their own food, butchering their own hogs, and making their own beer. Telling stories from our personal lives as children and adolescents gives our children a sense of their roots and a picture of how life was different in the "olden" days. They love hearing about our adventures and our misadventures.

I remember a story of an adventure I had with another neighborhood friend. There was a vacant house around the corner. Parts of it were boarded up. One day we decided to go inside! Even though it was clearly off limits, we ventured in. We looked around downstairs and then we climbed up the stairs, looking at the empty rooms, the wallpaper falling off the walls, the loose boards… Suddenly, we heard the sounds of a person downstairs! We froze in our tracks. Peering over the edge of the staircase we saw a head of hair, dark brown, with a cap that we thought for sure was that of a policeman. We knew we were in trouble! A voice called us to come down right now! When we looked up at the person we met at the bottom of the stairs, it was my friend's mom! Thank goodness! She gave us a good talking to and sent us off to play.

How to begin? Begin with a description of the house you lived in as a child. Include your neighborhood and the neighbors around you that you remember. Chances are, there were a few characters in the neighborhood. What were the seasons like where you grew up? Did you ever get lost? What did you read? What sports or games did you enjoy? Did you play a musical instrument? Where did your family go on vacation? What did you do there? Did you go to camp in the summer? What was it like for you?

These topics are waiting to be made into stories from your life that your children will enjoy. Make a few notes or an outline, if you want, earlier in the day. You will find that you remember more and more as you tell the stories from your youth. Be sure to add in humor, and make up some events that you wished had happened. Create a larger than life character that entered your life. My sisters and I never tired of hearing about my father's adventures on the back of a whale. It's a story!

# A Story Creating Model for Children Age 8 and Older

For 8-year-olds and older, the children might write a story about "How the Dog Came Indoors" using the cat story above as a model.

In the classroom, that could be a project in which the children work together in groups of two or three to write the story. Divide the class into groups (choose the groups so you have a good mix of capable and less capable children in each group) and let them chat together for about 15 minutes. Then ask them to write the bare bones of the story down on paper. That means to briefly state in short phrases (no sentences required) what happens in the order it happens like a list down the page. Then have two groups sit together. One group tells their version of the story by taking turns telling it to the other group until it is told. Then the second group takes their turn. Then have them go back and write the story out with more detail, filling in some description. Children of 8 and older can create an interesting tale using such a great model!

At home, sit with your child of 8 or older and write the story of How the Dog Came Indoors! This is a great activity to do over several days or perhaps during a weekend when you are "snowed in." Follow the suggestions above. Story creating with children is great fun. Use the story exercises found earlier in the chapter to give your child the opportunity of reviewing the story and making the experience of the story richer and more satisfying.

# Riddles!

Riddles are fun, challenging and appeal to the budding intellect of children from age 7 and up. They can be a "story starter" or "warm-up" that you use to change the space at home or at school and prepare everyone for the story. Children enjoy making them up, too; and may surprise you with their inventiveness. Here are a few to get you started.

I am 3, I am 1
Over the hills I do run
You can pick me; I don't mind
and in Ireland I'm easy to find!
What am I? (shamrock)

At night they come without being fetched
By day they are lost without being stolen.
What are they? (stars)

As red as a heart, as round as a rose
If you squeeze me too tight
I'll drip on your clothes.
What am I? (tomato)

Small and limp, I fit in your hand
When you blow into me, I expand.
Bigger and bigger until you stop,
If you're not careful, I will pop!
What am I? (balloon)

First I was yellow, I was yellow all right.
Then I was turned to snowy white.
I jumped and jumped when I grew hot
The more I jumped the bigger I got!
What am I? (popcorn)

Green as grass
White as snow
Red as blood
Black as mud.
What am I? (black berry)

What is it that you can keep
After giving it to someone else?
(your word)

I'm warm when you come in
And all of me is skin.
My sister is always with me
To keep me company.
What am I? (socks)

What walks all day on its head,
never complains and holds up a shoe?
(a nail in a horseshoe)

What gets wet when drying? (a towel)

The more you take, the more you leave behind.
(footsteps)

What goes 'round and 'round the wood,
But never goes into the wood?
(The bark of a tree)

A cloud was my mother,
The wind is my father,
My children are the rivers,
A rainbow is my bed,
The earth my final resting place.
What am I? (rain)

It stands on one leg
with its heart in its head.
What is it? (cabbage)

What holds water,
Yet is full of holes? (sponge)

Though it is not an ox, it has a horn;
though it is not an ass, it has a pack;
Wherever it goes, it leaves a silver trail.
What is it? (a snail)

Thirty white horses upon a red hill
Now they stamp, Now they champ,
Now they stand still
What are they? (teeth)

A shoemaker makes shoes without leather.
With all four elements put together:
Water, fire, earth and air;
Every customer takes two pair
(Blacksmith-horseshoes)

As I was going o'er London Bridge
I heard something crack;
Not a man in all England
Can mend that.
What was it? (ice)

As I was going to St. Ives,
I met a man with seven wives;
Each wife had seven sacks,
Each sack had seven cats,
Each cat had seven kits:
Kits, cats, sack sand wives,
How many were going to St. Ives? (one)

You follow me to school,
But I leave you at the gate.
What am I? (a road)

You use it from your head to your toes,
The more it works, the thinner it grows.
What is it? (soap)

Who knows these four brothers?
One can eat without ever being satisfied.
One can run without ever being tired.
One can drink without ever being drunk.
One can whistle, but none likes his tune.
(Fire, Water, Earth, Air (wind))

| YYUR | (Too wise you are, |
| YYUB | Too wise you be, |
| ICUR | I see you are |
| YY4 me | Too wise for me.) |

What smokes, but cannot chew?
(chimney)

Two geese before a goose,
And two geese behind a goose; How many
geese are there? (three)

Two legs sat upon three legs
With four legs standing by;
Four then were drawn by ten:
Read my riddle ye can't, how ever much ye
try. (Milkmaid sitting on a three-legged stool,
milking the cow)

There are two small windows:
One person looks out of them,
And the whole world looks in.
What are they? (eyes)

Something I tell with not a word,
I keep it well, though it flies like a bird.
What is it? (time)

We are little creatures,
All of different voice and features;
One of using lass is set,
One of us you'll find in jet.
The other you may see in tin,
And the fourth a box within.
If the fifth you should pursue,
It can never fly from you.
(The vowels: A,E,I,0,U)

There is a room with eight corners.
In each corner sits a cat.
Before each cat sit seven cats.
How many cats are in the room? (eight)

There is a thing that nothing is,
And yet it has a name.
It's sometimes tall and sometimes short;
It joins our walks, but never talks,
And plays at every game.
What is it? (a shadow)

The fiddler and his wife,
The piper and his mother,
Ate three half cakes, three whole cakes
And three-quarters of another.
How much did each get?
(If the fiddler's wife was the piper's
mother, each one got ½ + 1 + ¼ =1¾)

It runs all day and never walks,
Often murmurs, never talks.
It has a bed, but never sleeps,
It has a mouth, but never eats.
What is it? (a river)

One can bear it,
Two can share it,
But for three
It can never be.
What is it? (a secret)

It travels across the ocean
It will return over the sea
It will tell a tale,
And utter not a word.
What is it? (letter)

Forty teeth have I complete,
Yet I've never learned to eat;
Sometimes black and sometimes white
I cannot even bite!
What am I? (comb)

I am, as you'll agree with me,
The funniest thing in land or sea.
My mouth is bigger than my head,
I always stay within my bed,
Yet funnier still I often rise.
Now, answer that, you solvers wise!
Yet, though in bed I always stop,
You'll see me rescind neck and crop,
Through the valley, down the hill,
In fact, I'm very rarely still.
Now, what is this, please answer me;
This funniest thing in land or sea? (river)

# Activities for 7/8 Year-Olds

Children at age 7/8 should be given more responsibilities around the house and classroom. This is an ideal age for getting involved in team sports, musical instruments and other artistic and physical activities. Here is a great activity you can do with your children or students at this age. This is a developmental movement activity that requires the child to cross the midline with each hand numerous times. Crossing the midline is essential for brain stimulation and development. **

## Hey, My Name is Joe! (Ages 7 and Up)

**A developmental movement activity that children enjoy...**

I have seen several versions of "Joe" and do not know the source of any of them! It's great fun and one that children can do one-on-one with an adult or as a class. Begin swaying side-to-side and stepping in an easy left right rhythm. Then add the speaking. Step left on Hey and right in the pause and then left again on "name" and right on "Joe". Continue with the easy left right movement and add the words in to fit your rhythm.

L    R    L    R    L    R    L R

Hey,   my name is Joe and I work in a button facto-ry.

        L    R    L    R

One day my boss said, "Joe, are you busy? I said, "No".

   L    R      L    R

Then push this button with your right hand.

Continue stepping in the same rhythm adding the movement of your right arm. You do this by bending your right arm up at the elbow and while holding the elbow waist high on your right side so you can swing your forearm down in front of you to where your hand is level with your tummy and back up again.

Repeat the two first lines again, and, instead of repeating line three, and say: "Then push this button with your left hand."

Now the left hand does exactly what the right hand is doing as you repeat the first two lines again. The two hands work in such a way that one hand is in the up position while the other hand is in the down position (horizontal to your waist).

Repeat the first two lines again with both hands moving in rhythm, and say: "Then push this button with your right foot."

Your right foot now moves across your body to touch the floor lightly in front of your left foot. It does this at exactly the same time as your right hand pushes its button. Then add the left foot in tandem with the left hand.

Repeat the first two lines again with both hands and your right foot moving in rhythm and say: "Then push this button with your left foot."

Once you have both hands and both feet moving together you can enjoy this for one or two repetitions (in silence with just the hands and feet moving to the rhythm, then...

Speak the first two lines with both hands and both feet moving and say: "Then push this button with your head!"

Now nod your head in the same rhythm as the movement of your hands and feet. Repeat the first two lines again and when Joe is asked if he is busy, say loudly, "YES!" And that's the end!

There are variations on Joe. I learned several versions from teachers in different countries. It seems to have traveled around! And, as with telling a story, it is good to set the stage for the movement activity by telling a little story about life in a factory where the workers repeat the same repetitive motions over and over again for hours. You can generate a great conversation around this theme. Perhaps, you worked in a factory like I did. After you have told the story, then begin the movement. Once they know it, have several children come forward to lead the class. This exercise offers you, as teacher or parent, a chance to see who gets confused or struggles to keep the rhythm going. Have a child help another child by standing side by side with them. These kinds of movement exercises strengthen coordination, build rhythmic sense, and help with right-left integration. And, they are lots of fun! A story in action!

## **Why is crossing the midline important?

The ability to cross the midline is important on the physical level as well as on the brain level. On the brain level, a lack of midline crossing may indicate that the left and right sides of the brain (the left and right hemispheres) are not communicating well together.

The left and right brain hemispheres communicate across a mass of tissue called the corpus callosum. Because each hemisphere carries out different tasks, it is important for each hemisphere to communicate with the other across the corpus callosum in order to coordinate learning and movement.

On a physical level, when your child spontaneously crosses the midline with the dominant hand, then the dominant hand is going to get the practice that it needs to develop good fine motor skills.

If your child avoids crossing the midline, then both hands will tend to get equal practice at developing skills, and your child's true handedness may be apparently delayed and fine motor skills may not be as good as they could be.

# CHAPTER 13

## The 9-Year Change

### The Eagle

by Alfred Lord Tennyson

*He clasps the crag with crooked hands;*
*Close to the sun in lonely lands,*
*Ring'd with the azure world, he stands.*
*The wrinkled sea beneath him crawls;*
*He watches from his mountain walls,*
*And like a thunderbolt he falls.*

Albert Einstein: "The most beautiful thing we can experience is the mysterious. It is the source of all true art and science."

When Tom (a 9-year old child of sanguine temperament) smiles, his whole face lights up. His eyes are always in motion, taking in every aspect of the situation at hand. He is a keen observer who enjoys helping others to solve problems. He is the first one on the scene when someone is hurt or needs help. He just seems to know what others need and is ready on the spot to help set up the baseball field or organize the stage for a play. He laughs easily and when something unusual happens or plans change, he goes with the flow. You could say he is unflappable. Everyone is his friend. Sometimes, though, it is hard for Tom to stay focused on the task at hand. He can easily become distracted by what is going on all around him. He forgets to get his homework done and "forgets" to do his chores! He needs a gentle hand to remind him and a smile to encourage him to stick to the task and not be distracted and head off on another project before the one at hand is finished.

217

Lately, Tom has been feeling sad. He is uncomfortable with this strange feeling and he can't find the source of his sadness. He is despondent and finds it more difficult to focus. These unfamiliar feelings annoy him. He feels vulnerable and uncomfortable in himself. His self-confidence and buoyancy in life seem to have vanished overnight.

Tom has always fallen asleep easily. These days it's become more difficult and when he is finally asleep, he's been having nightmares. He's been noticing more details about everything. Just the other day he looked at both of his parents and then looked at himself in the mirror and began to wonder if he was adopted. He asked his mother about it the other evening before bed. She was surprised and even a bit shocked. Where could he have gotten that idea? She told him the story of his birth and he relaxed and seemed to fall asleep more easily that night.

## The Change in the Child Around Age 9 or 10

What is happening to Tom happens to every child sometime between the age of about 9 and 10 years old. This is the 9/10-year change. Some children experience it more obviously than others. Around age 9 or 10 the child's sense of time and self-awareness mature to a new level. Prior to this change, the child lives fully in the present. Gradually, the past, present and future separate within the maturing consciousness of the child. For some children this shift is gentle and almost imperceptible. For others, a sense of loss and sorrow or even discomfort and confusion can occur.

One of the most mysterious realms we adults experience is the inner realm of the self. As we reflect on the experiences we have had in our lives, we are free to allow them to change us or not. We are free to embrace and integrate them or to reject them. In our world of thinking we are continually separating the past, the present and the future clearly and effortlessly. We say we "learn" from our mistakes and it is true that we have this ability for we can imagine different outcomes of our actions. We feel regret and sorrow when we recognize our shortcomings and errors in judgment. We are constantly checking in with our past experiences and making judgments about future decisions based on those experiences. As contemporary human beings we seek to explain and come to terms with the dualism of an inner and outer life. We strive to integrate our past experiences with our present situation in an effort to fashion our future.

In contrast, children before age 9 or 10 live in the present; they do not yet have an inner experience of the past and the future as we do. There is a buoyancy and quality of wonder in their moment-by-moment experience of the present. Regret and sorrow for what one has done requires the ability to think about the past as separate from the present. We've all noticed how the young child easily shifts and moves through bumps along the road. They seem to be able to let go of the past easily, and that is normal.

Children who have very active imaginations and have a strong connection to nature can wake up one morning and feel the world has abandoned them. Some children feel overwhelmed or just plain sad. Some children feel this loss and become more emotional for a time. Some experience nightmares. Children, who went to sleep easily before the 9-year change, may now repeatedly call to the parents to stay with them until they fall asleep. Mood swings are common, and fits of temper and crying may occur at the slightest provocation and for no apparent reason.

This new perspective is one of being more of an observer of the world rather than a part of it. This change also heralds the birth of one's conscience. Children become more deeply aware of the effect of their deeds on others. During this transition children who were happy and lighthearted can become withdrawn and irritable. Each child is unique and moves through this exciting and challenging time in his or her own way. The antidote is knowledge, patience, and understanding on the part of the adults, and a good story at the end of the day helps put things in perspective, too.

Often, in the life of a child, a dramatic experience of loss and/or a premonition of the future occurs during the 9th or 10th year. Sometimes, children will meet someone who inspires them and/or they will get an intimation of what they will do in the future. Not only do such events herald the change, they often help the child move through the change and even support the child moving towards future possibilities. If we look at the biographies of well-known individuals, we can see this pattern at work.

**Albert Einstein** was born in 1879. He experienced early speech difficulties, yet overcame this handicap and became a top student. In 1889, at age 10, he met Max Talmud who was a friend of his father's. That meeting initiated a 6 year relationship with the family in which Talmud came to dinner weekly and guided Einstein through many educational interests and pursuits. He introduced him to key texts in science, math, and philosophy, including Kant's *Critique of Pure Reason* and Euclid's *Elements*, which Einstein called the "Holy Little Geometry Book."

**Susan B. Anthony**, an American Civil Rights leader, who focused on women's suffrage, was born in 1820. She was a very precocious child, having an avid curiosity about the world around her. At age 10, she met Mary Perkins, a teacher who inspired her with a progressive view of womanhood. This meeting planted the seeds that would lead her into her future work.

At the age of nine, **Abraham Lincoln's** mother died. Later, his father married Sarah Bush Johnston. Lincoln became very close to her and called her "mother." She inspired him to follow his heart and served as a source of inspiration to him all her life.

Take a few moments right now to think back on your life around age 9 or 10. Did your family move to a new house? Did you change schools? Was a sibling born? Did some friend or family member or pet die? Do you remember having nightmares or anxiety about separating from your parents? Perhaps you will recall an experience that speaks of this change. In my own life, I recall two seminal events. My first pet, a soft gray cat with white markings on paws and tail, Puss n' Boots, was struck by a car and died. That same year, my best friend, a child of nine himself, died of illness. These experiences of death had a profound effect on me. It was not a negative effect but, rather, an awakening to the reality of death being a natural part of life. In retrospect, I am indebted to these events, as they helped to deepen my respect and love for life and enkindle a wonder at what might happen in the afterlife.

As a teacher, I witnessed a group of children passing through this phase. Over the course of third and fourth grade, each child became more observant and more critical. They asked more discerning questions. One child began to draw in perspective in the fourth grade indicating changing powers of perception. They noticed all my mistakes and told me about them without any self-consciousness whatsoever! They shared their opinions about any and all changes in the classroom. They wanted to have a say in how things were done. It was an exciting time of awakening. Friendships shifted and groups of children who had been very close now drifted towards other children seeking new friendships. What was lost? Some children felt a loss of connection to the world around them more than others. Some became more sensitive and cried more easily than before. Parents reported that nightmares were common. Some children who had always fallen asleep easily became uncomfortable being left alone at bedtime. They needed more attention as part of the bedtime routine. The intimacy created by sharing a story helps to relax and reassure the child. The content of the story helps the child to understand this phase. Each child is unique. Yet these are common experiences that indicate a new step in awareness is being made. The child of this age needs extra attention and understanding. This too shall pass!

As I pointed out, it's at this age that the conscience is born. Prior to this inner shift right and wrong are blurred and children experience them as being outside the self. After the change, children feel the responsibility for their actions arising from within themselves. This awareness of self-responsibility is the birth of conscience. This new self-awareness can rest heavily on the child's shoulders, as the conscience matures. I have a dear friend who remembers the day she did not take a library book back on time. She did not tell her parents. She felt very guilty for weeks and weeks. She stopped going to the library. She truly thought something terrible would happen because she had made such a mistake. Her conscience was born! As it turned out, her mother found the book and together they returned it. The librarian thanked her!

Children at age 9-10 often begin to make up stories that border on lies as they experiment with this newfound awareness. Before this age, they may tell a story about something they made up, but it is not the same as consciously lying. At 9/10, the lie becomes available. Children inwardly feel what it is like to tell a lie consciously for the first time.

Children of this age often want to do volunteer work or give their allowance to a cause that protects endangered species or helps less fortunate children who perhaps don't have enough to eat. These heartfelt longings come from deep within the child's new sense of fairness, and we honor those feelings by finding ways for the child to help other people and animals.

It's natural for children at this age to be very interested in how things work and how things are made. Cooking, farming, gardening, knitting, or working with tools to build a birdhouse, for example, help them to connect with the creative powers now being born within the self. Such projects help children connect to the day-to-day tasks of living on the earth, an experience that is satisfying and fulfilling.

Regular chores that give children a feeling of connectedness to the life of the family support them at this age. (Even if they insist they don't want to do it, they need it—and they know this.) The inner sense of growing self-responsibility makes this a good time for them to have their own pet for which they alone are responsible. Involving them in family projects, in which they learn new tasks and skills, is essential. All of these activities support children in finding a new sense of their place in the outer world as they deepen the inner experience of connection that exists between human beings and nature.

## Stories for the 9-year change

Stories appropriate for the 9-Year Change include stories from the Old Testament, Creation Stories from many cultures, and Folk Tales. In addition, the books of Laura Ingalls Wilder books are a treasure not to be missed.

Stories that nurture, reflect, and embody this inner change include stories from the Old Testament told with humor. Why the Old Testament? These classic tales explore the image of a polarity between the Hebrew People and God, the higher authority. We each have an inner, higher authority, if you will, and, since the children of this age are beginning to awaken to their conscience, their own higher inner authority, these stories offer a mirror of that inner shift. The Old Testament stories tell a similar tale again and again. The higher authority, God, instructs the people; they do what is recommended for a while but then they disobey. They suffer the consequences and have to start again. They are on a journey to the Promised Land and can only get there through experiencing trials and tribulations created by making many mistakes. These stories weave a wonderful tapestry of humor, drama, trial, and overcoming that give children of this age a digestible picture of hubris and, at the same time, a sense of a higher authority that stands at the ready to help. Children understand the struggles of the Hebrew people and see parallels to life on the playground at recess.

Creation Stories are a particular kind of myth, and are found in every culture. Some involve wondrous gods and goddesses; others involve great spirits or mysterious animal helpers. They have common themes that are colored by the culture out of which they arose. They are apropos for 8- and 9-year-olds who, in the third and fourth grade, are very interested in where things come from and how things work. Creation stories help children understand, on an intuitive level, that we are all connected to one another in mysterious ways and that we are truly, in the end, brothers and sisters all over the earth.

Hearing creation stories from around the world offers a look into how other cultures thought about how the world came into being. Having a discussion about the differences between cultures, i.e., how they see and experience the world, is of interest at this age. These stories carry us back to ancient times in far away places. Children enjoy the unfamiliar imagery and many a good discussion can ensue.

Another wonderful group of stories for this age is the Laura Ingalls Wilder collection. Beginning with *Farmer Boy*, Ms. Wilder describes life on the farm and the life of a specific family moving west in the early years of the settling of the American West. This exciting and heart-warming collection of stories has nurtured generations of children. Filled with adventure, humor, challenge, and overcoming, they feed children of this age who are seeking to understand the world around them in a new way. The Wilder family's connection to the land and the rhythms of the seasons demonstrates a healthy relationship between humans and the earth. The stories inspire self-responsibility, generosity, and satisfy the adventurous spirit of the imagination. They are an example of how it is possible to feel supported by the outer world. These are stories to read aloud together.

Here is a collection of Creation Stories and Folk Tales for you to tell to your children or students.

# The Enchanting Song of the Magical Bird (Age 9 and Up)

### An African Folk Tale

*(Child's developing inner awareness, wisdom of childhood, differences between children and adults, community problem solving.*

One day a strange bird arrived in a small village that nestled among low hills. From that moment on, nothing was safe. Anything the villagers planted in the fields disappeared overnight. Every morning there were fewer and fewer sheep and goats and chickens. Even during the day, while the people were working on the lands, the gigantic bird would come and break open their storehouses and granaries, and steal from them their winter food supplies.

The villagers were devastated. There was misery in the land – everywhere was the sound of wailing and the gnashing of teeth. No one – not even the bravest hero of the village – could get his hands on the bird. It was just too quick for them. . They hardly ever saw it: they just heard the rushing of its great wings as it came to perch in the crown of the old yellowwood tree, under its thick canopy of leaves.

The headman of the village tore out his hair in frustration. One day, after the bird had plundered his own livestock and winter supplies, he commanded the men to sharpen their axes and machetes and to move as one against the bird. "Cut down the tree; that is the answer," he said.

With axes and machetes ground to gleaming razor edges, the men approached the great tree. The first blows landed heavily and bit deep into the flesh of the trunk. The tree shuddered, and from the thick, tangled leaves of its crown the strange and mysterious bird emerged. A honey-sweet song came from its throat. It reached into the hearts of the men and spoke of fabulous, far-off things that never would return. So enchanting was the sound that the machetes and the axes fell one by one from the hands of the men. They sank to their knees and stared upward in longing and yearning at the bird that sang for them in all its brilliantly colored splendor.

The men's hands became weak. Their hearts became soft. No, they thought, so beautiful a bird could never have caused such damage and destruction! And when the sun sank red in the west they shuffled like sleepwalkers back to the headman and told him there was nothing, but nothing that they could do to harm the bird.

The next morning the young men took their gleaming axes and machetes and set off for the tree. The first blows again landed heavily, digging deep into the flesh of the trunk. And, just as before, the green canopy of the tree opened and the strange bird appeared in all its multihued finery. Once again the most wonderful melody echoed across the hills. The enchanted young men listened to the song that spoke to them of love and courage and of the heroic deeds that awaited them. This bird could not be bad, they thought. This bird could not be wicked. The young men's arms became weak. The axes and machetes fell from their hands, and they knelt like the older men before them, listening in a trance to the song of the bird.

When night fell, they stumbled, bewildered, back to the headman. In their ears still sounded the enchanting song of the mysterious bird. "It is impossible," said the leader of their group. "No one can withstand the magical power of the bird."

The headman was furious. "Only the children remain," he said. "Children hear truly and their eyes are clear. I will lead the children against the bird."

The next morning the headman and the children of the tribe went to the tree where the strange bird was resting. As soon as the children let the tree feel the bite of the ax, the leafy canopy opened and the bird appeared just as before – blindingly beautiful. But the children did not look up. Their eyes stayed on the axes and machetes in their hands. And they chopped, chopped, chopped to the rhythm of their own music.

The bird began to sing. The headman could hear that its song was beautiful beyond compare, and he could feel the weakness in his hands. But the children's ears could only hear the dull, regular sounds of their axes and machetes. And no matter how enchantingly the bird sang, the children continued to chop, chop, chop.

Eventually the trunk creaked and cracked apart. The tree crashed to the ground and with it fell the strange and mysterious bird. The headman found the bird where it lay, crushed to death by the weight of the branches.

From everywhere the people came charging. The hardened older men and the strong young men could not believe what the children with their thin arms had accomplished!

That night, the headman declared a great feast to reward the children for what they had done. "You are the only ones who hear truly and whose eyes are clear," he said.

"You are the eyes and ears of our tribe."

## Lazy Jack (Age 9 and Up)

*(Laziness, Ingenuity, Awakening to Self-Responsibility)*

Once there was a boy whose name was Jack, and he lived with his mother on a dreary common. They were very poor, and the old woman made her living by spinning, but Jack was so lazy that he would do nothing but bask in the sun in the hot weather, and sit by the corner of the hearth in the wintertime. His mother could not persuade him to do anything for her. And was obliged at last to tell him that if he did not begin to work for his porridge, she would turn him out to get his living as he could.

This threat at last roused Jack, and he went out and hired himself for the day to a neighboring farmer for a penny, but as he was coming home, never having had any money in his possession before, he lost it in passing over a brook.

"You stupid boy," said his mother, "you should have put it in your pocket."

"I'll do so another time," said Jack.

The next day Jack went out again, and hired himself to a cow keeper, who gave him a jar of milk for his day's work. Jack took the jar and put it into the large pocket of his jacket, spilling it all, long before he got home.

"Dear me," said his mother. "You should have carried it on your head."

"I'll do so another time," replied Jack.

The following day Jack hired himself again to a farmer, who agreed to give him a cream cheese for his services. In the evening Jack took the cheese, and went home with it on his head. By the time he got home the cheese was completely spilled, part of it being lost and part matted with his hair.

"You stupid boy," cried his mother. "You should have carried it very carefully in your hands."

"I'll do so another time," replied Jack.

The day after this Jack again went out, and hired himself to a baker who would give him nothing for his work but a large tomcat. Jack took the cat, and began carrying it very carefully in his hands, but in a short time puss scratched him so much that he was compelled to let it go. When he got home, his mother said to him,

"You should have tied it with a string, and dragged it along after you."

"I'll do so another time," replied Jack.

The next day Jack hired himself out to a butcher, who rewarded his labors by the handsome present of a shoulder of mutton. Jack took the mutton, tied it to a string and trailed it along after him in the dirt, so that by the time he had got home the meat was completely spoiled. His mother was this time quite out of patience with him for the next day was Sunday, and she was obliged to content herself with cabbage for her dinner.

"You ninnyhammer," said she to her son. "You should have carried it on your shoulder."

"I'll do so another time," replied Jack.

On the Monday, Jack went once more, and hired himself to a cattle keeper, who gave him a donkey for his trouble. Although Jack was very strong, he found some difficulty in hoisting the donkey on his shoulders, but at last he accomplished it and began walking slowly home with his prize.

Now it happened that in the course of his journey home with his prize, he passed by the home of a rich man whose only daughter was deaf and dumb. She had never laughed in her life, and the doctor said she would never recover until someone made her laugh.

Many tried without success and at last the father in despair offered her in marriage to the first man who could make her laugh. Jack was passing with the donkey on his shoulders, the legs sticking up in the air; and the sight was so comical and strange, that she burst out into a great fit of laughter, and immediately recovered her speech and hearing.

Her father was overjoyed, and fulfilled his promise by marrying her to Jack, who was thus made a rich gentleman. They lived in a large house, and Jack's mother lived with them in great happiness until she died.

# Crow Brings the Daylight (Age 9 and Up)

An Inuit Myth retold by S. E. Schlosser, in the public domain
*(A Creation Story, Trickery, Bravery, Stinginess)*

Long, long ago, when the world was still new, the Inuit lived in darkness in their home in the fastness of the north. They had never heard of daylight. It was Crow who first explained what daylight was. Crow traveled back and forth between the northlands and the southlands, but they did not believe him.

Many of the younger folk were fascinated by the story of the light that gilded the lands to the south. They made Crow repeat his tales until they knew them by heart.

"Imagine how far and how long we could hunt," they told one another.

"Yes, and see the polar bear before it attacks," others agreed.

Soon the yearning for daylight was so strong that the Inuit people begged Crow to bring it to them. Crow shook his head. "I am too old," he told them. "The daylight is very far away. I can no longer go so far." But the pleadings of the people made him reconsider, and finally he agreed to make the long journey to the south.

Crow flew for many miles through the endless dark of the north. He grew weary, and almost turned back. But at last he saw a rim of light at the very edge of horizon and knew that the daylight was close.

Crow strained his wings and flew with all his might. Suddenly, the daylight burst upon him with all its glory and brilliance. The endless shades of color and the many shapes and forms surrounding him made Crow stare and stare. He flapped down to a tree and rested himself, exhausted by his long journey. Above him, the sky was an endless blue, the clouds fluffy and white. Crow marveled at the wonderful scene.

Eventually Crow lowered his gaze and realized that he was near a village that lay beside a wide river. As he watched, a beautiful girl came to the river near the tree in which he perched. She dipped a large bucket into the icy waters of the river and then turned to make her way back to the village. Crow turned himself into a tiny speck of dust and drifted down towards the girl as she passed beneath his tree. He settled into her fur cloak and watched carefully as she returned to the snow lodge of her father, who was the chief of the village people.

It was warm and cozy inside the lodge. Crow looked around him and spotted a box that glowed around the edges. Daylight, he thought. On the floor, a little boy was playing contentedly. The speck of dust that was Crow drifted away from the girl and floated into the ear of the little boy. Immediately the child sat up and rubbed at his ear, which was irritated by the strange speck. He started to cry, and the chief, who was a doting grandfather, came running into the snow lodge to see what was wrong.

"Why are you crying?" the chief asked, kneeling beside the child.

Inside the little boy's ear, Crow whispered: "You want to play with a ball of daylight." The little boy rubbed at his ear and then repeated Crow's words.

The chief sent his daughter to the glowing box in the corner. She brought it to her father, who removed a glowing ball, tied it with a string, and gave it to the little boy. He rubbed his ear thought-fully before taking the ball. It was full of light and shadow, color and form. The child laughed happily, tugging at the string and watching the ball bounce.

Then Crow scratched the inside of his ear again and the little boy gasped and cried.

"Don't cry, little one," said the doting grandfather anxiously. "Tell me what is wrong."

Inside the boy's ear, Crow whispered: "You want to go outside to play." The boy rubbed at his ear and then repeated Crow's words to his grandfather. Immediately, the chief lifted up the small child and carried him outside, followed by his worried mother.

As soon as they were free of the snow lodge, Crow swooped out of the child's ear and resumed his natural form. He dove toward the little boy's hand and grabbed the string from him. Then he rose up and up into the endless blue sky, the ball of daylight sailing along behind him.

In the far north, the Inuit saw a spark of light coming toward them through the darkness. It grew brighter and brighter, until they could see Crow flapping his wings as he flew toward them. The people gasped and pointed and called out in delight.

The Crow dropped the ball, and it shattered upon the ground, releasing the daylight so that it exploded up and out, illuminating every dark place and chasing away every shadow. The sky grew bright and turned blue. The dark mountains took on color and light and form. The snow and ice sparkled so brightly that the Inuit had to shade their eyes.

The people laughed and cried and exclaimed over their good fortune. But Crow told them that the daylight would not last forever. He had only obtained one ball of daylight from the people of the south, and it would need to rest for six months every year to regain its strength. During that six-month period, the darkness would return.

The people said: "Half a year of daylight is enough. Before you brought the daylight, we lived our whole life in darkness!" Then they thanked Crow over and over again.

# Maui Fishes Up the Islands (Age 9 and Up)

## Polynesian

*(Creation Story, Overcoming exclusion)*

Maui was the youngest of all his brothers. He wanted to go fishing with his older brothers, but they refused to take him with them. He had no fishhooks of his own and often lost the ones they lent him.

One day Maui decided he would try to make his own fish hooks. In those days fishhooks in Polynesia were made of bone. He visited his aunt who knew about making many things and asked her how to make a fish hook. She told him he needed to visit the underworld to learn the proper way to make fishhooks. So Maui journeyed into the earth to the underworld and there he met an old wise woman. Half of her was bone and half of her was flesh. He asked her to help him make the best fishhooks. She gave him her jawbone and told him it was the perfect shape for a fishhook. Maui thanked her and gave her a necklace he had made from shells. She told him the jawbone would help him catch the biggest fish in the sea.

When Maui returned home, his brothers were out fishing. Maui asked his mother for one of her sacred birds. "Why do you need this bird?" she asked. He showed her his new hook and explained that he needed powerful bait for such a special hook. His mother gave him the bird and now he was ready to fish. He ran down the beach and waited for his brothers. They returned and told him they had not caught any fish. Maui saw his chance. He showed them his new hook and told them where to paddle. They paddle far out to sea that day and threw in their lines, but caught nothing. "We must go further out" Maui told his brothers.

The brothers paddled and paddled. Finally, they became angry. "Maui, there are no fish to show for all your talk. And as for your clever hook, it hasn't even touched water. Why did we listen to you? We're going home!"

Quickly, Maui let down his line. He lowered the magic hook made from the jawbone of his ancestress. Attached to the hook was the sacred bird his mother had given him for bait. It went down into the depths to the very bottom of the great sea. There it passed in front of an ancient being called Old One-Tooth. Old One-Tooth holds down the land at the floor of the sea. When the hook came by with the bird on it, Old One-Tooth took it into his mouth. Some say Maui's sister Hina-of-the-Sea was there at the time and it was she who secured the hook to Old One-Tooth's jaw. Maui's line grew taut. He tied it to the canoe and told his brothers to paddle fiercely. They used all their might. They paddled as they had never paddled before. The weight of their catch grew heavier and heavier. Maui's paddle surged in the water and he sang a magic chant that went something like this:

*"Oh Sacred Lands beneath the Sea arise, arise! Face the Sun!*
*The powers of the Sea bid it! The Powers of the Sky bid it!*
*Sea foam shall dance around you.*
*Do not sulk below, Arise! Face the Sun."*

The brothers looked back to see a great island rise up out of the water. It was covered with mountains and trees. One of the brothers was so shocked he dropped his paddle. Just then the line broke. The great island stopped moving and stayed in place. Then, a few smaller islands rose up and settled in nearby. These sacred islands were teeming with life! Colorful birds, flowers of brilliant shades of red and yellow and blue and fruits of all shapes and sizes abounded. The waters surrounding the islands were teeming with fish of all shapes and sizes.

It was to these islands that the peoples of Polynesia came and settled. They are a strong and proud people who still today honor and give thanks to Maui for fishing up their sacred homeland from the floor of the sea.

# Pangu Creates the World (Age 9 and Up)

## Chinese Creation Story
*(Steadfastness, Selflessness)*

When time began there was a dark emptiness of confusion and chaos. No form, nor shape, nor space. Heaven and Earth were as one. Day and night were not separated. The sun and the moon were not, and the millions of stars that inhabit the night sky were not. A dark mass like a giant egg floating aimlessly on the currents of the sea was all there was. Deep in the darkness of this chaos, the spark of life caught the first creature of the universe. Pangu was born.

Pangu slept and did not stir for thousands of years. On and on he slept: a sleep without movement or dreams. Yet, as he slept, he grew. He grew and grew until his vastness filled the hollow of the egg. When he awoke, he found himself trapped against the ceiling of the shell. He forced his arms against the shell and with a great blow he shattered the shell and the dark mass inside floated out. Its lighter parts floated upwards and became the sky. The darker, heavier parts sank downwards and became the earth.

Pangu observed this and was afraid that the sky and earth might miss each other and not come together again. So with his mighty arms and hands he pushed the sky upward, a little bit everyday. And at the same time he pounded and pummeled the earth with his feet until it became a compact mass beneath him. The sky eased upwards slowly and Pangu grew into that space, taller and taller in order to hold the sky up. He stood erect like a giant pillar holding the earth and sky apart. For an eternity he stood there, till the elements of earth and sky grew solid and firm, each on fixed in its own place. They would never close together again.

This mighty task took many thousands of years to complete. Pangu grew old and weary from his toil. Slowly, his great body sank to the earth, spread out over all its lands. Soon, the only sound in the whole world was the quiet rhythm of the breath of the sleeping Pangu. Deeper and deeper into sleep he journeyed. Slowly his body changed and formed the world, as we know it today. His breath became the wind and his voice became the roar of thunder and the puff of clouds. His right eye became the bright fire of the sun while his left eye gleamed gently from the moon.

His chest became the mountains that still hold up the sky and his legs and arms extended the long mountain ranges that mark the edge of the flat plains. His blood poured forth to create the rivers that gave life and his skin became the soil of the earth.

Every part of Pangu had its purpose. The long hairs on his head and body became the trees and plants and flowers; his bones were soon the minerals and jewels of the earth. His sweat became the rain and the dew and the parasites. The tiny creatures that live on his skin became the fish and the birds and all the animals. And, even the dry flecks of skin that fell from his body were transformed. They became the human beings that inhabited the world.

The great Pangu gave everything he had to the world and to the people who live in it. His body is still the earth's roots, his breath its spirit. So, in this way, the noble Pangu brought creation to birth.

# The First Marionette (Age 9 and Up)

## A Hindu Legend of Ancient India
*(Creativity, an Object Story)*

Long, long ago Lord Shiva and Lady Parvati were walking through the bazaar gazing at the handy work of the artisans of ancient India. There were poets speaking poems, dancers dancing, singers singing, hand embroidered cloths of silk and satin; it was a feast for the senses.

They came upon a carpenter's table on which sat two dolls fashioned of wood with jointed and pegged limbs including their hands and feet.

"Let us put our spirits into those dolls," said Lord Shiva. They did, and the two dolls began to dance.

Soon a crowd gathered. "Why, they look almost alive," an old woman, gasped. Children laughed and clapped their hands. When Lord Shiva and Lady Parvati withdrew their spirits, the dolls slumped to the ground.

"Oh, don't stop!" the disappointed people cried. Lord Shiva said, "Carpenter, see if you can make them move!"

The carpenter tied pieces of string to each of the dolls' jointed limbs. When he lifted the strings, the dolls slowly rose, at first moving awkwardly, then, as he gently pulled on the strings, they began to dance.

Lord Shiva smiled, "When you put your spirit into them, you, too, can bring them to life."

# The Rumor (Age 9 and Up)

*(Gossip, Rumors, Fear, Panic)*

One warm afternoon, a hare was resting under a banyan tree. He thought, "I wonder what would happen if the earth were to break up?" Just at that moment he heard a "thud" followed by a rumbling sound.

"It's happened," thought the hare, "the earth is breaking up!"

He jumped up and ran and ran and ran.

"Where are you going and why are you running so fast?" asked a hare who crossed his path.

"The earth is breaking up!!" shouted the hare. "You should run, too."

The second hare ran so fast he overtook the first hare.

"The earth's breaking up, the earth's breaking up!" he shouted to other hares as he flew past.

Soon thousands of hares were scampering through the forest. Other animals became caught up in the panic. As word spread from one to another, soon everyone knew that the earth was breaking up.

It was not long before the whole jungle was on the move. Insects, reptiles, birds, badgers, foxes, wild ponies, monkeys and four-footed animals fled in wild disorder and their cries of terror filled the air.

A lion standing on a hill saw the animals coming and wondered what was going on. He hastened down the hill and positioned himself in front of the horde.

In his most commanding voice he called for them to stop. His commanding presence stemmed the rising tide of panic among the animals.

"The earth is breaking up!" shrieked a parrot, alighting on a rock near the lion.

"Who says so?" the lion roared.

"I heard it from the monkeys," cried the parrot.

The monkeys said they had heard it from the tigers, who said their informants were the elephants, who gave their source as the buffaloes. The buffaloes had heard it from the snakes. The snakes pointed at the hares. The hares pointed to one another until the one who started it was identified.

"What makes you think the earth is breaking up?" the lion asked.

"I heard it cracking with my own ears, sire," squeaked the hare, trembling in fear.

The lion investigated the sound the hare had heard and found that it was caused by a large coconut falling from a tree. It had landed on a pile of rocks, causing a minor landslide.

"Go back to your homes," said the lion to the animals who were now looking very foolish.

"The earth's safe. Next time, check out a rumor before acting on it!"

## Poetry and Alliteration for This Age Group

Speaking poems and verses out loud with emphasis improves clarity of speech and strengthens the sense for rhythm in language. Alliteration is the rhythmical repetition of sounds. It is different than rhyme in that the sounds can occur throughout the line of the poem and nothing has to rhyme.

*Blow, breezes, blow!*
*Flow, rivers, flow!*
*Shine, sun, shine!*
*And grow, flowers, grow!*

*Bears that look for berries early*
*Find bigger, better berries surely.*
*But bees must wait 'til buds are open*
*Before they buzz among the blossoms*

### Simple Simon

*Simple Simon met a pie man going to the fair.*
*Said Simple Simon to the pie man,*
*"May I taste your wares?"*
*Said the pie man to Simple Simon,*
*"Show me first your penny."*
*Said Simple Simon to the pie man,*
*"Indeed, Sir, I haven't any."*

Have your children or students make up their own alliterative sentences such as the following:

— Shut the shutter before it makes you shudder.
— A big bug bit the little beetle, but the beetle bit the big bug back.
— When the canary keeled, the coal miners left the cave.
— Friendly Fred fed the ferrets first.
— Busy Betty baked brownies before breakfast.

# CHAPTER 14

## 10 to 11 Years Old

*To make a Prairie it takes a Clover*
*And one Bee.*
*One Clover and a Bee*
*And Revery.*
*The Revery alone will do*
*If Bees are few.*
Emily Dickinson

## Characteristics of the Child at 10-11 Years Old

Mary is a tall and willowy 11-year old girl. She gazes slightly down as she walks. She loves to read and think about the stories she reads. Her favorite color is blue. She has one best friend in whom she confides. She enjoys writing. Sometimes, she gazes out the window wistfully. She can be a bit sad about a book she has read. When she walks, she doesn't shuffle, but her feet barely leave the ground. She remembers conversations almost verbatim and is always the first one to learn a new poem or her part in a play. She keeps many of her thoughts to herself, and is often silent and contemplative. She is a good friend, loyal and sympathetic. She is someone to be trusted. Her parents wish that she would share more of her life with them. She has a rich inner life and tells them she wants to become a writer. She loves mythology and revels in the drama and challenge faced by the characters. History is her favorite subject.

From the age of 10 to 11, the child is inwardly seeking to discover wisdom and knowledge that offer an expanding imaginative context in which to find his or her rightful place in the world. Now keenly aware of differences between herself and others, the child's interest is sparked by the challenge and delight of group dynamics in a classroom, club, or sports team. This age group is seeking camaraderie and connection and enjoys hearing a story as part of a group and being able to discuss it and write about it. They are developing a more objective viewpoint that allows them to stand apart like the mythical gods as an observer who has a perspective that is different from the main characters. Children at this stage of development move back and forth between total immersion in the story and standing back from the story, reflecting on it. Experiencing an inner playfulness between these two perspectives strengthens the child's growing powers of discernment. Children of 10-11 are preparing for another shift in inner awareness as their self-perception matures and their relationship to the world changes. Receiving guidance through the metaphorical context of stories is a healthy way for them to live out their dreams of adventure as they grapple with inner questions.

## The Cry for Myth

Rollo May in his book on mythology, *The Cry for Myth*, describes how every culture has a unique mythology to explain how the world was created and to define the role of the human being on earth. A myth is an expanded metaphor of the life of a people over ages of time. Therefore, it is usually longer than a wonder tale, a fable or a folktale. Every culture has its own myths. Myths portray how to live a life of service to others, and Rollo May asserts that mythology nourishes us by offering a metaphorical context for life. Without such stories, we can become lost in the day-to-day struggles that life presents us. Within the myth, we meet the hero or heroine. Rollo May points out that: "The hero carries our aspirations, our ideals, our beliefs. In the deepest sense, the hero is created by us; he or she is born collectively as our own myth. This is what makes heroism so important: it reflects our own sense of identity, and from this our own heroism is molded. This person is the myth in action, a role model who represents the ethical and moral stance required of the individual in society, and upon whom are projected the highest aims of the community."

While fairy tales, fables, and biographies describe the challenges of individuals in great detail and clarity, myths are the sagas of a people rather than an individual. Myths carry us back into ancient times. They are long sagas that were told around the fire night after night by storytellers who knew them by heart.

In every culture, myths reflect the geography of the homeland, and the customs and idiosyncrasies of that culture in the personas of both the gods and human beings portrayed. Myths offer a metaphor for living a life in harmony with the gods that is both humorous and poignant. Myths are stories of the creation of the world and the inhabitants who populate it, rule it, and work in it. They tell of battles with dragons and demons, heroes and villains who challenge one another. Beyond the world of people is a world populated by gods and goddesses who stand watch over the people, guiding them, helping them, and, sometimes, creating obstacles for them to overcome.

Mythology places the individual seeking self-knowledge in the context of a great cultural journey—the journey of a people as they face challenges and celebrate triumphs through the ages.

How do myths suit children of 10 and 11 years old? They are exciting tales balanced on the knife-edge between the believable and the unbelievable. Rich with fascinating metaphors, they challenge children to ponder, question, and wonder. The heroes venture forth to find an elixir, a boon for the people, and become caught up in a journey that is full of adventure and unexpected twists and turns along the way. Help comes from strange and surprising sources, usually when least expected.

## Stories for 10-11 Year-Olds

When we think of mythology, we recall the stories of the ancient Greeks, Romans, and tales from the Far East—Persia, Egypt, and India. A lesser-known group of myths are The Norse Myths, a wild and wonderful collection of tales from Scandinavia. You might imagine that some rather unique and dramatic stories would arise from that striking landscape and culture, a land of dramatic contrasts: deep fjords and towering mountains, bright and sunny summers, dark and snowy winters. For children at age 10-11, the dramatic landscape and rambunctious stories are just right.

## Norse Myths

At the beginning of this saga, the end of the age of the Norse gods and their world is foretold: the story of Ragnarok. The tales then follow in an historical order beginning with a creation story. Knowing about the end right from the beginning leads children to a deeper understanding of the past, present, and future. In the chapter on children of age 9/10, we discussed the change in their awareness of time and explained how their experience of the past, present, and future is becoming more clearly differentiated in a conscious way during this phase of life. We further mentioned that they lose the experience of being at one with the world during this transition. In part, this is why using this literary form of telling the end of the tale at the beginning is appreciated and even relished by children of this age. This age group is experiencing the past, present, and future in a more differentiated way; therefore, they are fascinated by the challenge of using this new awareness to understand the Norse Myths.

Children enjoy the tension that this foreknowledge creates as the stories progress slowly towards the culmination: Ragnarok. I believe it is an empowering and validating experience, as I notice that they particularly relish the option of standing back a bit to reflect on the story, using their new powers of thinking and their deepening understanding of time.

The cosmos in Norse mythology consists of several worlds that flank a central Tree of Life, Yggdrasil. The upper world circle is home to the Norse gods, the land of Asgaard. The middle world (Earth) is the realm of the men and women, the land of Midgaard. The Lower world is the realm of the giants, the land of Jotunheim. Three sisters, known as the three Norns, sit at the base of the Tree of Life. They are the keepers of the Past, the Present, and the Future, and they spin the thread of life for each person when she or he is born. There is a great wall that protects Asgaard from the giants. The Bifrost Bridge connects Asgaard to the other worlds and Heimdal is the guardian of that bridge. Odin, the All-father, together with his wife Freya are the wise leaders of the gods who protect the balance between the three worlds. In contrast to Odin stands Loki, the Trickster, the Teller of Lies. Loki acts as a catalyst for good and for evil, both a helper and a hinderer. Many a lively discussion can be had about the motives behind his actions and his character. Odin and Loki often stand in opposition to one another creating a dynamic tension throughout the saga. Iduna is the goddess who tends the apple orchard in Asgaard. Her apples are no ordinary apples. She gives one to each of the gods and goddesses every day for these apples are the elixir of life. They keep the gods immortal. Without them, the gods would age and die. Hodor is the blind god with a kind heart. Thor with his hammer, Mjelnior, protects the land of the Aesir gods from the giants. Thor has red hair and is hot tempered. He keeps his hammer with him at all times. Little is told of the lives of the humans who live in the middle realm known as Midgaard. In the lower realm, also live the gnomes, who dig in the earth. They are blacksmiths and create many wondrous tools and gifts for the gods. As you can imagine, a dramatic stage is set in which these humorous and lively tales come to life, suiting the child of this age well.

The bulk of the tales revolve around encounters between the gods and the giants. The gods are all knowing and self-centered. The giants are very strong physically, but not very intelligent. This polarity creates humor, tension, and drama throughout the saga.

At this age, children are diving deeper into the complexity of relationships. This stage of childhood is accompanied by myriads of questions having to do with fairness, honesty, betrayal, and forgiveness. The Norse Myths portray the myriad of human qualities while employing grand imagery and lively humor. Each god or goddess personifies a particular human quality. Often, a god's name conveys a feeling, mood, or idea that suggests the kind of character he or she is. Loki, the Trickster, the Teller of Lies, (that is his full name) uses his cleverness for his own gain. We all know people like this, and the children recognize in Loki aspects of one another as well as family members, family friends, and relations. Odin, the All-father, sacrificed one of his physical eyes to attain knowledge and gain an inner eye of discernment and seeing into the future in order to guide his people. We all know people who sacrifice for the sake of others.

The child of 10-11 relishes the cleverness of Loki and admires the steadfastness and uprightness of Odin. These characters are archetypes, and each has his greater and lesser moments in the tales. The child gains many gifts from these wonderful myths. The stories are filled with hilarity and surprise and call forth questions about honesty, faithfulness, and deceit. For children whose sense of humor is maturing and whose ability to laugh at themselves is awakening, the Norse Myths offer a safe way to look at themselves from the outside for the first time. The dynamic interplay of humor and drama throughout the myths strikes a welcome chord.

Being able to stand outside the story and watch the unfolding of events is exciting. Foreshadowing offers a new perspective that is challenging and satisfying. The ability to stand back and evaluate situations, assess the character of the individual gods and goddesses, and "see" into the future of the story is a delight and a training for children as they struggle to understand and come to terms with their own lives in light of their new powers of observation and thinking. As a metaphor for this stage of development, the Norse Myths hit the mark!

The following two Norse Myths are a complete story. Tell them in the order they are written here. Discuss the first story at length over several days, retelling parts of it with your students or children before moving on to the second story. Gather questions about the story. Draw some pictures and write a paragraph about the story with your students or child. Then tell the second story. Many a fascinating conversation can be had about the polarities offered in these stories. For example: fairness – injustice; physical prowess – intellectual prowess; honesty – untruth. Discover others, and, as you work with the story, you will find the children know more than you might imagine.

These are long stories. Feel free to read them if telling them seems daunting. The review process as described above is important, as it allows time to reflect and offers time to ask questions about the story and come to some insights about the story's meaning and purpose.

# The Wall of Asgaard (Age 10 and Up)

## Norse Myth
*(Fairness, Trickery, Greed, Loss of Innocence, Injustice)*

ALWAYS there had been war between the Giants and the Gods—between the Giants who would have destroyed the world and the race of men, and the Gods who would have protected the race of men and would have made the world more beautiful.

In the beginning, the Gods climbed up to the top of a high mountain. They decided to build a great City for themselves that the Giants could never overthrow. The City would be called "Asgaard," which means the "Place of the Gods". They chose to build it on a beautiful plain that sat on the top of that high mountain. To protect their new city, they decided to build the highest and strongest wall that had ever been built. This wall would extend around the entire city.

One day as they were just beginning to build their halls and their palaces a stranger appeared, walking towards them. Odin, the Father of the Gods, spoke to him saying, "What do you want on the Mountain of the Gods?"

"I know what is in the mind of the Gods," the Stranger said. "The Gods intend to build a great City here. I cannot build palaces, but I can build great walls that can never be overthrown. Allow me build the wall round your City. You will not regret it.

"How long will it take you to build a wall that will go round our City?" said the Father of the Gods.

"A year, O Father Odin," said the Stranger.

Now Odin knew that if a great wall could be built around their new City, then the Gods would not have to spend all their time defending Asgaard, their city, from the Giants. He also thought that if Asgaard were protected, he himself could go amongst men and teach them and help them. He thought that no payment the Stranger could ask would be too much for the building of that wall.

Odin brought the Stranger to the Council of the Gods, and he swore before them all that in a year he would have the great wall built. Then Odin made oath that the Gods would give him what he asked in payment if the wall was finished to the last stone in a year from that day.

The Stranger went away and came back on the morrow. It was the first day of summer when he started work. He brought no one to help him except a great horse. Now the Gods thought that this horse could only drag blocks of stone for the building of the wall. But the horse did more than this. He set the stones in their places and mortared them together. Day and night, by light and dark the horse worked, and soon a great wall was rising round the palaces that the Gods themselves were building.

"What reward will the Stranger ask for the work he is doing for us?" the Gods asked one another.

Odin went to the Stranger. "We marvel at the work that you and your horse are doing for us," he said. "No one can doubt that the great wall of Asgaard will be built up by the first day of summer. What reward do you claim? We would have it ready for you."

The Stranger turned from the work he was doing, leaving the great horse to pile up the blocks of stone. "O Father of the Gods," he said, "O Odin, the reward I shall ask for my work is the Sun and the Moon, and Freya, who watches over the flowers and grasses, for my wife."

Now when Odin heard this he was terribly angered, for the price the Stranger asked for his work was beyond all prices. He went amongst the other Gods who were then building their shining palaces within the great wall and he told them what reward the Stranger had asked. The Gods said, "Without the Sun and the Moon the world will wither away." And the Goddesses said, "Without Freya all will be gloom in Asgaard."

They would have let the wall remain unbuilt rather than let the Stranger have the reward he claimed for building it. But one who was in the company of the Gods spoke. He was Loki, a being who only half belonged to the Gods; his father was the Wind Giant.

"Let the Stranger build the wall round Asgaard," Loki said, "and I will find a way to make him give up the hard bargain he has made with the Gods. Go to him and tell him that the wall must be finished by the first day of summer, and that if it is not finished to the last stone on that day the price he asks will not be given to him."

The Gods went to the Stranger and they told him that if the last stone was not laid on the wall on the first day of the Summer not Sol or Mani, the Sun or the Moon, nor Freya would be given him. And now they realized that the Stranger was one of the Giants.

The Giant and his great horse piled up the wall more quickly than before. At night, while the Giant slept, the horse worked on and on, hauling up stones and laying them on the wall with his great forefeet. And day after day the wall around Asgaard grew higher and higher.

Now, you can imagine that the Gods had no joy in seeing that great wall rising higher and higher around their palaces. The Giant and his horse would finish the work by the first day of summer, and then he would take the Sun and the Moon, Sol and Mani, and Freya away with him.

Loki was not disturbed. He kept telling the Gods that he would find a way to prevent him from finishing his work, and thus he would make the Giant forfeit the terrible price he had led Odin to promise him.

It was three days to summertime. All the wall was finished except the gateway. Over the gateway a stone was still to be placed. And the Giant, before he went to sleep, bade his horse haul up a great block of stone so that they might put it above the gateway in the morning, and, thus, finish the work two full days before summer.

It happened to be a beautiful moonlit night. Svadilfare, the Giant's great horse, was hauling the largest stone he ever hauled when he saw a little mare come galloping toward him. The great horse had never seen so pretty a little mare and he looked at her with surprise.

"Svadilfare, slave," said the little mare to him and went frisking past.

Svadilfare put down the stone he was hauling and called to the little mare. She came back to him. "Why do you call me 'Svadilfare, slave'?" said the great horse.

"Because you have to work night and day for your master," said the little mare. "He keeps you working, working, working, and never lets you enjoy yourself. You dare not leave that stone down and come and play with me.

"Who told you I dare not do it?" said Svadilfare.

"I know you daren't do it," said the little mare, and she kicked up her heels and ran across the moonlit meadow.

Now the truth is that Svadilfare was tired of working day and night. When he saw the little mare go galloping off he became discontented. He left the stone he was hauling on the ground. He looked round and he saw the little mare looking back at him. He galloped after her.

He did not catch up to the little mare. She went on swiftly before him. She galloped over the moonlit meadow turning and looking back now and then at the great Svadilfare, who came heavily after her. Down the mountainside the mare went, and Svadilfare, who now rejoiced in his liberty and in the freshness of the wind and in the smell of the flowers, followed her with joy. With the morning's light they came near a cave and the little mare went into it. They went through the cave. Then Svadilfare caught up on the little mare and the two went wandering together, the little mare telling Svadilfare stories of the Dwarfs and the Elves.

They came to a quiet grove of trees and they stayed there together, the little mare playing so nicely with him that the great horse forgot all about time passing. While they were playing together in the grove the Giant was going up and down, searching for his great horse. He had come to the wall in the morning, expecting to put the stone over the gateway and so finish his work. The stone that was to be lifted up was not near the gateway and when he called for Svadilfare, his great horse did not come. He went in search of him. He searched down the mountainside and he searched far across the earth, as far as the realm of the Giants. But he did not find Svadilfare.

The Gods saw the first day of summer come and the gateway of the wall stand unfinished. They said to each other that if it were not finished by the evening they need not give Sol and Mani to the Giant, nor the maiden Freya to be his wife. The hours of the summer day went past and the Giant did not raise the stone over the gateway. In the evening he came before them.

"Your work is not finished," Odin said. "You forced us to a hard bargain and now we need not keep it with you. You shall not be given Sol and Mani nor the maiden Freya."

"Only the wall I have built is so strong I would tear it down," said the Giant. He tried to throw down one of the palaces, but the Gods laid hands on him and thrust him outside the wall he had built. "Go, and trouble Asgaard no more," Odin commanded.

When Loki returned to Asgaard, he told the Gods how he had transformed himself into a little mare and had led Svadilfare, the Giant's great horse, to a cave far away. The Gods sat in their golden palaces behind the great wall and rejoiced that their City was now secure, and that no enemy could ever enter it or overthrow it. But Odin, the Father of the Gods, as he sat upon his throne was sad in his heart. He was sad that the Gods had in the end used trickery to get their wall built. He was sad that oaths had been broken, and that a blow of injustice had been struck in Asgaard.

# Iduna and Her Golden Apples (Age 10 and Up)

## Norse Myth
*(Steadfastness, Imagination is the elixir of life)*

In the ancient land of Asgaard there was a garden. In that garden there grew a tree and on that tree there grew shining golden apples. Anyone who ate of them every day did not grow a day older. The Norse Goddess Iduna tended the garden and the golden apples. No one else could pluck them off the tree and if she were not there to tend the garden then the trees would begin to die. Iduna never left her garden.

Each day Iduna picked one apple for each of the gods and goddesses. One by one they would come to the garden to receive their apple from Iduna. Beside the garden stood her golden house and each day her husband Bragi told her a story that never ended.

Now it happened that one day Odin, the All-Father God, went to the land of men to watch over their doings. Loki, the Trickster, the Teller of Lies, went with him. For a long time they traveled through the world of Men. At last they came near Jotunheim, the land of the Giants.

It was a bleak and empty region. There were no growing things there, not even trees with berries. There were no birds, and no animals. As Odin, the All-Father, and Loki, the Trickster went through this region hunger came upon them. But in all the land they saw nothing that they could eat.

At last, Loki came upon a herd of wild cattle. Loki crept quietly towards them and caught hold of a young bull and killed it. He cut up the meat, lit a fire and put the meat on spits to roast it. While the meat cooked, Odin, the All-Father, sat a way off thinking on what he had seen in the world of men.

Loki kept the fire roaring, but when the meat was taken off the spits and Odin cut it, it was still raw and uncooked! Loki thought he had not made the fire hot enough and set it blazing with more wood. He took a plate of the cooked meat to Odin.

Odin cut into the meat only to find that it was still raw! "Is this a trick of yours, Loki?" he asked. Loki was so angry at the meat being uncooked that Odin realized he was not playing a trick. A third time he put the meat on the fire to cook and every hour he checked it, and it remained as raw as the first time they took it off the fire.

Now Odin understood that the meat must be under an enchantment. He strode off hungry but feeling strong. Loki continued to cook the meet until at last he fell asleep.

Dawn came and Loki was stirring the fire to life when he heard a whirr of wings above him. There he saw a mighty eagle circling round and round above his head.

"Can you not cook your food?" screamed the eagle.

"I cannot," said Loki.

"I will cook it for you if you will give me a share of it," screamed the eagle.

"Yes, come and cook it!" cried Loki.

The eagle circled lower and lower until he was above the fire. He flapped his great wings making the fire blaze hotter and hotter. A heat that Loki had never felt came from that burning blaze! In a minute he pulled the meat from the spits and saw that it was fully cooked.

"My share, my share," screamed the eagle. He flew down and grasped a large piece of meat and instantly devoured it. Then he grasped another piece, and then another! It looked to Loki that he would be left with nothing for his dinner.

The eagle grabbed the last piece. Loki was furious. Taking up the spit he struck the eagle with it. Loki heard a clang as if he had struck metal. The wood of the spit stuck to the breast of the eagle. Loki held on and suddenly the eagle rose into the air. Loki was carried up with him.

Before he knew what had happened Loki was being flown toward Jotunheim, the Realm of the Giants. The eagle screamed, "Loki, I have thee at last. You cheated my brother of his reward for building the Wall of Asgaard. Know now that Thiassi the Giant has captured you. O Loki, most cunning of the dwellers in Asgaard."The eagle flew off leaving Loki alone on the frozen ice. Loki felt as if he were bound to the iceberg by chains of cold. After a day, Thiassi returned.

Would you like to leave the iceberg?" he asked Loki.

"Yes!" cried Loki with tears freezing on his face.

"You will be set free once you bring me the shining apples of Iduna."

"I cannot get Iduna's apples for you, Thiassi," said Loki.

"Then stay upon the iceberg." And Thiassi flew off. When Thiassi returned

he asked Loki again for the apples. Loki explained that this was an impossible task. The giant called upon Loki to use his cunning.

"Well, Iduna is a simple woman and perhaps I can trick her to go outside the wall of Asgaard with her apples. She never lets an apple out of her hand except when she gives one to a God or Goddess to eat," replied Loki.

"Make it so that she will go beyond the wall of Asgaard," said the Giant. "If she does, then I shall get the apples from her. Swear by the World-Tree that you will lure Iduna beyond the wall of Asgaard. Then I shall let you go."

"I swear it by Yggdrasil, the World-Tree, that I will lure Iduna beyond the wall of Asgaard if you will take me off this iceberg."

The Thiassi changed himself into a mighty eagle and taking Loki in his talons, he flew with him over the stream that divides Jotunheim, the realm of the Giants, from Midgaard, the World of Men. He left Loki on the ground of Midgaard, and Loki made his own way back to Asgaard.

Odin had returned to Asgaard and told the gods about Loki's attempt to cook the enchanted meat. The gods were amused to think of Loki left hungry when he was such a cunning fellow. When they saw him return they took him to the Feast Hall and gave him the best food and wine. When the feast was over the gods went to Iduna's garden which they did every day after their main meal.

There sat Iduna in the golden house that opened onto her garden. She was the picture of innocence, goodness and beauty. She had eyes as blue as the sky and she smiled as if she were recalling the happiest times of her life. The basket of shining apples was beside her.

To each god and goddess she gave a golden apple. Each of the gods rejoiced as they ate their apple thinking that they would never become a day older. Odin, the All-Father spoke the runes that were always said in praise of Iduna. Then the Dwellers of Asgaard left the garden and returned to their shining houses.

Loki remained behind. He sat in the garden, watching the fair and simple Iduna. After awhile she spoke to him saying, "Why are you still here, wise Loki?"

"To gaze upon your apples," said Loki. "I am wondering if the apples that I saw yesterday are as shining as the ones in your basket."

"There are no apples in the world as shining as mine," cried Iduna.

"The apples I saw were more shining," said Loki. "It's true! And they smelled so delicious!

Loki's words troubled Iduna. Her eyes filled with tears. "Surely Loki, there cannot be apples more shining or delicious than mine!"

"Come then, and see," said Loki. "Just outside Asgaard is the tree that has the apples I saw. Iduna, you who never leave your garden, know nothing of he world outside Asgaard. Come and see!

"I will come, Loki," said Iduna, the fair and innocent.

Iduna went outside the wall of Asgaard. She went to the place Loki had told her where the apple tree grew. She looked this way and that, but saw no tree. Suddenly she heard a whirr of wings above her. Looking up she saw a mighty eagle flying towards her. She fled back toward the gate of Asgaard, but the eagle swooped down and lifted her up. She was carried away! Away from Asgaard she flew with the eagle, over Midgaard, toward the rocks and snows of Jotunheim. Across the river that flows between the world of Men and the Realm of Giants they flew.

At last the eagle flew into a cavernous hall in a mountain. The hall was lit by fires that shot up from the earth like columns of light. The eagle loosened his grip on Iduna and she sank down on the ground. The feathers of the bird fell away and there stood the Giant.

"Oh, why have you carried me off from Asgaard and brought me to this place," Iduna cried.

"I want to eat your shining apples, Iduna," said Thiassi, the giant.

"That will never be, for I will not give them to you," said Iduna.

"Give me the apples to eat, and I shall carry you back to Asgaard."

"No, I cannot. I have been trusted with the shining apples that I may give them to the Gods only."

"Then I shall take the apples from you," said Thiassi. And he took the basket from her hands and opened it. But when he touched the apples they shriveled under his hands. He left them in the basket and he set the basket down, for he knew now that the apples would be no good to him unless Iduna gave them to him with her own hands.

"You must stay with me here until you give me the shining apples," said the giant.

Poor Iduna was frightened: she was frightened of the strange cave and the fire that burst out of the ground and of the giant. But more than any of these she was frightened to think what would happen to the gods of Asgaard if she were not there to give them the shining apples to eat.

The Giant came to see her again. Iduna would not give him the shining apples. There in the cave she stayed, day after day, each day refusing to give an apple to the Giant. In her dreams she began to see the Dwellers of Asgaard growing older. Each day, she saw them going to her garden to be given a shining apple. She knew the changes that were coming over them.

Every day Odin and Thor, Hodur and Baldur, Tyr and Heimdal, Vidar and Vali, Frigga and Freya, Nanna and Sif visited her garden, but there was no one to pluck the apples for them. A change began to come over the Gods and Goddesses. They no long walked lightly. Their shoulders became bent; their eyes no longer were as bright as dewdrops. And when they looked upon one another they saw the change. Age was coming upon the Dwellers in Asgaard.

They knew that the time would come when Frigga would be gray and old, when Sif's golden hair would fade; when Odin would no longer have clear wisdom and when Thor would not have strength enough to raise and fling his thunderbolts. And the Dwellers in Asgaard were saddened by this knowledge. It seemed to them that all brightness had gone from their shining city.

Where had Iduna gone? The Gods searched for her through out the World of Men. But no trace had they found. Odin summoned Hugin and Mugin, his two ravens that flew through the earth and through the Realm of Giants and knew all things past and all things that were to come. Hugin and Mugin came and one sat on his right shoulder and one sat on his left shoulder and they told him deep secrets: they told him of Thiassi and of his desire of the shining apples that the Dwellers in Asgaard ate and of Loki's deception of Iduna, the fair.

What Odin learnt from his ravens was told in the Council of the Gods. Then Thor the Strong went to Loki and laid hands upon him.

"What do you want with me, O Thor?" asked Loki.

"I would hurl you into a chasm in the ground and strike you with my thunder," said the strong God. "It was you who took Iduna from Asgaard."

"O Thor," said Loki, "Do not crush me with your thunder. Let me stay in Asgaard. I will strive to win Iduna back."

"The judgment of the Gods," said Thor, "is that you, the cunning one, should go to Jötunheim, and by your craft win Iduna back from the

Giants. Go or else I shall hurl you into a chasm and crush you with my thunder."

"I will go," said Loki.

From Frigga, the wife of Odin, Loki borrowed the dress of falcon feathers that she owned. He dressed himself in it and flew to Jötunheim in the form of a falcon. He searched through Jötunheim until he found Thiassi's daughter, Skadi. He flew before Skadi and he let the Giant maid catch him and hold him as a pet. One day the Giant maid carried him into the cave where Iduna, the fair and simple, was held.

When Loki saw Iduna there he knew that part of his quest was ended. Now he had to get Iduna out of Jötunheim and away to Asgaard. He stayed no more with the Giant maid, but flew up into the high rocks of the cave. Skadi wept for the flight of her pet, but she ceased to search and went away from the cave.

Then Loki flew to where Iduna was sitting and spoke to her. Iduna, when she knew that one of the Dwellers in Asgaard was near, wept with joy. Loki told her what she was to do. By the power of a spell that was given him he was able to change her into the form of a sparrow. But before she did this she took the shining apples out of her basket and flung them into places where the Giant would never find them.

Skadi, coming back to the cave, saw the falcon fly out with the sparrow beside him. She cried out to her father and the Giant knew that the falcon was Loki and the sparrow was Iduna. He changed himself into the form of a mighty eagle. By this time sparrow and falcon were out of sight, but Thiassi, knowing that he could make better flight than they, flew toward Asgaard.

Soon he saw them. They flew with all the power they had, but the great wings of the eagle brought him nearer and nearer to them. The Dwellers in Asgaard, standing on the wall, saw the falcon and the sparrow with the great eagle pursuing them. They knew who they were—Loki and Iduna with Thiassi in pursuit.

As they watched the eagle winging nearer and nearer, the Dwellers in Asgaard were afraid that the falcon and the sparrow would be caught and then Iduna would be carried off by Thiassi. They lighted great fires upon the wall, knowing that Loki would find a way through the fires, bringing Iduna with him, but that Thiassi would not find a way.

The falcon and the sparrow flew toward the fires. Loki went between the flames and brought Iduna with him. And Thiassi, coming up to the fires and finding no way through, beat his wings against the flames. He fell down from the wall and was never seen again.

Thus Iduna was brought back to Asgaard. Once again she sat in the golden house that opened to her garden. Once again she plucked the shining apples off the tree she tended, and once again she gave them to the Dwellers in Asgaard. The Dwellers in Asgaard walked lightly again, and brightness came into their eyes and into their cheeks. Age no longer came over them. Their youth came back and light and joy were again found in Asgaard.

## An Interpretation of the Norse Myth about Iduna

Let's take a look at how we could interpret this story. What are the key images, questions, and metaphors? What is it that keeps us young? What keeps us from inwardly dying? The apples of Iduna are a metaphor. Let's explore it. For me imagination is the elixir of life. It is what keeps us alive and thriving. We use it to create something new, solve a problem, and to step into one another's shoes.

Imagination: the elixir of life!
Imagination: the birthplace of invention…
Imagination: the creation of something out of nothing…

We value it,
We revere it
We honor it

But, do we truly understand it and how to pass it along to the next generation?

If the imagination is not used, it becomes dull and does not develop and mature. In fact, in some cases, it dies. Our ideas become old; we rehash our younger days and youthful dreams and ideals and wish we could go back...

We age inwardly.

What is the secret to the cultivation of the imagination, to the nurturing of the imaginations of the next generation? I believe it is a matter of exercising it, using it, picking up the apple of the imagination and eating it, digesting it and using it to create something new.

It is not such a simple matter. It is easy to forget about it, be distracted by our day-to-day demands of life. It requires effort to use it, and persistence and regular practice to develop it. Each and every day, we must eat the apple of the imagination or our imaginations will slowly whither and die.

If we look at the history of ancient civilizations, we find a pattern of a youthful energetic societies that bring forth new ideas and then, at some point, reach a peak and begin to degenerate, to rehash old ways of doing things: to die. The imagination has been lost or stolen. It can be stolen by complacency, idleness, fear, doubt, lack of discipline, just about anything that distracts us and keeps us from our highest pursuits.

In the story of "Iduna and Her Golden Apples," the giant Thiassi finds a way to steal Iduna and her apples. The apples are eaten daily by the gods of Asgaard, keeping them young and alive. Without the apples of the imagination, the gods begin to wither. Thiassi wants what the gods have and contrives to get it. He threatens Loki, and Loki tricks Iduna into stepping outside the garden of Asgaard. Soon, the gods see one another aging rapidly and losing the will to live. But Loki, the trickster, the teller of lies, who is responsible for getting the apples for Thiassi, also brings them back along with Iduna.

Thiassi is outwitted by Loki. Thus, he who allowed the theft has redeemed himself by using his imagination to get Iduna and the apples back to Asgaard.

It's a story worth contemplating. It is the imagination that keeps us young inwardly and engaged with life and on fire with creativity. It is an essential part of our humanness. The giant, who is an image of the immature human being, is that part of us that acts on impulse only and expects to get everything he wants without doing the inner work. He can truly become a giant in our psyche.

Children love these images and metaphors at age 10. The stories are humorous; the characters of the Norse gods and heroes are larger than life. The predicaments that the gods find themselves in let us know that they are not so perfect. In fact, they are downright human. The world of the Norse gods and heroes delights and challenges the 10-year-old child. The variety of characters and the clarity of their personalities make for clear metaphors and humorous adventures.

## Other Mythologies from Ancient Civilizations

Traditionally mythology begins with the Norse Myths that are told in the fourth grade at age 9 or 10 (4th grade US). Mythology also accompanies the study of the ancient civilizations of India, Persia and Greece in the 5th grade (ages 10 – 11). Telling myths from ancient India, Persia and Greece enlivens the history of those periods. Finally, we reach the Romans in 6th grade at ages 11-12 and tell some Roman Myths.

Myths are long and exciting tales that are told over a period of days. Charles Kovacs collected and wrote wonderfully crafted versions of ancient myths from each of these cultures. His books are now back in print. Find them online by googling Charles Kovacs. We have included a few myths in each of the chapters mentioned above to inspire you to journey into the land of mythology. See the bibliography for collections of these important and enduring sagas.

## The Old Woman and the Rice Fields (Age 10 and Up)

Based on a Japanese Folktale

*(Present-Mindedness, Courage, Taking Drastic Action in the Face of Great Danger)*

Once there was a wise old woman who lived up on a mountain, far away in Japan. All round her little house the mountain was flat, and the ground was rich; and there were the rice fields of all the people who lived in the village at the mountain's foot far below. Mornings and evenings, the old woman and her little grandson, who lived with her, used to look far down on the people at work in the village, and watch the blue sea which lay all round the land, so close that there was no room for fields below, only for houses. The little boy loved the rice fields, dearly, for he knew that all the good food for all the people came from them; and he often helped his grandmother to watch over them.

One day, the old woman was standing alone, before her house, looking far down at the people, and out at the sea, when, suddenly, she saw something very strange far off where the sea and sky meet. Something like a great cloud was rising there, as if the sea were lifting itself high into the sky. The old woman put her hands to her eyes and looked again, hard as her old sight could. Then she turned and ran to the house. "Yone, Yone!" she cried, "bring a brand from the hearth!"

The little grandson could not imagine what his grandmother wanted with fire, but he always obeyed, so he ran quickly and brought the brand. The old woman already had one, and was running for the rice fields. Yone ran after. But what was his horror to see his grandmother thrust the burning brand into the ripe dry rice, where it stood.

"Oh, Grandmother, Grandmother!" screamed the little boy, "what are you doing?"

"Quick, set fire! Thrust your brand in!" said the grandmother.

Yone thought his dear grandmother had lost her mind, and he began to sob; but a little Japanese boy always obeys, so though he sobbed, he thrust his torch in, and the sharp flame ran up the dry stalks, red and yellow. In an instant, the field was ablaze, and thick black smoke began to pour up the mountainside. It rose like a cloud, black and fierce, and in no time the people below saw that their precious rice fields were on fire. Ah, how they ran! Men, women, and children climbed the mountain, running as fast as they could to save the rice; not one soul stayed behind.

And when they came to the mountain top, and saw the beautiful rice-crop all in flames, beyond help, they cried bitterly, "Who has done this thing? How did it happen?"

"I set fire," said the old woman, very solemnly; and the little grandson sobbed, "Grandmother set fire."

But when they came fiercely round the old woman, with "Why? Why?" she only turned and pointed to the sea. "Look!" she said.

They all turned and looked. And there, where the blue sea had lain, so calm, a mighty wall of water, reaching from earth to sky, was rolling in. No one could scream, so terrible was the sight. The wall of water rolled in on the land, passed quite over the place where the village had been, and broke, with an awful sound, on the mountainside. One wave more, and still one more, came; and then all was water, as far as they could look, below; the village where they had been was under the sea.

But the people were all safe. And when they saw what the old woman had done, they honored her above all others for the quick wit which had saved them all from the tidal wave.

# The Golden Dagger (Age 10 and Up)

*(Inspiration, The beginning of Farming)*

Long, long ago in the land of ancient Persia the people lived a nomadic life. The people moved from place to place following the animals that they hunted for their food. It was a hard life.

One day, a great leader came to the people, King Hushang. He showed the people how to become herdsmen. Over time their herds of sheep and cattle grew and multiplied. Then, in their dreams he showed them how to tame wolves to become the very first dogs. The god of ancient Persia gave the people the gift of fire. And the people were no longer hungry or cold. The people tamed horses to carry their burdens as they moved from place to place.

The god of those people was called Ahura Mazda, the God of Light. He spoke to the people in dreams. He was the god who showed them how to make fire. After King Hushang died, the new king, King Djemshid, noticed that the herds of cattle and sheep were growing. The people had to move more often from place to place to find fresh grasses to feed the animals.

One night King Djemshid had a dream. In this dream he saw the god Ahura Mazda holding a golden dagger in his hand. Suddenly, Ahura Mazda, the god of light, stabbed the dagger into the ground, into the earth. When he drew the dagger out again a great green stalk grew up from the earth. Hanging from the stalk were golden grains of wheat. Then, Ahura Mazda gave King Djemshid the golden dagger.

When King Djemshid woke up the next morning he could not stop thinking about his dream. What was that dagger? How could it make things grow out of the earth? What was Ahura Mazda trying to tell him in his dream? Then, suddenly, he knew what to do. He made a dagger like the one he saw in the dream, but he made it bigger. It was the first plow. He used it to cut through the earth and break up the clods of soil until they were soft and he could plant seeds from the grasses that grew nearby. Then he had another idea.

He took some rope and tied a cow to the plow and he plowed the earth! The first furrows on earth were now ready to be planted. He gathered seeds from the wild grasses that grew nearby and planted them in the furrows. These were something like the seeds we call wheat, today.

His people wondered about this. The next spring the seeds sprouted and in the summer the field was full of golden grains of wheat. The King showed the people how the grains could be ground into flour and how the flour could be made into bread. They people learned to build plows out of wood. These "golden daggers" allowed them to plow the earth, sow the seeds, harvest the grains, grind the grains and make them into bread.

That is the story of the herdsmen of ancient Persia who became farmers. A farmer stays by his fields and builds a home. He no longer wanders from place to place like a nomad. Over time all the peoples of the earth learned to make plows, till the earth, grow crops and make bread. But the Persians were the first, and it all began when Ahura Mazda showed King Djemshid the golden dagger in a dream.

## The Wise Peasant and the King (Age 10 and Up)

Adapted from Charles Kovacs' rendition, public domain.

**There is a great math puzzle at the end of this story for your students to solve.**

*(Bravery, Greed, Cleverness, Dishonesty, Manipulation)*

Long ago in the land of India there lived a king who loved to ride his horse through the countryside. Every morning he would have one of his horses brought to him and he would sally forth into the wood surrounding his palace. As luck would have it, this day a bird suddenly rose up as they passed a field. It startled the horse and the horse bolted. The king could do nothing to control the wild galloping of the crazed horse. It was all he could do to hold on.

Fortunately, a brave peasant working in a nearby field saw the king struggling with the crazed horse and left his field to help. He ran as fast as he could and when the horse crossed his path he grabbed the reins and using all his strength brought the horse to a standstill.

The king who was shaken up by the wild ride felt indebted to the peasant and thanked him profusely. "My dear man, you have saved my life. I, as your king, wish to reward you for your deed. Please come to my castle tomorrow to receive your reward."

The peasant went home to his wife and with pleasure he told her the story. Together they dreamed about what they might do with the reward. Early the next morning he set off for the palace and arrived at the gate.

There a soldier stopped him from entering and asked what business he had at the palace. The peasant explained that the King was expecting him for he was to receive a reward for rescuing the King.

The soldier smiled and explained that the peasant could not enter unless he, the soldier, allowed him to do so. Therefore, since he was a poor man, he required the peasant to share his reward with him.

The peasant said he would be happy to give the soldier a few gold coins.

But the greedy soldier replied, "Oh no, I want no less than one sixth of your total reward." The poor peasant could not do other than to agree.

He went through the gate and into the great palace. There, he was met by the King's general who was dressed in a fine uniform.

"And what is a poor peasant doing here in the palace," he inquired.

The peasant explained once more why he had come to see the King.

"Well," said the general, "in that case you must see the King's secretary. I am the only one who can take you there. Therefore, you must give me a share of your reward."

"Good heavens," said the peasant. "It seems that everyone here wants a bit of my reward. How much do you want"?

"One third," said the general. "If you don't pay me what I want, I will not take you to see the King's secretary and you will not have any reward at all."

"Very well," replied the peasant. "You shall receive one third."

The general took the peasant to the King's secretary and explained why the peasant had come. As soon as the general left, the secretary said:

"My good fellow, without me you cannot see the King at all. If I don't go to the King to request your audience with him, you will not receive your reward. Therefore, for doing this great service I request one half of your reward."

"Very well," agreed the peasant "I will promise you half of the reward the King gives me and I hope you will enjoy it."

The secretary rose and went into the great hall where the King sat with his courtiers. He explained that a peasant was in the hallway and expecting a reward.

"Bring him in!" cried the King. "This man saved me from breaking my leg or even from breaking my neck, and no reward is enough for him."

At last, the peasant was brought before the King. "Well, my friend," spoke the King warmly, "You are most welcome here. You are a brave and kind man and truly you saved my life. Please tell me what reward you wish to have."

"Thank you, great King, for your generosity and kindness," said the peasant. "I request that your guard at the gate and your general, and your secretary be present when I receive my reward."

"Of course," said the King, a bit surprised. And he called for the three to be brought forth.

When they had arrived, the King said, "Now tell us your reward."

"Dear King, I have a strange request."

"Be that as it may," said the King, "just tell me. If I can get it for you will.

"What I wish for is 60 strokes with a cane on my back."

"Are you crazy," said the King.

"You promised to give me what I asked for, did you not? " replied the peasant.

The King had indeed promised, but he felt confused by the request. Nonetheless he called for the man whose job was to punish lazy slaves, and in came a tall African man a long stout cane.

"Alright, this man is to be given 60 strokes right away!" cried the confused King.

"Just a moment, please," said the peasant. "I have promised to share my reward: the soldier at the gate of the palace gets one sixth; the general gets one third; and the secretary gets one half."

The King began to laugh, as he understood the wisdom of the peasant. How were the 60 strokes divided between the soldier, the general and the secretary? Were there any left for the peasant?

Then the King sent the peasant home with a bag of gold coins.

## The Fisherman and the Seals (Age 10 and Up)

*(Kindness, Forgiveness, Living in harmony with nature)*

There was once a fisherman who dwelt in a little township nigh to John-o'-Groat's House, and was wont to catch fish and seals. When he found that he could earn more money by hunting seals, whose skins make warm winter clothing, he troubled little about catching salmon or cod, and worked constantly as a seal-hunter. He crept among the rocks searching for his prey, and visited lonely seal-haunted islands across the Pentland Firth, where he often found them lying on smooth flat ledges of rock fast asleep in the warm sunshine.

In his house he had great bundles of dried sealskins, and people came from near and far to purchase them from him. His fame as a seal-hunter went far and wide.

One evening a dark stranger rode up to his house, mounted on a black, spirited mare with a grey mane and a grey tail. He called to the fisherman, "Make haste and ride with me towards the east. My master desires to do business with you."

"I have no horse," the fisherman answered, "but I shall walk to your master's house on the morrow.

Said the stranger: "Come now. Ride with me. My good mare is fleet-footed and strong."

"As you will," answered the fisherman, who at once mounted the mare behind the stranger.

The mare galloped eastward faster than the wind of March. Shingle rose in front of her like rock-strewn sea-spray, and a sand-cloud gathered and swept out behind them like mountain mists that are scattered before a gale. The fisherman gasped for breath, and the wind blew fiercely in his face as they rode on. The mare went fast and far until she drew nigh to a precipice. There, she halted suddenly.

Said the stranger: "We have almost reached my master's dwelling."

The fisherman looked round about him in surprise, for he saw neither house nor the smoke of one. "Where is your master?" he asked.

Said the stranger: "You shall see him presently. Come with me."

As he spoke he walked towards the edge of the precipice and looked over. The fisherman did the same, and saw nothing but the grey lonely sea heaving in a long slow swell, and sea birds wheeling and sliding down the wind.

"Where is your master?" he asked once again.

With that the stranger suddenly clasped the seal-hunter in his arms crying, "Come with me," and he leapt over the edge of the precipice. The mare leapt with her master.

Down, down they fell through the air, scattering the startled sea birds. Screaming and fluttering, the birds rose in clouds about and above them. Down the men and the mare continued to fall till they plunged into the sea, and sank. The light around them faded into darkness deeper than night. The fisherman wondered to find himself still alive as he passed through the sea depths, seeing nothing, hearing nothing, while moving swiftly. At length he ceased to sink, and went forward. He suffered no pain or discomfort, nor was he afraid. A feeling of wonder arose within him in the thick, cool darkness. At length he saw a faint green light, and as he approached the light it grew brighter and brighter, until the glens and forests of the sea kingdom appeared before his eyes. Then he discovered that he was swimming beside the stranger and that they had both been changed into seals.

Said the stranger, "Yonder is my master's house."

The fisherman looked, and saw a town of foam-white houses on the edge of a great sea-forest. A bank of sea-moss that was green as grass but more beautiful, and very bright covered the forest floor. There were crowds of seal-folk in the town. He saw them moving about to and fro, and heard their voices, but he could not understand their speech. Mothers nursed their babes, and young children played games on banks of green sea-moss, and from the brown and golden sea-forest came sounds of music and the shouts of dancers.

Said the stranger, "Here is my master's house. Let us enter." He led the fisherman towards the door of a great foam-white palace. It was thatched with red tangle, and the door was of green stone. The door opened as smoothly as a summer wave that moves across a river mouth. The fisherman entered with his guide. He found himself in a dimly lit room. There he saw an old grey seal stretched on a bed moaning with pain. Beside the bed lay a blood stained knife. The fisherman knew at a glance that it was his own knife. Then he remembered that, not many hours before, he had stabbed a seal, and that it had escaped by plunging into the sea, carrying the knife in its back.

The fisherman was startled to realize that the old seal on the bed was the very one he had tried to kill, and his heart was filled with fear. He threw himself down and begged for forgiveness and mercy, for he feared that he would be put to death. The guide lifted up the knife and asked: "Have you ever seen this knife before?" He spoke in human language.

"That is my knife, alas!" exclaimed the fisherman.

Said the guide: "The wounded seal is my father. Our doctors are unable to cure him. They can do nothing more without your help. That is why I visited your house and urged you to come with me. I ask your pardon for deceiving you, O man! But, as I love my father greatly, I had to do as I have done."

"Do not ask my pardon," the fisherman said.

"I have need of yours. I am sorry and ashamed for having stabbed your father."

Said the guide: "Lay your hand on the wound and wish it to be healed."

The fisherman laid his hand on the wound, and the pain that the seal suffered passed into his hand, but did not remain long. As if by magic, the wound was healed at once. Then the old grey seal rose up strong and well again.

Said the guide: "You have served us well this day, O man!"

When the fisherman had entered the house, all the seals inside the house, weeping great tears of sorrow; but they ceased to weep as soon as the fisherman laid his hand on the wound. When the old seal rose up they all rejoiced.

The fisherman wondered what would happen next. For a time the seals seemed to forget his presence, but at length his guide spoke to him and said: "Now, O man! You can return to your own home where your wife and children await you. I shall lead you through the sea depths, and take you on my mare across the plain that we crossed when coming hither."

"I give you thanks," the fisherman exclaimed.

Said the guide: "Before you leave there is one thing you must do. You must take a vow to never again hunt seals."

The fisherman answered: "I promise not to hunt for seals ever again."

Said the guide: "If ever you break your promise you shall die. I counsel you to keep it, and as long as you do so you will prosper. Every time you set lines, or cast a net, you will catch many fish. Our seal-servants will help you, and if you wish to reward them for their services, take with you in your boat a harp or pipe and play sweet music, for music is the delight of all seals."

The fisherman vowed he would never break his promise, and the guide then led him back to dry land. As soon as he reached the shore he ceased to be a seal and became a man once again. The guide, who had also changed shape, breathed over a great wave and, immediately, it became a dark mare with grey mane and grey tail. He then mounted the mare, and bade the fisherman mount behind him. The mare rose in the air as lightly as wind-tossed spray, and passing through the clouds of startled sea birds reached the top of the precipice. On she raced. The night was falling and the stars began to appear, but it was not quite dark when the fisherman's house was reached.

The fisherman dismounted, and his guide spoke and said: "Take this from me, and may you live happily."

He handed the fisherman a small bag and cried: "Farewell! Remember your vow." Then he wheeled his mare right round and passed swiftly out of sight. The fisherman entered his house, and found his wife waiting there. "You have returned," she said. "How did you fare?"

"I know not yet," he answered. Then he sat down and opened the bag, and to his surprise and delight found that it was full of pearls.

His wife uttered a cry of wonder, and said: "From whom did you receive this treasure?"

The fisherman then related all that had taken place, and his wife wondered to hear him.

"Never again will I hunt seals," he exclaimed. And he kept his word and prospered, and lived happily until he died.

# The Magnet (Age 10 and Up)

## From Natural Science Stories by Leo Tolstoy
*(Object Story, Discovery of the Magnet)*

In olden days there was shepherd whose name was Magnes. Magnes lost a sheep. He went to the mountains to find it. He came to a place where there were barren rocks. He walked over these rocks and felt that his boots were sticking to them. He touched them with his hand but they were dry and did not stick to his hand. He started to walk again, and again his boots stuck to the rocks. He sat down, took off one of his boots, took it into his hand and touched the rocks with it.

Whenever he touched them with his skin or with the sole of his boot, the rocks did not stick; but when he touched them with the nails they did stick.

Magnes had a cane with an iron point.

He touched the rock with the wood; it did not stick. He touched it with the iron end and it stuck so that he could not pull it off.

Magnus looked at the stone, and he saw that it looked like iron, and he took pieces of that stone home with him. Since then that rock has been known and has been called magnet.

# The Leopard, the Jackal and the Ram (Age 10 and Up)

A Fable from South Africa

"Kraal" is South African for house or home, a ram is a male sheep, and a jackal is a wild dog.

*(Fear, Cleverness, Trickery)*

Leopard was returning home one afternoon after a day of hunting. He came upon the kraal of Ram. He had never seen Ram before and approached him submissively.

"Good day, friend! What may your name be?"

"I am Ram!" said the other in a gruff voice. Then, striking his breast with his forefeet, he called out, "Who are you?"

"Leopard," answered the leopard, more dead than alive, and then, taking leave of Ram, he ran home as fast as he could.

Jackal lived at the same place as Leopard. He could see the fear in Leopard's eyes. Leopard spoke to Jackal,

"Friend, I am out of breath, and half dead with fright, for I have just seen a terrible looking fellow, with a large and thick head, and when I asked his name, he answered, "I am Ram."

"What a foolish fellow you are," cried Jackal, "to let such a nice dinner pass you by. Tomorrow we shall go and together shall eat it up."

Next day the two set off for the kraal of Ram, and as they appeared over the hill, Ram, who had turned to look around, saw them and immediately ran to his wife and said, "I fear this is our last day, for Jackal and Leopard are both coming against us. What shall we do?"

"Don't be afraid," said the wife, "but take up the child in your arms, go out with it, and pinch it to make it cry as if it were hungry." Ram did so as the Jackal and Tiger approached.

No sooner did Leopard cast his eyes on Ram then fear again took possession of him, and he wished to turn back. Jackal had provided against this, and made Tiger fast to himself with a leather strap, and said, "Come on," when Ram cried in a loud voice, and pinching the child at the same time, "You have done well friend Jackal, to have brought Leopard to eat, for you hear how my child is crying for food."

On these dreadful words, Leopard, notwithstanding the entreaties of Jackal to let him go, set off in the greatest alarm, dragging Jackal after him over hill and valley, through bushes and over rocks, and did not stop to look behind him until he brought himself and Jackal back to his place again.

So Ram escaped.

## The Need for Heroes and Role Models

Today, perhaps more than ever, children need heroes, both feminine and masculine. A hero is someone who is known for accomplishing a heroic task that includes overcoming incredible odds and obstacles both within him or her self as well as, in the world. In contrast, an idol is someone who is known for being popular. Today, there are many idols for children and adolescents to admire and emulate: rock stars, TV celebrities, sports figures, etc. Heroes are often less known. Seeking out heroes and telling their stories will inspire you and your children or students.

Every story has a hero, sometimes feminine, sometimes masculine. Paying attention to supporting characters who help the hero, or assume the role of the hero for part of the story encourages students to identify with them as well as with the hero. Having a discussion about the characters that spoke to "you" will give students an opportunity to share insights about the story and the significance of characters who may have played a more important part in the story than was obvious at first.

# CHAPTER 15

## The 12-Year Change

### The Arrow and the Song

Henry Wadsworth Longfellow

*I shot an arrow into the air,*
*It fell to earth, I know not where;*
*For, so swiftly it flew, the sight*
*Could not follow it in its flight.*
*I breathed a song into the air;*
*It fell to earth, I know not where;*
*For who has sight so keen and strong,*
*That it can follow the flight of song?*
*Long, long afterward, in an oak,*
*I found the arrow, still unbroke;*
*And the song, from beginning to end,*
*I found again in the heart of a friend.*

## The 12-Year Change: Crossing the Rubicon!

Jose is easy going. Nothing seems to bother him. His parents wish he would "wake up" a bit and "do something." In actuality, Jose gets everything anyone asks of him, either at home or at school, done on time and done well. He just doesn't seem to get excited about things. He has an easy smile and lots of friends. His parent's wonder if he has enough initiative. But in his own easy-going way, Jose helps many of the other children in his class by his calm manner, gentle smile, and steadfastness. He is a true friend. He doesn't waver. And once he has set forth on a project or journey, he holds fast until it is done. He has many friends, but no best friend. He likes it that way. While he is hardly ever ruffled by life's ups and downs, when he does get shaken out of his routine and familiar surroundings too suddenly, he can become distraught and even hysterical for a time. It takes calm firmness to help him come back around and deal with the situation.

Jose is twelve and is fascinated by science. He loves the scientific process, the methods scientists use to experiment and prove their theories. The logic of the process is comfortable to his way of thinking. When he was younger, he rarely spoke up in class, but now, he enjoys the challenge of logical thinking and uses it well to debate about scientific theories. He can get so excited about a theory that he becomes angry when someone else disagrees with his logic or his judgment of the results of an experiment.

At the age of 12, the young adolescent enters a sensitive period that, in times gone by, was welcomed and heralded as a time of sacred inner change. It was considered appropriate to mark this change with a ceremony, welcoming the child into the adult world. Ceremonies today that continue to honor that tradition include Bar and Bat Mitzvah's, confirmations, and initiation adventures often created by parents and teachers together to provide an outdoor challenge experience for the child at this age. It is an exciting time as the inner capacity we call judgment matures. This ability is what we use to make decisions, based on considering several points of view; to draw conclusions from our scientific experiments; and to discern what is right and wrong, based on an inner code of ethics. When we make a judgment and act upon it, we are solely responsible for the consequences.

A great story metaphor for the 12-year change is the story of Julius Caesar crossing the Rubicon. Caesar was returning from a great successful battle. He was leading his men into Rome. The tradition was that a general, upon returning from a battle, stopped at the banks of the Rubicon River on the outskirts of Rome to take off his battle gear, thus symbolizing his loyalty to the Emperor. Caesar did not do that! He crossed the Rubicon River in full armor and rode into Rome. Once he stepped into the river on horseback there was no turning back. He had broken every law. The 12-year change is the Rubicon of childhood. Childhood is ending and the journey ahead is fraught with new challenges. Children now experience themselves as individuals who are alone. They recognize their unique individuality as being utterly separate from anyone else. This is why traditionally, at this time of life, initiation ceremonies of various kinds took place in cultures around the world, welcoming the young person into the tribe, into the adult community. The complete story "Crossing the Rubicon" can be found at the end of this chapter.

In education, this is the time when science courses challenge students to observe experiments and then to draw their own conclusions based on their observations. Chemistry is a joy to teach to 6th graders who are eager to explore their new capacities of judgment. Gradually, the ability to discern and draw conclusions from one's own observations carries over into other areas of the young person's daily life. An understanding of and respect for the power of thinking awakens within the young person as he or she grapples with experiences in an effort to deduce concepts and draw conclusions.

Today's culture has made this particular age group a target for consumerism. Advertising focused on so-called "tweens" between 11 and 15 is booming, as advertisers are aware that this age group has disposable income burning a hole in their pockets. Naturally, they are drawn to the most modern electronic devices and hip clothing. Some of them have part-time jobs or chores for which they are paid and many have weekly allowances. Most children in America have their own cell phone at this age and many of them have access to a computer, through which they can participate in various social media websites.

Scientists used to believe that the number of neurons in the human brain was fixed in childhood and that no new neuron growth occurred in teens or adults. Not so, say scientists today. (*The American Academy of Child & Adolescent Psychiatry, www.aacap.org*) Young adults are busy adding neurons all through their teenage years. They need challenges as a stimulus to engage their growing powers of thinking.

This age group needs to be actively involved in experimenting, drawing conclusions, reading challenging and stimulating material, and applying their ideas in practical ways in the real world. Schools need to provide an environment that awakens the students' interest in a variety of disciplines. These difficult yet wonderful students also need challenge in their daily lives at home to further stimulate their brains as they continue to grow and expand. Problem solving skills can be developed through family projects and outdoor camping and hiking expeditions, for example.

Adding fire to this tumultuous time is an explosion of hormones. Most of us are aware of the hormone changes just from our observations of the adolescents around us, and from our own memories of that stage of our lives. And who hasn't reminded an adolescent boy that it is time to wear deodorant? The combination of hormone activity and a brain calling out for stimulating intellectual activity is a challenging one. Yet, it is an exciting prospect to realize that at age 12, and beyond, the brain is still expanding. How can we, as parents, teachers, coaches, and project leaders, spur them on?

Knowing this information guides us to offer more stimulating intellectual pursuits accompanied by physical challenges. Science projects, mathematical pursuits, creative writing projects, art projects, challenging outdoor activities, and community service projects offer opportunities that challenge the budding intellect of the adolescent.

A battle can ensue in the changing life of the adolescents as they struggle to balance desires and instincts, which are becoming increasingly more powerful and compelling, with ideals and passions for study. The exploration of the mind and the creation of a rich inner life of thinking must become a top priority. As adults, we must remain calm and present throughout this stage of development.

Sharing a great myth together in the evening over a period of days or even weeks, offers a stimulating and relaxing way to connect, as, together, you explore ideas and reflect on questions that have been around since time began. Stories take us into another world and bring us back refreshed and encouraged about who we are today. They can offer an intellectual challenge and an escape from the pressures of adolescence at the same time.

Since a new doorway into the world for the young person opens at this age, it must be met with sensitivity and patience on the part of parents and teachers. Teens of this age are definitely seeking guidance from the adults around them but will rarely openly admit it. They will walk around you and sometimes bait you into an argument just to see if you are interested enough to take the bait. Often boys from the age of about twelve will only want to engage in a conversation with their parents late at night when they are in bed. As surprising as this may seem, at that point in the day, they feel safe and less exposed and want to talk. Just when you thought your day was done!

Girls, on the other hand, will chatter and argue, testing their mettle against you and relishing the challenge. Boys tend to be more reclusive as they move further into adolescence. As one educator put it, boys play ball, and girls sit and gossip once the twelve-year change is in full swing.

Teens are full of unspoken questions. Who are my role models? Where are the adults who walk their talk? What is life about anyway? Where can I find meaning for my life? What is the most important thing they need at this critical time? Community! This is an age group that needs opportunities to use their rapidly developing intellectual capacities orally. These students benefit from bringing back the oral tradition through debate, conversation, and storytelling in the classroom, with friends, and at home. Simply making yourself available to listen (without judgment or even interjecting your ideas…. just deep listening) is a great gift to this age group.

Girls develop 1 to 1 ½ years earlier than boys. They begin to use language as a weapon. Gossip emerges as a new form of communication. The emotions of both sexes are overturning their sense of self and inner comfort, and they are literally oozing out of themselves. How do we help them bring a sense of order and calm into this chaotic time?

One antidote is to tell the stories of ancient history, particularly the stories of ancient Rome. Hearing these stories offers them a way to gaze upon the outer world objectively. Objectivity calms down the inner tumult of their budding adolescent emotions. Stories, both fiction and true, that provide examples of inner and outer structures are of interest. How people rule themselves today and in the past provide the kind of structural imagery they are seeking. They are particularly intrigued by how the Romans became masters of objective law. Stories and, in particular, biographies that accompany a study of the specifics of Roman political structure including the 12 tables (of laws), the 2 houses of government, and the checks and balances, which required that lawmakers work together and compromise with one another, offer them a picture of how they can develop their own inner checks and balances. Adding in a comparison of the U.S. system of checks and balances and biographies from the colonial period is also possible. A longing for intellectual stimulation that speaks to their imaginative power and calls upon their sense of morality and justice, can be met through story and, in particular, through biographical tales that deal with questions of man's responsibility to man.

Abstract thinking includes the ability to comprehend and express concepts, to draw conclusions based on observations and experience, and to comprehend metaphors and figures of speech. The capacity to use language that clearly expresses one's ideas and thoughts is developing at this age. Storytelling uses metaphors that adolescents can understand and discuss. Stories present complex relationships that challenge and stimulate the thinking capacity of this age group. Over time, imagery that is found in stories strengthens the writing capacity and builds the imagination at the same time.

The experience of hearing stories that are set in a time and place that the young people have never experienced expands their horizons as well as develops flexibility in thinking. Within the world of story, fresh concepts are presented, and complex relationships are experienced. Their feelings are stretched as the characters move through challenges to arrive at a new level of understanding. The overcoming of obstacles of all kinds and the presence of helpful people and animals gives them confidence that help will come when needed if they are open to it. Additionally, stories offer a venue for discussions that develop abstract thinking.

A study of the history of the world's religions that features them in the order in which they arose, i.e., Judaism, Hinduism, Buddhism, Christianity, and Islam, offers this age group an opportunity to use their new powers of judgment to compare and contrast the belief systems and the cultures of the ancient world. These studies also meet their inner longing to know more about the greater world around them: its wondrous achievements, as well as, its failures.

Underneath the myths of various cultures there lie secrets of how a specific culture perceived the world, how the people thought and used their imaginations to make sense of their world. Myths offer us, as modern people, an experience of seeing into the past metaphorically: a way to walk in the shoes of another culture in another age. Biographies of leaders from all walks of life down through the ages throughout the world also satisfy and stimulate the new capacity of judgment ripening in the child at this age.

**Nothing great was ever accomplished without enthusiasm!**

– Ralph Waldo Emerson

I once knew a teacher who had her students stand up and chant that phrase loudly in rhythm while moving their arms and stamping their feet to that rhythm. I tried it. The teenagers loved it. Figure out a stamping and swaying movement with your feet and then add your arms and try it with your children or students. It is very energizing! You feel enthused and the words make sense as they rock into your heart. Get energized and get together.

Other challenges for this age group might include taking on a new discipline, i.e., ballet, sports, dance, debate, choir, or exploring a form of artistic expression like pottery, painting, or blacksmithing. Experiencing group challenges via camps, sports, and musical groups (bands, orchestra, choir) fills a social need while providing a personal challenge.

Giving your 12-year-old more responsibilities around the house and garden is also stimulating. Expect an argument over this; that's part of the teenage "persona." Inwardly, they will feel recognized by you and appreciate your trust in their ability to carry out more complex tasks. Responsibility is a buzzword for this age group. Trust is implicit in the concept of responsibility. The 12-year-old is interested in questions of trust. Do you trust *me*? Are *you* worthy of *my* trust? Is *he* worthy of my trust? Adolescents are explorers of sorts, and as they explore and compare their life experience to those of others in their neighborhood, or school, as well as, through myths and folk tales, they learn more about who they are becoming. Their inner world expands to meet their outer world.

See "Story Suggestions by Age Group" in Part IV of this book for a list of myths and other stories for the 12 year old.

# Stories for the 12-Year-Old

Okay, math teachers and lovers, this story is for YOU! The first time I heard this story was during a teacher interview. I was watching a woman, who turned out to be a master teacher, tell this story. She worked it out on the board with the children as she wended her way through the story. We hired her!

Draw it on the board in a way that makes sense to you, and your students will begin to understand the concept of geometric progression as the story unfolds!

## A Grain of Rice

### A Mathematical Folktale
*(Greed, Fear, Deception, Cleverness, Justice, and a math puzzle!)*

Long ago in India, there lived a Raja who believed he was wise and fair, as a Raja should be. The people in his province were rice farmers. The Raja decreed that everyone must give nearly all of his or her rice to him. "I will store the rice safely," the Raja promised the people, "so that in time of famine, everyone will have rice to eat, and no one will go hungry." Each year, the Raja's rice collectors gathered nearly all of the people's rice and carried it away to the royal storehouses.

For many years, the rice grew well. The people gave nearly all of their rice to the Raja, and the storehouses were always full. But the people were left with only enough rice to get by. Then one year the rice grew badly and there was famine and hunger. The people had no rice to give to the Raja, and they had no rice to eat. The Raja's ministers implored him, "Your highness, let us open the royal storehouses and give the rice to the people, as you promised." "No!" cried the Raja. How do I know how long the famine will last? I must have the rice for myself. Promise or no promise, a Raja must not go hungry!"

Time went on, and the people grew more and more hungry. But the Raja would not give out the rice. One day, the Raja ordered a feast for himself and his court—as, it seemed to him, a Raja should now and then, even when there is famine. A servant led an elephant from a royal storehouse to the palace, carrying two full baskets of rice. A village girl named Rani saw that a trickle of rice was falling from one of the baskets. Quickly she jumped up and walked along beside the elephant, catching the falling rice in her skirt. She was clever, and she began to make a plan.

At the palace, a guard cried, "Halt, thief! Where are you going with that rice?"

"I am not a thief," Rani replied. "This rice fell from one of the baskets, and I am returning it now to the Raja."

When the Raja heard about Rani's good deed, he asked his ministers to bring her before him.

"I wish to reward you for returning what belongs to me," the Raja said to Rani. "Ask me for anything, and you shall have it."

"Your highness," said Rani, "I do not deserve any reward at all. But if you wish, you may give me one grain of rice."

"Only one grain of rice?" exclaimed the Raja. "Surely you will allow me to reward you more plentifully, as a raja should."

"Very well," said Rani. "If it pleased Your Highness, you may reward me in this way. Today, you will give me a single grain of rice. Then, each day for thirty days you will give me double the rice you gave me the day before. Thus, tomorrow you will give me two grains of rice, the next day four grains of rice, and so on for thirty days."

"This seems to be a modest reward," said the Raja. "But you shall have it."

And Rani was presented with a single grain of rice.

The next day, Rani was presented with two grains of rice.

And the following day, Rani was presented with four grains of rice.

On the ninth day, Rani was presented with two hundred fifty-six grains of rice. She had received in all five hundred and eleven grains of rice, enough for only a small handful. "This girl is honest, but not very clever," thought the Raja. "She would have gained more rice by keeping what fell into her skirt!"

On the twelfth day, Rani received two thousand and forty-eight grains of rice, about four handfuls.

On the thirteenth day, she received four thousand and ninety-six grains of rice, enough to fill a bowl.

On the sixteenth day, Rani was presented with a bag containing thirty-two thousand, seven hundred and sixty-eight grains of rice. All together she had enough rice for two bags. "This doubling up adds up to more rice than I expected," thought the raja. "But surely her reward won't amount to much more."

On the twentieth day, Rani was presented with sixteen more bags filled with rice.

On the twenty-first day, she received one million, forty-eight thousand, five hundred and seventy-six grains of rice, enough to fill a basket.

On the twenty-fourth day, Rani was presented with eight million, three hundred and eighty-eight thousand, six hundred and eight grains of rice—enough to fill eight baskets, which were carried to her by eight royal deer.

On the twenty-seventh day, thirty-two Brahma bulls were needed to deliver sixty-four baskets of rice. The Raja was deeply troubled. "One grain of rice has grown very great indeed," he thought. "But I shall fulfill the reward to the end, as a Raja should."

On the twenty-ninth day, Rani was presented with the contents of two royal storehouses.

On the thirtieth and final day, two hundred and fifty-six elephants crossed the province, carrying the contents of the last four royal storehouses—Five hundred and thirty-six million, eight hundred and seventy thousand, nine hundred and twelve grains of rice.

All together, Rani had received more than one billion grains of rice. The Raja had no more rice to give. "And what will you do with this rice," said the Raja with a sigh, "now that I have none?"

"I shall give it to all the hungry people," said Rani, "and I shall leave a basket of rice for you, too, if you promise from now on to take only as much rice as you need." "I promise," said the Raja. And for the rest of his days, the Raja was truly wise and fair, as a Raja should be.

To use this story, tell it first. Then work out the math on the board with the students for the first few days. Then have the students work in pairs to figure out the quantities of rice for each day. It's a great story to use for introducing the exponential properties of numbers, working with multiplication, and understanding mathematical concepts in 5th and 6th grade.

# The Hermit and the Elephant (Age 12)

## A Story from Ancient India

*(The power of prayer and focus.)*

Long ago in Ancient India there were men who left their homes and families and went to live as hermits in the forest. They dedicated their lives to prayer and meditation. By focusing their full attention on prayer they would forget the world around them. When it rained, they didn't notice it. When the sun baked the earth, they sat still and did not move. When the winds of winter blew, they remained calm and focused. Through this practice they learned to give all their time to prayer. However, when these hermits prayed it was quite hard work.

It was this complete concentration on one task, so that nothing else entered the mind, which gave such a man special powers. Even today there are hermits in India who still have these powers. Now, there once was a hermit in a remote village who was revered by the Indian peasants of that village, and treated with great respect. The hermit sat beside the road through the village and the peasants walked carefully around the holy man and, from time to time, they would put a bowl of milk or a bowl with a little rice beside him.

The wild animals that live in the forests of India – the tigers, elephants, snakes and monkeys – stay away from the villages where people live because they don't like the smell of human beings. Elephants live in herds. The elephants that belong to the same herd help each other when there is any danger. No one knows why, but sometimes one elephant in the herd misbehaves. He kicks and hurts the other elephants with his tusks and pushes them away when they go to drink in the river.

Eventually, the other elephants have had enough and the whole herd turns against him. They attack that elephant, and they would throw him down and trample him to death if he did not run away. After being chased away, he is not allowed back in the herd. A lone elephant like this is called a rogue elephant. Once a rogue elephant knows he cannot come back to the herd, he goes mad with fury. He runs through the forest trumpeting wildly and trampling down everything that gets in the way. All the animals flee from his path, even the tigers.

Now it happened that early one morning when the people of that village were leaving their huts to go to work in the fields, a very loud trumpeting was heard in the distance. The children of the village stopped playing as the sound grew louder and louder. Suddenly a huge rogue elephant with fiery red eyes came charging from the woods onto the road. The people scattered in all directions to get out of its way. Mothers and Fathers quickly gathered up their children. But there was one small toddler still in the road as the rogue elephant came rumbling down into the village.

In all the commotion, everyone had forgotten the hermit. As the elephant drew nearer, the hermit arose and walked slowly and quietly into the middle of the road just in front of the child. The elephant kept charging when suddenly he stopped just three feet from the hermit. The holy man had not moved at all. He stood absolutely still with his gaze focused on the elephant.

Everyone in the village held their breath while the elephant and the holy man looked at each other. After a long time or a short time, the elephant turned away. The wildness had gone out of him, and he walked slowly and quietly back into the forest. The hermit sat down in the road again as if nothing had happened.

# Julius Caesar and the Crossing of the Rubicon (Age 12)

## Roman History

*(Ambition, Irreversible Decisions)*

Since ancient times the Rubicon River marked the northern-most boundary of the city of Rome. One of the oldest laws in Rome was that a Roman general could not lead his troops in full armor across that river and then on into the city. He must lay down his armor and so must his troops before crossing the Rubicon River. It was an act of treason to lead your army across the river in battle gear.

Treason was punishable by death. It was a serious offense not only against the Roman government but also against Roman society. For hundreds of years all Roman generals had respected this law.

In 49 B.C. Julius Caesar was proving to be one of the most remarkable generals in Rome's history. He had led his troops into Gaul, the part of the world we now know as France. After battling with the native peoples of Gaul he succeeded in defeating them and had become their ruler.

Pompey, the other surviving consul of the First Triumvirate, was also leading a vast Roman army to the east and south of Rome successfully conquering the peoples there. He was now in Spain, which was fairly far away in an age when men traveled on foot and by horseback when Caesar approached the Rubicon. The two powerful generals were becoming jealous of one another. Pompey had married Caesar's daughter, Julia.

However, when she died in childbirth the blood ties between the two men were broken. Pompey was from the aristocratic class while Caesar was a common man. Each was beloved by the class of people he represented.

It is said that Caesar hesitated as he approached the River Rubicon. As the army milled around the camp, a man began to play upon a pipe. The soldiers gathered round. A trumpeter joined in and then ran to the riverbank still trumpeting his horn! Someone shouted, "Advance!" and Caesar cried out "Let us go where the omens of the

Gods and the crimes of our enemies summon us! THE DIE IS NOW CAST!

And with that the trumpets blew and Caesar led his army to cross the Rubicon! There was no turning back. The deed could not be undone. He and his army had broken one of the oldest laws of Ancient Rome.

The call went out to Pompey to return at once to defend the Senate from Caesar.

Pompey and his army met Caesar and his army on the outskirts of Rome. This was the beginning of a struggle for power over the Roman Empire between Caesar and Pompey.

# That is Good! (Age 12 and Up)

## A wisdom tale from Ancient India
*(Optimism)*

Long, long ago a great King of India ruled wisely and well. He had a minister who was always ready to advise and help him and who was known for his wisdom. However, the advisor had one habit that annoyed the King. Whenever anything happened, he always responded with the same comment, "That is good, that is good."

One day the King was hunting when his horse was startled by a large snake. The King was thrown from the horse and dragged some distance. In the process his foot was cut and he lost his big toe. His minister who accompanied him always, knelt beside him to inspect the wounds and said, "That is good, that is good."

"How can you say, That is good?" cried the King in a rage.

What kind of a minister are you? You are dismissed from my service immediately."

"That is good," said the minister, "That is good." And off he went to pack his bags.

The King returned home and his foot healed minus the toe. He was ready to try his luck at hunting again and set off on his favorite horse. He chased after a wild boar and soon after he became lost from his hunting party. As he came around a bend in the road he was ambushed by the tribal people who lived in the wild. He was tied up and taken back to their village.

This particular tribe had a custom of sacrificing their prisoners to their god. They prepared him for the sacrificial celebration by washing and decorating him. The celebration began with music and dancing as the King was led to the slaughtering place like a goat. The king was shaking with terror from head to foot. He nearly fainted when the priest of the tribe came towards him waving a long knife. The priest danced around him, inspecting him from every angle. Suddenly, he motioned for the music and dancing to stop. "This man is no good," he said. "He has been cut." He pointed to the missing toe on the foot of the King. "We cannot sacrifice to our gods something that has already be cut," cried the priest. The priest slashed the vines that bound the King's hands and legs and set him free. The King limped back to the palace as quickly as he could.

Back in the safety of his palace, the King remembered his minister and called for him. He told him the story of his capture and release. "You were right. It was good that my toe was lost. Because of it, I was not sacrificed by the tribal people. But why did you say, 'That is good,' when I fired you from your post?"

"There is always something good that comes of things, your highness," replied the minister. "If I had not been fired, I would have been with you that day when you were captured by the tribal people. Because I have all my toes, I would have been next in line for the sacrifice."

"You are truly right, my friend," said the King. "That was good. It was good indeed, and so is your wisdom. You shall advise me always."

And he did. And it was good.

# The Three Questions (Age 12 and Up)

Leo Tolstoy

*(Wisdom, Being Present in the Moment)*

There was once a king who decided that if he knew who the most important people in world were, and what the most important thing to do was, and when the best time to do each thing was, that he would certainly be the finest king ever to rule the land. Although he had asked his advisers, none had been able to give him a good answer to these questions.

At last he decided to ask the advice of a wise hermit. The king dressed in the clothes of a commoner and set out for the forest. When he neared the hermit's hut, he ordered his knights to stay back at a distance, and he rode the last section of trail alone.

The king found the hermit digging in his garden. The old man greeted him but continued digging. The king told the hermit that he had come to find answers to his three questions. The hermit listened but gave no answer and continued working. The king observed that the hermit was frail and elderly and that the work was very difficult for him. The king offered to take over the digging, and the hermit allowed it.

The king dug for one hour. Then he repeated the question, but the hermit did not answer. He worked again for another hour, and then repeated his questions with the same results. This continued for a few more hours until the sun began to sink low in the sky. Finally the king got discouraged. "I came to you for answers wise man. If you have none, tell me and I will return home."

Just them someone came running up the path. They turned to see a man with his hands pressed to his stomach and blood flowing from between them. He dropped to the ground at the king's feet.

The king and the hermit knelt down and began tending to the man. The king washed and bandaged the man's wounds. The blood continued to flow so he kept having to change bandages. The king also helped the hermit to get fresh water, and to help the man to drink.

Finally the man slept and did not wake until the next morning. The king too slept upon the ground, waking often to watch over the man. In the morning the man woke up and looked at the king.

"Forgive me," he said to the king.

"You have nothing for me to forgive you for," the King answered. "Oh, but I do," he said. "You were my enemy, and I had sworn to take revenge on you for killing my brother and taking my land. I knew that you were coming here today and I decided to kill you on the trail. But when you did not return for many hours I left my hideout to find you. Your guards recognized me and wounded me. I escaped them but I would have bled to death if you had not cared for me. I meant to kill you but now you have saved my life. If I live I shall gladly serve you for the rest of my life." The king was so happy to have been reconciled with an old enemy that he immediately forgave him and promised to return his land. Then the king called for his knights to carry the man back to his castle to be cared for by his own doctor.

After the wounded man had gone, the king asked the hermit once more if he would not give him the answer to his question.

"Your questions have already been answered." the hermit replied.

"But how?" the king answered, perplexed.

"How?" repeated the hermit. "If you had not taken pity on my weakness yesterday and helped me instead of returning home, that man would have ambushed and killed you on the trail. Therefore, the most important time was when you were digging my garden beds; and I was the most important person; and the most important thing to do was to do good for me. Later, when the man came running to us, the most important thing to do was to care for him. If you had not bound up his wounds he would have died without making peace with you. Therefore the most important person was that man, and what you did was the most important thing, and the right time was the time when you were doing it.

"You see, the most important time is always the present moment. It is the only time that is important because it is the only time that we have control over. The past we can only look back on and wish that we had done differently. The future we can only imagine. The most important person is always the one you are with in the present moment, and the only important deed is the deed that does what is best for others."

At last the king understood. He returned to rule wisely one moment at a time.

## Being Yourself (Age 12 and Up)

### Hasidic Tale
*(Be Yourself)*

A long time ago the wise Hasidic master, Rabbi Zusya still lived on the earth. He had a group of devoted students with whom he shared the ancient wisdom from the Hasidic tradition. His students loved him and they were aware now that he was aging and might not be with them much longer. Rabbi Zusya, himself, was aware that his time on the earth was coming to an end. So he gathered his students together one last time.

Hesitantly, one of his students spoke up and asked the great teacher what he was most afraid of about dying.

"That is an easy question," he smiled as he replied, "I am most afraid of what will happen after I die. I am afraid of what I will be asked when I get to heaven."

Now the students were sitting on the edge of their seats, amazed at this reply.

"What will they ask you?"

"They will **not** ask me, Zusya, why were you not more like Moses?"

"They will **not** ask me, Zusya, why were you not more like Solomon?"

"They will ask me, "Zusya, why were you not more like Zusya?"

This wonderful tale can lead to a discussion about being oneself. Being oneself is sometimes challenging. Writing a response to this story could begin with the question, "What is it like to be you?" Further questions could include:

When do you feel most like yourself? When do you feel least like yourself? How could you change yourself so that you would feel more like yourself? What could you do to feel more like yourself? What do you dream of doing in the future? Think about the next six months, twelve months, two years, and five years. What kinds of activities could you be doing now that might help you do what you want in the future?

# The Wolf and the Gypsy (Age 12 and Up)

*(Wisdom, Friendship, & Reconciliation of Former Enemies)*

A pack of wolves was led by a sly old beast that had seen many dangers in his long life. He had spat in death's eye many a time, yet emerged triumphant from all his fights.

That old wolf knew the forest laws, knew the forest did not spare the weak, knew also that one day he would be too old to lead the pack. Then they would not spare him.

Though his old wounds prevented him from hunting as well as in his younger years, he still got by with cunning, and always ran on ahead to seek out the prey.

But one cold winter the hunting was lean; and for the first time he saw contempt in the pack's gray eyes. No longer were young wolves afraid of him; they knew he was getting old. The entire pack had patiently awaited this moment when it could turn on its once strong leader, as was the habit of the pack.

It was then he made up his mind.

Waiting until deepest night, the old wolf rose silently and began to slink away, distancing himself from the hungry wolves.

They sensed his flight and took up pursuit. They were not as wise in forest lore as he. He kept just ahead of them, making for a clearing where he knew a lone gypsy's cottage stood.

At one time that gypsy, too, had been leader of a pack. What a mighty gypsy pack it had been! He had led his gypsies down many tracks. He had been wise and bold and his guidance had saved the gypsies from many a misfortune.

The time came, however, when old age had withered the leader's strength. He could feel it in his bones: he was not strong enough to hold the reins, to keep young braves in check.

One time, when the clan was wintering in a village and the gypsy families were quartered in huts, the old chief summoned up his remaining strength and stole away to build himself a cottage in the forest. And that spring, when the gypsy band moved off the chief was not with them; he remained alone in the forest. No one had seen him, so it was thought that he must have fallen victim to hungry wolves or vanished into a snowdrift.

He did run into wolves. Yet though he was quite unarmed, the wolf pack did not touch him: their leader had forbidden it. The old man knew not why.

So the gypsy lived alone amidst the towering wood. He feared no one and when one night he heard an eerie wolf cry near his hut, he lit a torch and opened the door. The yellow-flecked gray eyes of the old wolf stared up at him, as if asking for aid. At the margin of the trees he could see the wolf pack waiting to attack. But as he swung his torch, the wolves slunk back, merging with the gloom. He held the door and the wolf entered his hut.

The two old-timers, the gypsy and the wolf, looked fondly at each other; the gypsy patted the old leader's furry head as he lay meekly at his feet by the warm fire.

# The King of the Fish (Age 12 and Up)

*(Compassion, Self-Responsibility, Overcoming Obstacles, Friendship)*

Davey hated fish. He didn't like the taste of fish, he didn't like the way their cold eyes stared right into you, and the smell of them made him sick. Times were hard and Davey needed a job. And that's how it happened that Davey took a job working on a fishing boat. He chopped off the heads and the tails of all the fish that the fisherman caught.

Now one day he and the fisherman were out on the sea when suddenly the fisherman threw a fish over to Davey. It was the most beautiful fish he had ever seen. It sparkled in the sunlight. All the colors of the rainbow glinted on its radiant body. Davey had never seen such beauty and he didn't have the heart to kill it. So, when he thought that the fisherman wasn't looking, he quietly slipped the fish over the side of the boat and into the sea. Unfortunately, the fisherman turned around just in time to see him do it. "What have you done?!" he screamed at Davey and rowed back to shore. "Don't come back."

Davey was a sorry sight as he slowly walked home. His head hung and he wondered what he would do now. Then he sensed that someone was walking beside him. I don't know how, but Davey knew it was the Devil. Maybe it was the horns sticking out of his head or the talk poking out of the back of his trousers. I don't know.

"Hello Davey", said the Devil. "I hear you have had some bad luck lately."

"You could say that", replied Davey.

"Davey, I have a proposition for you," said the Devil. "I've got the most beautiful cow in the world and I will lend her to you for three years. She will give you the creamiest milk you have ever tasted in your life and more than your family could ever possible manage to drink. But I will come back for her when the three years are up and ask you three questions. If you can't answer those questions, Davey, then you'll have to come back to Hell with me."

Davey thought about this for a while. He'd never been too sure he was going to Heaven anyway, so he agreed. There was a puff of smoke, and the Devil disappeared. And there, in front of Davey stood the most beautiful fawn colored Jersey cow staring at him with its big brown eyes. From that time on Davey's luck changed. For once in his life the Devil had told the truth and the cow gave the loveliest, creamiest milk and more than his family could ever possibly manage to drink. They started to make butter, cheese, yoghurt, and whatever they could think of to use up that milk. But they had so much left over that they decided to sell some. With the extra money the bought some chickens, geese, a goat and they even opened a restaurant.

All of this took time and Davey realized time was running out. He thought, "Maybe the Devil has forgotten me...then again, maybe not.

"Perhaps they'll be easy questions.... perhaps not."

Davey started to read the Encyclopedia. A few weeks later he was still on the A's. A few more weeks and he was on the B's. Davey's time was running out. The day arrived and Davey was in the restaurant waiting for one last customer to finish his meal. Suddenly there was a crash of thunder, and a tremendous flash of lightning and there before him stood the Devil.

Now the Devil loves to show off. He'd polished his skin until it was glowing red, he'd sharpened his horns until they glinted, his tail was lashing from side to side and he was stabbing the air with his trident.

"Hello Davey, ready for my three questions, are we?"

"Bbbb but... struggled Davey. He tried to sink into a hole in the ground, and then suddenly realized where it led to and quickly stood up again. Meanwhile, the stranger in the corner stood up and walked over to Davey and said:

"Yes, he is. That's your first question over; you've got two left."

"Davey, will you tell him to butt out of it?" said the Devil, exasperated.

"No, he won't. That's your second question over, you've got one left," replied the stranger.

"And who the Blazes are you anyway?" yelled the Devil, now furious.

"I'm the King of the Fish and Davey saved my life three years ago today. Your three questions are up, your cow's around the back."

The Devil, well he was so furious at being outwitted, he walked straight out of that restaurant and never came back. He was so angry he forgot to take his cow with him!

## The Tiger and the Coal Peddler's Wife (Age 12 and Up)

### Korean

*(A tale of a woman's courage and compassion)*

Deep in the mountains lived a young couple that supported themselves by digging and selling coal. It was a hard life and a lonely one for their nearest neighbor was many miles away. Still they were very happy. They were awaiting the birth of their first child that was due any day now.

Early one morning the man headed out to the nearest village. It was market day and he was planning to sell a load of coal and buy supplies that they needed. Just as he was coming into the village a rainstorm suddenly poured from the sky. There were few people who came to the market. So he went door-to-door to sell his coal. By the time he had sold it all and had bought all the supplies they needed, it was too dark and too late for him to go home.

Meanwhile, his wife gave birth. And at the same time their dog gave birth to three puppies.

The woman lay in bed, cuddling the baby and sleeping off and on. When it became dusk and her husband had not returned, she began to worry. She was hungry and knew that she must eat in order to nurse the baby. She got up out of bed and began preparing seaweed soup.

She heard something outside the door and thinking that it was her dear husband, threw open the door to greet him. And there staring at her was a very large tiger.

She was overcome with fear but knew she must protect her child. She tried to stay calm; out of the corner of her eye she saw the puppies. Quickly she grabbed one of them and threw it at the tiger. " Here's some meat for you!"

The tiger caught the puppy in its mouth, gulped it down and looked at the woman hungrily.

"Here! Take this!" she shouted, throwing it another puppy.

The tiger gulped it down and stared at the woman.

She looked at her faithful dog and its remaining puppy. She couldn't bring herself to give the puppy to the tiger. Glancing around she noticed some cotton. She quickly wrapped it around a hot coal from the cooking fire and tossed it to the tiger.

As with the puppies, the tiger caught it in its mouth and quickly gulped it down. Its eyes became gig and it opened its mouth as though it were choking. I ran a few steps this way and that. Then it fell forward on its front legs and then over on its side. The woman watched its body shake and become still.

Her husband returned home early the next morning wand was alarmed to see a dead tiger in front of his house. But his alarm turned to relief when his wife met him at the door with their newborn son in her arms.

The man sold the tiger skin for a good sum of money and from then on they lived more comfortably.

# Marduk, the Fearless One (Age 12 and Up)

## Ancient Babylonian Myth
*(Creation Story, Courage)*

In about 4,000 BC there was a great city known as Babylon. The walls surrounding the city were so wide that a chariot could be driven atop the walls. The Babylonians had discovered how to decorate the outside walls of their great city with colored enameled bricks. This same clay could be fashioned into jars and pots, and bowls. This was the beginning of pottery.

The people of that time grew their hair long and the men also had long beards. They had dark skin and dark hair. Their hair was curled and frizzy and oiled to make it look shiny and to catch the light of the sun. The men also wore very high hats, long cloaks down to their ankles and a long shawl that covered the left arm. The other end was fastened under the right arm, leaving it free to move and gesture. The women wore similar cloaks and wore a cloth over their heads that also covered most of their face. It was thought impolite for a woman to show her face in public.

The buildings of Babylon looked like boxes stacked one on top of the other. The building at the base was the largest with each succeeding building atop it getting smaller and smaller. There were seven such box-like buildings with the smallest one on top. Each of these buildings was a temple for the gods of Babylon. How did these temples come about?

At the beginning of the world there was no order or rhythm. There was only chaos and the Lord of Chaos was a dragon named Tiamat. Tiamat loved chaos and disorder and he wanted the world to stay untidy and wild without any shape or form.

The gods looked down upon the chaos and began to sing. The harmonies they created were so remarkable that the whole world began to ring. Out of the chaos the harmonies brought order into being. In this way shapes and forms of beauty and rhythm began to emerge. The mighty dragon destroyed this creation and vowed to destroy further creations of the gods.

The gods trembled with fear.

Ea, the god of the dawn had a brave and adventuresome son, Marduk. When the gods came together to discuss what could be done, Marduk boldly stepped forward and said, "I will fight the dragon and end this tyranny forever."

To show his power, Marduk took his cloak off his shoulders and commanded it to disappear. Then he gave another command and the cloak reappeared. Ea, his father, and the other gods praised him as the bravest and strongest of them all.

Marduk made a great net, and armed himself with bow and arrows and a mighty club. He then spoke the words of a magic spell. At his command, a howling storm swept him up into the air to the lair of the dragon. The dragon crouched outside his cave. His scaly body gleamed and flames flickered from his eyes and nostrils. When he saw a huge storm approaching carrying the young god Marduk, Tiamat roared. His roars carried his terrible magic spells. The spells would destroy anyone who had any trace of fear.

Marduk had no fear. His courage surrounded him like a great shield. Tiamat's evil spells could not break through the strength of his courage. Quickly, Marduk threw his great net over the dragon. As the monster snarled and opened his huge jaws to tear the net to shreds, Marduk commanded the wind to fly into Tiamat's mouth. It blew through Tiamat's mouth and down into his body. While the dragon twisted and turned with pain, Marduk lifted his mighty club and shattered the monster's head. The people rejoiced at Marduk's brave deed.

# CHAPTER 16

## 13 to 14 Years Old

### Sonnet 109 by William Shakespeare

*O! never say that I was false of heart,*
*Though absence seem'd my flame to qualify.*
*As easy might I from myself depart*
*As from my soul, which in thy breast doth lie:*
*That is my home of love: if I have rang'd,*
*Like him that travels I return again,*
*Just to the time, not with the time exchang'd,*
*So that I myself bring water for my stain.*
*Never believe, though in my nature reign'd*
*All frailties that besiege all kinds of blood,*
*That it could so preposterously be stain'd,*
*To leave for nothing all thy sum of good;*
*For nothing this wide universe I call,*
*Save thou, my rose; in it thou art my all.*

Students in 8th grade (U.S.) appreciate the Sonnets of Shakespeare. Comparing the language of the Sonnets to the way we might express such events and feelings today meets their growing interest in matters of the heart.

Here is an additional poem that I find mirrors the adolescent experience of the wonder within that is so difficult to talk about. While they often feel heavy like the clay jug, in contrast the burgeoning self is rich and tender. This is a poem they find intriguing.

### This Clay Jug, by Haffiz

*Inside this clay jug*
*There are canyons*
*And pine mountains*
*And the maker of canyons and pine mountains*
*All seven oceans are there and hundreds of millions of stars*
*The acid that tests gold is there*
*And the one who judges jewels*
*And the music from the strings no one touches*
*And the source of all water*
*If you want to know the truth, friend*
*I will tell you the truth*
*The god whom I love is inside.*

## Characteristics of the Child at Age 13 to 14

Annie is 13. She is a fireball. Her hand is always up to answer a question in class. She challenges herself to do her best in everything. She can become very self-critical if she feels she has not achieved what she thinks she should. She often holds leadership positions in the clubs and after school activities she enjoys. She is a fierce competitor who thrives on competition especially in basketball and track. Annie is very observant and quick to judge. While Annie is often right, she has a hard time admitting it when she is wrong. She loves history and math. Writing is more of a challenge for her, as it requires more patience than she sometimes is able to give. Annie finds it curious how much she enjoys poetry and especially the sonnets of Shakespeare. She admits that she is intrigued by the themes and the structure of the sonnets. She relishes the complexity of the language that Shakespeare employs. She feels calmed by the rhythms and the way the stories they tell resolve themselves so clearly. And yes, she dreams of a love like the one described in Sonnet 109.

Annie has many friends, but sometimes she alienates them when she insists on getting her way too frequently. They become annoyed with her because she is so quick and so often correct that it makes them feel less capable. Annie doesn't always get the social cues around her because she is so committed to getting the job at hand done to the best of her ability. Her standards are high and she can become judgmental when she feels others are not doing their best.

When children reach the age of 13-14, 8th or 9th grade in the U.S., they are interested in societal structures. How did societies develop? What is the relationship between the kind of society that developed and the landscape in which it developed? What was education and training like in that culture? The idea of an apprenticeship to learn a skill is intriguing. Building projects, and art and craft projects offer possibilities for self-expression. Community service projects go hand in hand with practical activities of all kinds.

An inner awakening is occurring that can be compared to the awakening during the Renaissance. Drawing in perspective was a new form of art that emerged during that period. It required a different kind of thinking and way of looking at the world. Students at this age enjoy learning perspective drawing and will respond to a study of the art of the period. They are also inspired by biographies of artists like DaVinci, Michelangelo, and Brunelleschi.

A study of historical societal structures captures their imaginations. For example, the journey to knighthood included a series of prescribed steps: page, squire, and knight. The guilds that developed in each of the trades during the Middle Ages also included a journey to mastery: apprentice, journeyman, master. Sharing biographies of individuals engaged in these professions is a sure-fire way to inspire their interest.

At 13, an adventurous outdoor challenge that calls upon the students' inner strength, patience, and wisdom to accomplish it either individually or in a group builds self-reliance and confidence. Self-reliance and self-trust go hand in hand. Rites of passage were commonplace in many cultures around the world for centuries. Today, we need to create them in our communities to mark this remarkable moment in the life of our young people.

Physics, the study of the laws behind the physical world, is another antidote to the many distractions that come towards this age group. Through training in objective observation, a new way of thinking is achieved. Penetrating the laws behind the physical world gives students ground under their feet.

How does one discriminate the essential from the non-essential in one's life? Reading and discussing biographies of artists, politicians, poets, farmers, and peasants, is stimulating and rife with such juicy questions. Examples of dealing with inner and outer challenges played out in a biography are engaging and life affirming. Sharing your favorite biographies with your child opens the door for a lively conversation and could lead to an exploration of your own biography from an objective point of view that your son or daughter will appreciate.

Story material for this age is objective, historical, **and** imaginative. *The Lord of the Rings* by J.R.R. Tolkien is a remarkable journey into a world that poses a myriad of questions similar to those being asked by the child of 13-14. The language is challenging, the imagery enlivening and stimulating, and the plot gripping. Even if the young person has seen the films, the books offer such rich imagery and exquisite language that they should not be missed.

I have collected a number of folk tales that children of this age enjoy. The folk tale genre occurs in all cultures, offering lively tales of challenge, overcoming, and trickery. See the end of this chapter for several stories and the appendix for book titles.

Children in early adolescence often enjoy the chance to revisit stories that are old favorites from earlier childhood. Encourage this! As they awaken to the feeling of the loss of innocence that adolescence brings, they enjoy being carried on the wings of imagination back to an earlier time in their life through such stories. This is not really nostalgia, as adults know it. They experience it as an opportunity to revisit a literary landscape that is beloved and familiar from a new perspective. Like visiting an old friend, a beloved story brings refreshment, and confidence arising out of familiarity. Revisiting allows the young person to relax and to let go, for a time, of the new persona that he or she is now developing. Entering the world of imagination through story builds a calm trust in the future, for as the stories remind us, the future is solidly grounded in the past.

From time to time, we all need a change of pace! Teenagers need to move! Here is an energizer that works and takes you around the world in a few minutes. I've done this with 8th, 9th, and 10th graders as a warm up before beginning an English or History lesson. It comes from a piece of music called *The Geographic Fugue* by Ernst Toch. This rockin' stomping version is one I learned from Jan Blake, a storyteller from the UK.

## The Geographic Fugue

### By Ernst Toch
*A rhythmic variation*

*Begin by creating a stepping rhythm, swaying from side to side from the left foot to the right foot so that Trinidad begins with the left foot striking the ground on "Trin"and the right hits the ground just after the last syllable "dad." There is one left step and one right step in each line until you reach Tibet. The left step happens on Yes! And there are three more steps in that line. In the next line, step left on Yes! And step three times on Tibet, Tibet, Tibet. In the next line, the left step and emphasis is on "sa" in Nagasaki and on "ha" in Yokohama. Play around with it until you figure it out! The underscores will help identify where the steps occur.*

Trinidad __
And the big Mississippi
And the town Honolulu
And the lake Titicaca
The Popocatepetl is not in Canada
Rather in Mexico, Mexico, Mexico
Canada, Malaga, Rimini, Brindisi
Canada, Malaga, Rimini, Brindisi
Yes! Tibet, Tibet, Tibet,
Oh Yes! Tibet, Tibet, Tibet,
Nagasaaaki __ and Yokohaaama __
Nagasaaaki __ and Yokohaaama __
Oh Yes! Tibet, Tibet, Tibet,
Oh Yes!

Some students will want to look up the cities and countries mentioned. Great idea! There is a great YouTube version that will show you the rhythm I am describing. Just google: "The Geographic Fugue."

## Stories for Adolescents, Ages 13-14.

Stories appropriate for adolescents at this age include Folk Tales and Biographies.

### The Chess Game (Age 13 and Up)

#### A Zen Story
*(Compassion and Concentration)*

A young man went to a remote monastery and said to the abbot: "I am disillusioned with life and wish to attain enlightenment to be freed from these sufferings. But I have no capacity for sticking at anything. I could never do long years of meditation and study and austerity. I should relapse and be drawn back to the world again, painful though I know it to be. Is there any sort of way for people like me?"

"There is," said the Abbot, "If you are really determined."

"Tell me what you have studied. What have you concentrated on most in your life so far?"

"On nothing of any importance. My family was rich and I didn't have to work. I suppose what interested me the most was chess. I spent most of my time mastering that game."

The abbot thought for a moment, and then he called for his attendant and asked him to find the monk who was a master of chess. The monk who was the master of chess then came in with a chessboard and the abbot set up the pieces. The abbot then asked for a sword to be brought. He showed it to the monk and the young man.

"Oh monk," said the Abbot, "you have vowed obedience to me as your abbot, and now I require it of you. You will play a game of chess with this youth, and if you lose I shall cut off your head with this sword. But I promise you will be reborn in paradise. If you win, I shall cut off the head of this man: chess is the only thing he has ever tried to master and if he loses he deserves to lose his head."

They looked at the abbot's face and saw that he meant it: he would cut off the head of the loser.

They began to play. With the opening moves the youth felt the sweat trickling down to his heels as he played for his life. The chessboard became the whole world; he was completely focused on it. At first he fell behind his opponent, but there came a moment when his opponent made a poor move and the youth seized the opportunity to launch an attack. As his opponent's position weakened, the youth stole a look at him. The monk's face was intelligent and sincere, reflecting his years of austerity and effort. The youth chose to make an error and then another until his position was ruined and he was left defenseless.

The abbot suddenly leaned forward and upset the board. The two players were mystified.

"There is no winner and no loser," declared the abbot. "There is no head to fall here. Only two things are required." He turned to the youth and said, "Today you have learned both compassion and complete concentration. You were completely concentrated on the game, but then in that concentration you felt compassion for your brother and were willing to sacrifice your life for him. Now stay for a few months with us to pursue your training in this spirit and your enlightenment is sure." The youth took the abbot's advice and grew wise under his guidance.

## Mastering the Sword (Age 13 and Up)

From the Hagakure by Yamamoto Tsunetomo
*(Overcoming fears)*

A man once went to the master swordsman Yagyu Munenori and asked to become his pupil. The master said to him, "I would teach you, but you already appear to have mastered the sword. Who was it that you studied under?" When the man answered that he had never studied fencing, the master said, "I have trained many over the years, even the Shogun himself! You cannot fool me." But the man persisted, and so the master sat in thought for a time before saying, "If you say it is so, then I will believe you; but I am certain you are a master of *something*, if not the sword. What is it?"

The man answered, "If you insist, there is one thing that I would consider myself master of. When I was a boy, I wanted to be a samurai when I grew up; but I was also terrified of death, which is not becoming of a warrior. I spent many years contemplating mortality, and eventually it was no longer a concern to me. Could this be what you're referring to?"

The master shouted, "That's it! I knew I hadn't made a mistake: you see, in order to master the sword, you must also master death. No matter how well they swung a sword, none of my students have ever understood this. I have nothing to teach you: you are already a master."

## Teaching by Example, Mahatma Gandhi (Age 13 and Up)

*(Wisdom)*

Once, there lived a mother whose son was addicted to eating large quantities of sugar. She was worried about his health and tried many times to break him of his addiction without success. Finally, in desperation, she decided to bring her son to the great leader, Mahatma Gandhi, and ask him for help.

When she had finally met with Gandhi and explained the situation, he said to the mother and her son, "Come back to me in two weeks, and I will speak to your son then."

In two weeks the mother and her son returned, and Gandhi took the boy and gravely told him, "Do not eat sugar. It is bad for your health."

The mother was upset, and asked, "If that is all you were going to say, why did you not say it two weeks ago?"

Gandhi explained, "Two weeks ago, I was still eating sugar myself."

# Mero's Bride (Age 13 and Up)

## A Myth from Asia

*(Love, patience, overcoming selfishness)*

Kuan Yin was a great spiritual teacher from the Far East. She studied the traditions of Taoism and Buddhism. She dedicated her life to helping others and to serving the highest truths. Her legacy of selfless service lives on and still today she is seen in rare moments when help is needed.

A long time ago, a fisherman's daughter was born on the outskirts of a tiny fishing village along the edge of a great river. One day she took some fish to market to sell. She had no trouble selling her fish, as she was such a kind child that everyone who met her felt better after knowing her. As she came into womanhood, she was so lovely that the folk of the village would stand in line to purchase her fish just so they could see her bright eyes and loving smile.

Now it happened that there was a young man in the village who was so taken by her kindness and beauty that he thought of nothing else but to have her for his bride. One day he gathered his courage and searched for her in the market. Suddenly there she was swaying like a lily in the wind as she walked. He stepped forward and he spoke bravely saying, "Fishermaiden, with all my heart I wish to be your husband. I vow to care for you my whole life." As she smiled at him kindly others in the crowded market place stopped to listen. Soon a number of young men were standing in line to speak their words of love to Kuan Yin. "Oh favored one, I, too, wish to be your husband." There were now dozens of them.

The Fishermaiden bowed her head and the crowd grew silent. She smiled and spoke clearly, "Ah, so many fine suitors, how could I possible choose? Can any of you recite the compassionate sutras of Kuan Yin?" The crowd grew silent. She received her answer. "I will marry the man who can recite these sutras in one month's time." She quietly slipped away into the crowd.

The young men of the village worked hard reading, studying and learning to recite the sutras of Kuan Yin. In a month's time the village gathered together to listen to the fruits of their labors. One by one they spoke the sutras and the villagers rejoiced. Then all were silent awaiting the gentle words of Kuan Yin.

She praised them for working so hard and speaking so well. Then she inquired, "Can one of you tell us about what the verses mean?" The young men were speechless. No one had thought of that. They had worked so hard just to learn them.

"In one month's time, if one of you can explain the meaning of the Sutras of the Venerable Kuan Yin, he shall be my husband."

All month the young men pondered what the sutras might mean. But they couldn't make much headway. One young man named Mero traveled far down the river and into the hills to seek a wise old sage. The wise sage held discourses each day. Gradually, Mero began to understand. At the end of the month Mero grasped the meaning of the sutras. When everyone gathered again at the market, Mero was the only one who could explain the sutras and he explained them magnificently. The fishermaiden smiled and said, "It takes a wise and compassionate heart to grasp the Sutras of Kuan Yin. I will be pleased to marry a man with such heart." She told Mero to come for her the next day at the little hut on the river's edge.

The next day Mero went as instructed. He knocked at the door and the fishermaiden's parents greeted him kindly. "We have been waiting for you," they said. "Come this way." They led him to a small room at the back of the house and told him to enter. He went inside to find his bride. But all he found was an open window. Outside the window he saw her footprints in the sand. He climbed through the window and followed the prints. They led all the way to the river's edge. There, Mero found a pair of glistening golden sandals. Instantly he knew that the fishermaiden was none other than the beloved Bodhisattva herself, the Venerable Kuan Yin. His heart swelled with humility and gratitude for the sacred teachings, which now burned in him. For without the mysterious interventions of Kuan Yin, he would never have discovered nor nurtured his higher gifts. Mero went on to become a great teacher, consulted by many far and wide for his wisdom and compassion He started each and every day with this prayer: Sainted Lady, thank you. Mystical Wife, Bodhisattva, Fragrant Lotus, Eternal Flame, Guiding Hand, Shining Pearl, thank you, thank you, for guiding me to my self and the greater truth." And that is the story of Mero's bride.

# A Drop of Honey (Age 13 and Up)

**There are several versions of this timely story from Burma and Thailand**

*(Responsibility, "An ounce of prevention is worth a pound of cure")*

A long time ago a king was standing on the balcony of his great palace eating honey on rice cakes with his chief adviser. They gazed down upon the busy street below. The king was laughing and enjoying the hustle and bustle of his people below. He was laughing when a drop of honey fell from his rice cake onto the railing.

"Oh great King, you have spilled a drop of honey. Do allow me to wipe it up for you," offered his advisor.

"Ah, pay no attention to that my friend," said the King. "It's not our concern. The servants will clean it up later. I do not wish to be disturbed just now."

The two continued talking and eating as the drop of honey slowly warmed in the sun and began to drip down the rail. At last it fell onto the street below.

Attracted by the smell of the sweet honey, a fly landed on it and began to eat it.

"Your Highness," the advisor commented, "the drop of honey has now landed in the street and is attracting flies. Perhaps we should call someone to clean it."

"Pay it no mind," answered the King, merrily. "It is not our concern.

Suddenly a gecko sprang out from under the palace, and ate the fly in one gulp.

Next a cat spied the gecko and pounced.

The cat playing with its food in the middle of the street caught the attention of a dog, who attacked it.

"Now, Sire, there is a cat and dog fight in the street. Surely we should call someone to stop it?" pleaded the adviser.

"Oh, pay it no mind, we have more important things to discuss, said the King. "Here come the cat and dog owners, they'll stop it. We don't need to get involved."

So the two continued to eat their honey and rice cakes and to watch the spectacle from their comfortable vantage point on the veranda overlooking the street.

Things were heating up now in the street. The owner of the cat began to beat the dog. This prompted the dog's owner to beat the cat. Soon the two were beating each other.

The king's good humor turned to anger as he watched the scene below. "I'll have no fight on my streets," he cried out and rose from where he sat. "Call my guards and have them stop this battle immediately."

The palace guards were summoned. But by this time the battle had grown. Friends of both parties had joined in the fray. They had tried to stop the fight but soon found themselves fighting one another. With the royal guards involved, the fight erupted into a civil war. Houses and shops were burned; the palace was set on fire and destroyed.

The kingdom was never returned to its former splendor, but new wisdom was gained in that country. To this day, it is understood that we are each responsible for our own actions whether they be small or large and if small problems are left unattended they will become large problems and a kingdom can be lost from a drop of honey not being attended to in good time.

This is a good story for teens to discuss. Several intriguing themes run through the tale: the question of responsibility, the question of dealing with a specific issue in a timely manner, and the question of avoiding getting involved in a given situation. Also, the story works well as a model for teens to use to write a short story.

## Hubris, Foolishness and a Lion (Age 13 and Up)

### A Folktale from India
*(Hubris, Arrogance, Foolishness)*

Once there were four friends who had grown up together in a small village in India. Three of them had the good fortune of going to school, while the fourth was a practical fellow with common sense.

One day the four friends were having tea together. One of them said, "Our village is small, and opportunities are few. We are so clever and well educated that we should travel the world to make our fortunes. There is no limit to what we can accomplish."

As they were planning to leave, one of the scholars said to the other two scholars, "I'm thinking that we three have had a wealth of experience. We have stayed up late night after night studying so we might distinguish ourselves through our studies. Our friend here is a fine fellow, but he is unschooled. Why should he be allowed to accompany us when he has so little to offer?"

The scholars mulled it over until they agreed that indeed their friend should come along, as he had been dear to them since childhood.

The next day they set off to visit grand cities and acquire more wisdom. They had not gone far when they came upon a heap of bones lying on the ground. One scholar specialized in bones. He said, "My friends, these are the bones of a lion. I can reassemble them in no time. We have a grand opportunity to put our schooling to work."

"Indeed," said the second scholar. "There is nothing I would like more that a chance to prove I can regenerate flesh and blood upon these bones."

"Brilliant," cried the third scholar, "And I have the technology to restore the creature to life."

So, the three scholars set to work using their specialized skills and great knowledge. The fourth fellow, lacking in book learning, said, "My friends, forgive me for I am not as learned as you, but is it wise to bring this animal back to life? Won't he be hungry and ferocious? Won't he look upon us as his prey?"

"Dear friend, how can you question the validity of our great endeavor?" said the first scholar.

The second said, "What good is our hard earned knowledge if it can't be put to good use?"

And the third said, "Think of how rich and famous we will be once we have defied death and brought this great creature back to life! Finally our wealth will equal our knowledge!"

"Well said," cried the other two scholars.

The unschooled fellow said, "Well if you must proceed, give me a moment to protect myself from the wild beast."

And he climbed up a tree just as the lion breathed its first breath.

The lion opened its eyes, rose to its feet, stretched its legs, tossed its mane and pounced upon the three scholars and ate them up.

Their unschooled friend waited in the tree until the lion had gone. He returned home alone and told his fellow villagers the whole story.

# The Warmth of a Fire (Age 13 and Up)

## A folk tale from the Middle East

*(Manipulation of language for one's own gain)*

*In the old days, when King David ruled, there was a poor man who had a dream of owning his own land. But he was a servant of a rich merchant. The merchant was so rich that he owned everything he wanted. But he was tired of everything he owned, and there was nothing new to amuse him.*

One cold night, the merchant called his servant to get wood for the fire. When the fire was blazing, the merchant asked: "I wonder how much cold a man can stand? Do you think it would be possible for man to stand all night on the highest peak of a mountain without blankets or clothing or fire?"

"I don't know," the servant replied. "But it would be a foolish thing to do."

"Perhaps, if he had nothing to gain by it," the merchant said. "But I bet a man couldn't do it."

"Master, I am sure a courageous man could stand naked on a mountain and not die of it. But as for me, it's not my business; besides, I have nothing to bet."

"Well," said the master. "Since you are so sure it can be done, I'll make a bet with you anyway. If you can stand among the rocks at the top of the mountain for an entire night, and not die, I will give you ten acres of good farmland with a house and cattle. Remember – no blankets or clothing or fire."

The servant could hardly believe what he heard. "Do you really mean your offer?" he asked.

"I am a man of my word," his master boasted.

"Then tomorrow night I will do it," accepted the poor man. "And afterward, for all the years to come, I shall farm my own land, and be my own master."

But he was worried, because the wind swept bitterly across that peak. He went to his wife and told her of the bet. The wife listened quietly until he had finished; she said, "Husband, I will help you. Tomorrow as the sun goes down, I will build a fire at the foot of the mountain. You will be able to see it as you stand on the peak. All night long you must watch the fire and think of its warmth. Think of me, your wife, sitting here and tending it for you. Think of the land we will farm. Do not close your eyes. Do not let the darkness creep upon you. If you do this you will survive, no matter how bitter the night wind."

The next day the poor man went back to his master's house. His heart was confident. He said, "I am ready." In the afternoon, he went to the mountain and climbed to the top. Servants went to watch him and report to the merchant. As night fell, the poor man took off his clothes and stood in the damp cold wind. At the foot of the mountain, his wife built a fire. It shone like a star in the blackness.

The wind turned colder and passed through his flesh and into the marrow of his bones. The rock on which he stood turned to ice. Each hour the cold numbed him more, until he thought he would never be warm. He kept his eyes upon the twinkling light far below. He remembered that his wife sat there tending his fire for him. Sometimes wisps of fog blotted out the light, and then he strained to see until the fog passed. He sneezed and coughed and shivered, but he survived. When the morning came, he put on his clothes and went down the mountain to claim his reward.

The merchant was astonished to see the poor man. He questioned his servants, "Did he stay all night without blankets or clothing or fire?"

"Yes," his servants answered. "He did all of these things."

"Well, you are a strong fellow," the merchant said. "How did you manage to do it?"

"Master, I endured by watching the fire at the foot of the mountain," he said.

"What! You watched a fire? I said no fire. You lose the bet! You own no land! You are still my servant!"

"But, Master, this fire was not close enough to warm me. It was far away."

The merchant said. "You didn't keep the conditions. It was only the fire that saved you."

The poor man was devastated. He went to his wife and told her what had happened.

She advised, "Take the matter to King David."

The poor man went to King David and complained, and the King sent for the merchant. Each man told his story. The servant said once more, "I endured by watching the fire at the foot of the mountain."

King David declared, "I find for the merchant because the servant did not comply with the terms of the wager; he used fire."

As the poor man and his wife left the palace in tears, they met Solomon, the son of King David. "Why do you weep?," he inquired. The poor man told his story.

Solomon said, "Don't worry. Justice will be done."

Some days later, Solomon sent invitations to a feast at the palace. Among the guests, he invited King David, the merchant, and the poor man and his wife. Solomon ordered a lamb to be slaughtered and preparations for the feast to begin.

On the day of the feast, the guests arrived and were seated. Time passed, and no food was served. King David asked his son, "When will the meal begin?"

"When the lamb is roasted," Solomon told his father.

Evening came and the guests began to grumble among themselves. It was very curious that no food was served. David went to the kitchen to find out about the delay. There he saw a fire in the hearth at one end of the kitchen, and at the other end of the kitchen, he saw the meat on a table – cold and uncooked. King David found his son and asked, "Why did you do this? Why did you invite us to a feast and then not roast the lamb? The fire is at one end and the meat at the other."

Solomon answered, "If the poor man was warmed by the fire at the bottom of the mountain while he stood at the top, then surely this lamb can be cooked by the fire which is only across the kitchen."

"My son, you are right," said the King.

Then he ordered the lamb to be put in the fire and roasted. Father and son returned to their guests, and King David filled all the wine glasses. He made a toast, "Here is a salute to my son, Solomon, who is wise enough to teach his father about the spirit of the law." Then he told about the dispute over fire and ordered the rich man to fulfill the agreement and give the servant the land, a house, and cattle. When the lamb was roasted, the feast began.

# The Squeaky Bed (Age 13 and Up)

One version of a universal story to help change one's perspective on how good or bad things are in life. The main character can be a woman or a man.

*(Perspective, Attitude)*

There was once an old woman who lived on a farm. She was very content with her life except for one thing. She didn't like her squeaky bed. All through the night, it made so many different squeaks and noises that she was finding it hard to sleep.

It happened one night that the squeaks grew so loud; it was more than she could bear. The next day, she went to visit a wise man in the village and told him her problem. The wise man sent her back to her farm, and told her to bring her cow in to live in the house. "Very strange," she thought, "but I will do as he says."

On reaching home, she called the cow inside, and that evening, as well as the bed squeaking, the cow was mooing all night. Back went the old woman to the wise man, and this time he advised her to go back to her farm and also bring in the sheep. On reaching home, she called the sheep inside. And that evening, as well as the bed squeaking and the cow mooing, the sheep were baaing all night long.

Back went the old woman to the wise man. This time, he advised her to bring in the donkey. On reaching home, she called the donkey inside. That evening, in addition to dealing with the squeaky bed, mooing cow, and baaing sheep, there was added the braying of the donkey all night long.

The exhausted woman returned to the wise man who told her that she ought to bring in the pig. Well, now she had to put up with the squeaky bed, mooing cow, baaing sheep, and braying donkey, she now had to listen to the grunting pig all night long.

She could hardly walk for lack of sleep, but back she went to the wise man, and he said the answer was to add the rooster. "Very strange", she thought, but she complied. When she got home, she called in the rooster. As you might have guessed, she now had to put up with the squeaky bed, mooing cow, baaing sheep, braying donkey, grunting pig, and now the crowing rooster as well.

The old woman couldn't stand it any longer. She had a terrible headache and hadn't slept for many days. She stumbled back to the wise man one more time and told him that she was going to tell all the villagers that he couldn't really be a very wise man since he had given such unhelpful advice.

The wise man begged the old woman to accept one more piece of advice from him – "Go home, old woman, take all the animals out of your house and let them go back outside where they belong." The old woman went home and put the cow, the sheep, the donkey, the pig and the rooster out of her house. That night and all the following nights, she slept deeply and soundly.

# The Origin of Strawberries (Age 13)

## A Cherokee Legend
*(Forgiveness, Love, and Compassion)*

When the world was new, there was one man and one woman. They were happy; then they quarreled. At last the woman left the man and began to walk away toward the Sunland, the Eastland. The man followed. He felt sorry, but the woman walked straight on. She did not look back.

Then Sun, the great Apportioner, was sorry for the man. He said, "Are you still angry with your wife?"

The man said, "No."

Sun said, "Would you like to have her come back to you?" "Yes," said the man.

So Sun made a great patch of huckleberries, which he placed in front of the woman's trail. She passed them without paying any attention to them. Then Sun made a clump of blackberry bushes and put those in front of her trail. The woman walked on. Then Sun created beautiful serviceberry bushes which stood beside the trail. Still the woman walked on. So Sun made apple trees, orange trees and mango trees. But the woman did not look at them.

Then Sun created a patch of beautiful ripe strawberries very close to her path. They were the first strawberries in the world. When the woman saw those, she stopped to gather a few. She tasted one and it was the sweetest berry she had ever tasted. As she gathered them, she turned her face toward the west. Then she remembered the man. She turned to the Sunland but could not go on. She could not go any further.

The woman picked some of the strawberries and started back home, away from the Sunland. Her husband met her and she handed him a strawberry. Then they went back home together.

# Biographical Tales

Telling tales from the biographies of historical and modern heroes is inspiring and builds confidence in the human spirit and its ability to overcome adversity and make a difference in the world.

History lessons come alive when peopled with true stories that take us on a journey to a different era through the eyes and heart of a human being who was part of that age.

Use this outline to craft your own tales of real-life characters and watch the faces of your students and your children light up with interest, and intrigue not only for the character you are bringing to life but also for the example of your creative imagination at work!

# Biographical Tale Outline

### Overview

Begin with a vignette from the life of the person you are introducing to your students or your children. Choose one that is dramatic, intriguing and grabs YOU. For example: a death, a shock, a failure, or a triumph. Then proceed with the biography going back to the beginning of the person's life and then moving forwards. Include a key turning point that changed everything forever in the life of that person. Work in a few light-hearted, humorous moments. Create a lively, imaginative character who is larger than life. Tell them what is most interesting to you about the person.

### Structure

1.  Begin with a direct quote from the individual. Choose one that is meaningful to you personally.

2.  Vignette—see above.

3.  . Give a brief description of person's childhood.

4. Mention several turning points at various stages in the life of the person which will often occur during development shifts and significant events, i.e., 9 or 10 years old, the 12-year change, adolescence, a family death, etc.

5. Describe encounters with mentors.

6. Describe key contributions, discoveries, and accomplishments.

7. Describe challenges faced and overcome including educational, social, political, and familial.

8. Describe moments of serendipity in which something occurred out of "nowhere" and changed the person's life or destiny forever.

9. Describe deep moments of inspiration, creation, or genius.

10. Include the years of hard work with seemingly little to show for it, moving through the dross to get to the heart of the matter.

11. What did the person have to overcome? For instance, their background, physical difficulties, loss of loved ones, other challenging events.

12. Conclude with another vignette from the later years of the person's life.

## Stories from the Years with My Adolescent Sons

When my children were young, we established a habit of closing each day together with baths and story time following down time after the evening meal. During the tricky years of adolescence, this changed dramatically, of course, because teens have busy lives and are often reluctant to share much with their parents. But I still sought and often found opportunities to reenter that world with them, as you shall see.

Sometimes we would tell each other stories of the day's experiences, but sometimes not, depending on their mood. Homework help was offered and sometimes occurred. Extracurricular activities filled the time between school and dinner. I was present for them and available to help if needed. I read longer, more complex books aloud that inspired lively conversations and debates. I believe the years of storytelling gave us all a context and a shared expectation for an evening time together either sharing our own stories or reading an exciting series of books like *The Chronicles of Narnia* or later, *The Lord of the Rings*.

I have raised sons. When they were in high school, I learned very little about their lives. "What did you do today?" "Nothing." "Oh, but surely, you did something interesting." "Uh, yeah." Or, simply a shrug of the shoulders. That was dinner conversation. Often, around 10 p.m., I would get a call from the bedroom. "Mom, could you bring me a glass of water?" My heart would rejoice! I would walk in with the water and sit there. I would listen. I learned not to give opinions unless asked specifically. My job was to listen without judgment. We never discussed this. It just was something we understood. I would be exhausted, but I would wait and listen. I would learn things that I would keep in my heart forever. I would offer support, "Let me know if I can do anything to help." "Okay." These were tender and treasured conversations where questions were posed, doubts expressed, and new insights revealed. Plans for the future as well as goals and dreams came up, too.

It was as if under the cover of night, the unspeakable could be shared. The next morning it was never discussed. Often the insights, questions, and doubts were simply too new and too vulnerable to be mentioned in the light of day. I am still grateful for these shared times with my sons during their teenage years. I know they felt I respected their privacy and valued their inner thoughts.

I believe that the years of storytelling naturally gave way to the teenage years of "real-life" story sharing. We knew one another's ways of being well from the years of nightly encounters during story time, and that habit of a regular evening time of sharing, helped us find new ways to relate as the years went by.

Today, more than ever before, in all the long ages of time, we need stories. In a time of constant stimulation via screens of all shapes and sizes from cell phones and computers, I-pads and I-pods, to online educational programs and homework assignments, a pause at day's end for a robust and spicy cup of story is ballast for parent and child alike. Together, we remember who we are alone and who we are together. Stories open the space between us in a way that is free of judgment and expectation. We exchange words, images, imaginative adventures, and, often, a laugh or two! We forget the cares of the day and enjoy a time of play and wonder while transforming the bedtime routine from one of resistance to one of shared exploration and delight.

In summary, the evening story ritual gently ushers the young child over the threshold of sleep with tales of long ago, rich in imagery, tales that have been told in all cultures since the beginning of time. The older child is regaled with tales of the foibles of humorous characters in fables, legends, and folk tales. Such tales rub off the edges of the child's burgeoning personality and give voice to inner fears and doubts as they offer clear imagery for the way forward. Help always comes!

The caregiver or parent is offered closeness and a soft and loving interweaving of hearts as the story ritual space unfolds each evening. The story gives the child and the adult an excuse to openly connect, to co-create a place of shared vulnerability and loving interchange as another day comes to a close. When you are exhausted and at the end of your rope, a quiet moment at bedtime with a story is almost a celebration of another day together! Whew! We made it!

The evening storytelling routine became a beloved bedtime event for us to meet and share our lives and tall tales under the cover of night. In the teenage years, that habit remained, allowing us to connect at day's end just because it was what we had always done.

# CHAPTER 17

## … And They Lived Happily Ever After

Telling a story is a gift. It requires preparation, practice, and discipline. Therefore it is a sacrifice both in the commitment of preparation and in the letting go once it has been told. It is a journey into the past to collect just the right story and an adventure in the present as you make it your own.

When you tell a story you plant seeds that may lie dormant for a long time before bearing fruit. You may never see this fruit yourself. Some years later a student may approach you and tell you how much the story meant. Or your child may want you to help her remember a beloved story so she can tell it to her own children.

Telling a story builds a bridge between cultures. It creates an opportunity to speak heart to heart to your child or your students as you share human history. As you step into the oral tradition, you become a bit of an historian yourself, keeping alive the stories that have been handed down through generations. Other cultures become more real and understandable through the telling of one of their stories.

Storytelling stimulates your own imagination and will give you confidence to eventually create your own stories. You may find yourself using a favorite story as a jumping off place to add on further adventures of your own invention. Taking courage to create your own story is something your audience will intuitively appreciate.

Stories support and guide children and adolescents without moralizing or preaching. Bruno Bettelheim, in The Uses of Enchantment: The Meaning and Importance of Fairy Tales, noted that *"All good fairy tales have meaning on many levels; only the child can know which meanings are of significance to him at the moment. As he grows up, the child discovers new aspects of these well-known tales, and this gives him the conviction that he has indeed matured in understanding... This can happen only if the child has not been told didactically what the story is supposed to be about."* Stories speak to the individual as well as to the group. Stories can bring the past alive and create a bridge between today and long ago. Creativity is a buzzword today; one that suggests innovation, a new way of looking at an old problem, or a need that is satisfied in an utterly new way. Story-telling is creativity in action. Metaphor is the language of the soul, which is why stories can have positive effects without the need for any embarrassing pointing of fingers, punishments, or humiliations.

In this book, I have offered you the tools you need to help your children and your students move through the challenges of childhood and adolescence by employing the right story at the right time. I hope this book gives you the knowledge and confidence to pursue this journey with your children and students. Enjoy!

# Part 3

# Supplemental Information

# Story Meanings
# and Temperaments Reference Guide

This guide lists every story in the book in the order it appears, and provides some additional information regarding the meaning and use of each story. It should help you in your quest to select the right story for the right child at the right time.

## Stories for Ages 3 and up. Note: Temperaments don't apply at this age.)

**Sweet Porridge** – The power of knowing the right word to speak at the right time.

**The Golden Goose** – A good heart is more important than a clever mind. A good heart serves a person well in any circumstance.

**The Little Red House with the Star Inside** – Life is full of surprises; the beauty of nature; looking at something that is common or "everyday" from a whole new perspective.

**The Thick, Fat Pancake** – Sacrificing yourself for others in need.

**The Little Red Hen** – Hard work and determination are qualities we need to complete tasks and achieve what we want for ourselves in life. Involving others and sharing our bounty with them brings joy and friendship.

**The Rooster and the Bean** – Determination and not giving up lead to completing the task and having new experiences. There are people ready to help you if you are willing to ask them and to return the favor. Tasks that seem daunting and overwhelming can be made possible by asking for help from others, thanking them for it and being willing to help them in exchange.

## Stories for Ages 4-5 (pre-school) (Note: Temperaments don't apply at this age.)

**The Bored Little Child** – Boredom appears at age 4-5. Friends are bored together in this tale, and discover that they can make new games to play together and thus overcome their boredom.

**Dolly Duck** – A boredom story with ducks as the main characters. They too overcome their boredom together.

**The House That Jack Built** – The community of people and animals that we are a part of helps us in ways we often forget. This story in verse reminds us of the many ways we are linked together and dependent upon one another.

**The Golden Key** – Life if full of surprises; hard work often has unexpected rewards.

**The Shining Loaf**–Human beings are interconnected in multiple ways that we often forget. Our actions affect the health and well being of others. Kindness and generosity are cumulative and bring their own reward. Taking action to solve a problem that seems impossible leads to self-growth.

**The Elves and the Shoemaker** – Kindness towards others brings happiness. Hard work and not losing hope bring help in the end and sometimes in a surprising and unexpected way; the darkest night always comes before the dawn.

**The Three Brothers**–An environmental wonder tale where the animals speak to humans who will listen and care for them. A gentle reminder of how we are dependent on the animals and they are dependent on us. Being kind to animals even when your own needs are great has surprising rewards.

**Nature Stories** – The Fish and the Fresh Water Clam, The Squirrel and the Toad, The Lizard and the Snail. These delightful tales are conversations between the two animals listed in each title. Written by Jacob Streit and now in the public domain, they describe encounters between animals that are true to the nature of each animal. Beloved by children ages 5–7.

# Stories for Ages 6-7 (First and Second Grade)

For ages 6 and up, additional notes are provided regarding the temperaments that are most evident in the stories to help you narrow selections to those appropriate for children of a specific temperament. Remember that any story can be told for any temperament by finding a place in the story to add details that appeal to a child of a particular temperament. Also, telling a part of a story in a more melancholic, choleric, sanguine or phlegmatic mood is another way to incorporate temperaments into any story.

## The Frog and the Pail of Cream – All temperaments, but especially Melancholic

Singing a song or repeating a positive thought gives courage in the face of adversity.

## The Crystal Ball – Choleric

A complex tale that addresses betrayals and the overcoming of selfishness.

## The Queen Bee – All Temperaments

A delightful Fairy/Wonder Tale about three brothers who set out to find their fortunes. A story of environmentalism, jealousy, kindness and forgiveness.

## The Donkey – Phlegmatic

Hope, perseverance, overcoming limitations, patience, honesty

## Mother Holle – All temperaments

Mother Holle is a fairy tale that addresses laziness, lack of respect for others, trying to get something for nothing, and the virtue of industriousness and self-sacrifice.

## Stone Soup – All temperaments and especially Phlegmatic

A folk tale that addresses the virtues of a community working together in time of hardship and need as opposed to staying away from others and hording what little you do have. The power of one person to change the lives of many is another theme.

## The Three Billy Goat's Gruff – Children today are in a hurry to grow up. This story reminds them that being patient and waiting

until they are really ready to try the two-wheeler bike makes sense on many levels.

**How Paper Came to Be – All temperaments and especially Sanguine**
A story to address how paper was first created by human beings. Serves to show the sacrifice of nature and the many steps that are taken by many people to provide us with things we use everyday. Fosters reverence and appreciation for nature and human beings.

**How the First Flute Came into the World – Melancholic**
Another example of how a new creation came into the world. The sacrifice of nature and the wisdom of creation are two of the themes. The beauty of music and the creativity of the human being working in harmony with nature are also themes in this tale.


## Stories for Ages 7–8 (Second and Third grade)

**St. Valentine – Melancholic**
A kindhearted man who lives life to the fullest and helps others wherever he is. An example of the power of faith in something greater than oneself, and sacrificing one's self for one's beliefs.

**The Rescue – All temperaments**
Innocence and determination can solve a problem. A humorous tale that allows the child hearing the tale to experience that she knows more than the adult hero of the tale. Great for any age!

**The Woodcutter and Hodja Nazrudin – All temperaments**
Addresses laziness, trickery, bullying, and the use of wisdom to show the misdeed clearly to all.

**The Hare and the Tortoise – Sanguine, Phlegmatic, Choleric**
This story addresses inflated self-importance, feelings of superiority, bragging vs. knowing oneself and one's strengths, and patience and steadfastness.

**The Fox and the Crow –All temperaments**
Addresses flattery as a form of manipulation and trickery.

**The Lion and the Mouse – Choleric, Sanguine.**
There is wisdom and power in all living creatures no matter their
size. Brute strength cannot solve all problems. Quick thinking and
steadfast use of one's gifts or skills can bring rewards. This story
is a good choice to address boasting, pride, bullying, and self-
aggrandizement, as well as steadfastness, kindness, and change of
heart.

**The Milkmaid and Her Pail – Sanguine**
This charming tale is about paying attention to the task at hand and
not becoming too distracted by dreams of the future.

**The Foolish, Timid Rabbit – All temperaments**
A humorous tale showing how rumors (like gossip) get started and
can quickly get out of control.

**The Three Fishes – All temperaments**
A tale of bragging and how it can lead to misfortune. The story
shows how friendship can help one get back on track.

**The Cat Who Came Indoors – All temperaments**
Ever wonder how cats came to be pets and live indoors? Here's an
intriguing answer.

**The Flying Squirrel, a folk tale–Melancholic**
An adoption story that is good for children who have experienced
loss or adoption. A story that inspires courage to be yourself.

**The Legend of the Big Dipper – Melancholic, Sanguine**
This story addresses steadfastness, generosity, kindness towards
strangers, and shows how one person can make a difference.

# Stories for Ages 9-10 (Third and Fourth Grade)

**The Enchanting Song of the Magical Bird –All temperaments**

What is it that children have that adults no longer possess? Innocence perhaps and less experience to stand in the way of doing what must be done.

**Lazy Jack – Sanguine**

An exploration of laziness! Jack is just plain lazy. This humorous tale shows the truth in a humorous and lively fashion.

**Wee Jack and the Old King – Choleric**

Sanguines and cholerics are next to one another on the temperament wheel. In this tale another side of Jack emerges as he challenges the King to a contest of wits! Great fun!

**Crow Brings the Daylight – All temperaments**

There's something for everyone in this creation story from long ago. But the trickery of Crow still shines through as he does his fine deed for others.

**Maui Fishes up the Islands – All temperaments**

This is a creation story with a twist. The youngest son proves his worth after being rejected by his older brothers. This is a great story to use to address bullying for both the bullies and victims of bullying.

**Pangu Creates the World – Phlegmatic, Melancholic**

This Chinese creation story stands in sharp contrast to the legends of Maui. Pangu is a dreamer and his visions become reality as he dreams them into being. Good for daydreamers and imaginative thinkers. What you believe and conceive, you can achieve.

**The First Marionette – Phlegmatic, Melancholic**

Doing your best to pour yourself into your projects can create something new in the world.

**The Rumor – Sanguine, Choleric**

Hare (or rabbit) and Lion stand in sharp contrast to one another in this humorous tale. Gossip and rumor can grow and create fear and needless suffering.

# Stories for Ages 10 – 11 (Fourth and Fifth Grade)

## The Wall in Asgaard – Choleric

This is a grand myth showing the relationship of the giants and the Norse gods–one that is full of trickery, and strife. The gods and giants have very different goals and values that are clearly portrayed and offer good fodder for lively follow-up discussions about what is fair and not so fair.

## Iduna and her Golden Apples – Melancholic

This is the follow-up story to The Wall in Asgaard. Iduna is the goddess who cares for the golden apples that each god eats every day to stay young. The story takes a look at youth and old age, honesty and dishonesty, as it weaves a tale about the imagination and how it must be nurtured every day by "eating the apple of life."

## The Old Woman and the Rice Fields – Choleric

A brave woman risks everything to save her village. This is a tale of courage, fearlessness, determination and forward thinking. One person by taking timely action can make a huge difference.

## The Golden Dagger – Sanguine

How did agriculture begin? How did people stop migrating and settle down in one place? This ancient myth from Mesopotamia offers the student a look into the far past when people first began to use tools.

## The Wise Peasant and the King –All Temperaments

A story of bravery, and cleverness set against dishonesty, greed and manipulation. The end of the story includes a fun math puzzle for your students or children to solve.

## The Fisherman and the Seals – All Temperaments

Seals have intrigued mankind for centuries with their expressive eyes and intelligence. A seal hunter comes to a deeper understanding of the life of seals. A compassionate tale of make believe and wonder. Environmentalism, friendship, compassion for all beings, overcoming selfishness.

### The Magnet – Phlegmatic

The story of how magnetic rock was first discovered. Observation and persistence lead to discovery. A Natural Science story.

### The Leopard, the Jackal and the Ram – All temperaments

There is more than one way to solve a problem. Keeping one's wits in the face of great fear offers the opportunity to solve the problem.

## Stories for the 12-year change (Sixth grade)

### A Grain of Rice – All temperaments

A delightful mathematical folktale is full of surprises as a young girl outwits a greedy king with her mathematical request for grain for her people. Courage, intelligence, kindness, and helping others in time of need.

### The Hermit and the Elephant – Phlegmatic

This tale shows the power of knowing yourself and being centered and balanced.

### Julius Caesar Crosses the Rubicon – All temperaments, especially Choleric

This historical adventure story is a metaphor of the 12-year change. Just like the 12-year-old, who now senses she can never go back to childhood, can never see the world in the same way but only through her newly awakened awareness and consciousness, Julius Caesar enters Rome by crossing the Rubicon River with his full warrior armor on! This had never been done before in the history of Rome, and Rome was never the same afterwards.

### That is Good – Melancholic

Believe it or not, life is good. Everything that happens is good. If you don't believe it, this story may convince you! A great story to write about, debate, and contemplate. Great fun, too!

### The Three Questions – All temperaments, especially Sanguine

What is the meaning of life? What is the most important thing to be doing with your life right now? A thought provoking tale that can lead to great classroom discussions at school, and warm discussions around the fireplace at home.

## Being Yourself – All temperaments

Rabbi Zusya poses a wonderful question about the importance of being oneself. Learning to know, trust and appreciate oneself is indeed one of the most important tasks of life.

## The Wolf and the Gypsy – All temperaments, esp. Phlegmatic.

At the end of life, one slows down and often makes friends of former enemies. A new perspective on life appears and former enemies become aware of common ground. This story is inspiring for the 12 year old who is becoming more sensitive to the feelings of others.

## The King of the Fish – Phlegmatic

A fisherman lets go of a beautiful fish that talks to him. He is then fired from his job. This story explores sacrifice, kindness and trickery and concludes with a dramatic surprise ending. A story rich in metaphor about growing up and becoming yourself. Help comes in surprising circumstances often when least expected.

## The Tiger and the Coal Peddler's Wife – Choleric

A woman who has just given birth to her first child hears a knock at the door. She opens it expecting to see her husband and is confronted by a tiger. Her resourcefulness and bravery will inspire your children and students.

## Ancient Babylon and Marduk, the Fearless–Choleric

A fiery warrior heads off to battle for his people. He uses his fearless will and his cleverness to defeat his enemy, a fierce dragon. An ancient tale from long ago, this story may be told with drama and fiery enthusiasm to this age group. Great for history lessons to bring the characters of history alive!

# Stories for Age 13-14 (Seventh and Eighth grade)

**The Chess Game – All temperaments**

This story speaks to youthful disillusionment with life, finding one's purpose, being challenged, and rising to the challenge.

**Mastering the Sword – All temperaments especially Phlegmatic**

Mastering something changes a person in profound ways. The mastery of one subject changes the way one perceives the world and the ease with which one is able to master other subjects.

**Teaching by Example – All temperaments**

Knowing how to teach requires deep immersion in one's subject. A word from a master teacher can have profound meaning for others.

**Mero's Bride –Melancholic**

This is a Burmese myth that teaches the virtue of study of ancient religious texts and the importance of love of something greater than oneself.

**A Drop of Honey – Sanguine**

This story addresses unexpected consequences of our actions and inactions. Ignoring something simple, putting off dealing with cleaning up after ourselves, doing our homework, or any number of procrastinations can lead to unexpected difficulty.

**Hubris, Foolishness and a Lion – All temperaments especially Choleric**

Education must be tempered by common sense. This is great story for teachers to tell students who have too much pride about their own gifts.

**The Warmth of a Fire – All temperaments especially Melancholic**

The manipulation of language for one's own ends. Greed, bravery, perseverance and fortitude, and not giving up.

**The Squeaky Bed – Melancholic**

**A woman (or a man)** –either can be used as the main character in this humorous tale about learning to appreciate what you have. Things could be always be worse!

**The Origin of Strawberries – All temperaments**

Strawberries look like hearts and maybe that's because in the beginning they were made to join two hearts together. This story addresses anger, jealousy, pride, and love.

*Author's Note: The guides provided above are just that, Guides! Use your own judgment and creativity to discern and tell just the right story at the right time. You know your children and your students well. Trust yourself to know when you have found the Right Story!*

# Analysis of Selected Stories in this Book

*Sweet Porridge* or *The Little Pot*. Read this story in Chapter 3. Knowing the right words to speak at the right time is one of the learning activities of the young child. The 3-year-old is immersed in the discovery of the power of language. Knowing the right word to speak at the right time satisfies the child's curiosity and burgeoning powers of persuasion.

There are only three characters in this gem of a fairy tale and they are all women: the mother, the child (the mother's daughter) and an older wise woman. The three stages of womanhood are represented: childhood, motherhood, and wise old age—the crone. The young child is the heroine of the story by remembering the right words to use for turning off the pot when her mother could not recall them.

The roll reversal is delightful for the child of 3 to 6 who will relish the humor of the situation. (Older children love this story too!) In this little story, the child is wiser than the adult. This mystery is one that we, as parents, know well. Who of us has not heard wise words from the mouths of babes?

To the young child, this story speaks of the power of words. The 2- and 3-year-old has discovered the power of the word *no*. Knowing the right words to speak to get what they want and to make sense of the world around them is the "work" of the young child. And what little child doesn't love helping around the house and achieving a task that the parent could not? That's what happens in the world when we know the right words that can change things. Words have the power to make things happen.

From another point of view, this story offers a picture of three stages of feminine development: The young child, who is both innocent and *wise because of her innocence*; the mother, who is the feminine archetype of motherhood; and the wise woman, who knows the sorrow of the child without being told. The wise woman is the keeper of the gift of knowledge. The young child has taken the initiative to seek help in the woods. The woods are a metaphor of the unknown, the outer world and the inner world of the self. The child displays courage and initiative in taking this step. The wise woman gives the child a gift in the form of a pot that cooks when the right words are spoken. The importance of speaking the right words at the right time is a topic of great interest to the young child. The child of this age is continually experimenting with language as she learns the secrets of its power. The child in the story makes good use of the gift given by the wise woman who has initiated the child into the wisdom of knowing the importance of speaking the right words at the right time.

At the end of the story, all is made right when the child returns, speaks the right words, and causes the pot to stop cooking. What is it in the mother that does not remember the right words? Why does the mother become hungry when the child is gone? What is the hunger she feels, and why does she need the child in order to receive nourishment?

The story speaks of the importance of the integration of each aspect of the feminine in order for health and balance to be achieved in one's life. It speaks of the turning of tables between the adult world and the world of the child and reminds us of the inherent wisdom that lives within each child. The story encourages us to seek that wisdom, respect it, and honor it. The story reminds us that help is always available but must be sought and usually takes an effort to find. Often, that wise helper is inside.... in the woods. It further tells us that the gift of the wise helper may not be as straightforward as we would like and may also bring its own challenges. Therefore, we must stay awake and not fall back into old patterns once we have become used to the new life the gift has brought us.

What does the story say to you? What is your favorite moment in the story? What do you love and what do you not like about the story? What would you change? Is there any aspect that annoys you? Looking under the skin of the story at your own reactions can lead you to a deeper understanding of what the story has for you. Take a moment right now and write for 10 minutes about the story. Put it down and read it again tomorrow. Jot down a few more thoughts. What did you notice this time that was not there yesterday? Working with a story in this way over several days can lead to surprisingly helpful insights. This work will lead you to a more open view of the myriad of possibilities that this story offers the young child.

Children often laugh out loud at the idea of the porridge filling up each house! They are delighted by the child's power over the pot. Children are very focused when they eat. Hunger, when it comes, consumes them and they appreciate having that desire satiated. The idea that the pot wanted to cook enough to feed the whole wide world seems perfectly right. Children have a sense of justice that often surprises adults. They enjoy the child's simple wisdom in recalling the right words: a wisdom that temporarily confounds the mother. They are becoming more aware of the consequences of their own actions at this age. No one is hurt. Everyone must eat his way home. It is a satisfying ending for a 3- 6-year-old.

Another question that I have for this story is what does it mean to eat your way home? Do we, as mature adults, notice and actively engage in (or pay attention to) the events of our daily lives well enough each day that we can say that we digest our daily experiences? At the end of the day have we eaten our way home? Do we take in what we encounter each day, receive its nourishment, and thereby make it part of ourselves? It's a question worth considering. Like all great wonder tales this one has a message for each one of us whether we be 3 or 63!

**The Rooster and the Bean.** Read this story in Chapter 7. This lively cumulative tale is about giving and receiving, making a sacrifice, and expecting nothing in return. In this humorous tale, the hen goes in search of water for the rooster who has swallowed a bean. Everyone from whom she asks help requires that she bring him or her a gift in return. Finally, she encounters the woodcutter. He gives her a gift and he requests nothing in return. The woodcutter's act of unselfishness is the catalyst that sets the story in motion to its ending.

The tale heads back in the direction from which it came. As the story moves towards its resolution, each character receives what he had requested and, in turn, gives the hen what she needs. Who is the woodcutter? As the supplier of the wood, he is the one who makes sure the fire, the warmth of life, is provided. The woodcutter and the chopping of wood are common images in fairy tales. Hansel and Gretel are left by a fire, while the parents chop wood. The boy who finds the Golden Key and the Iron Box while loading wood is another tale with the image of woodcutting at its center. The woodcutter when seen as the bearer of warmth calls forth the image of the heart in action.

This story is full of fun and delight. The cumulative tale is a "join in" tale. Encourage the children to join in with you repeating the familiar words, and helping you tell the story as it resolves itself. The images are from long ago and children accept them without question. Why does the river need a leaf from the lime tree? Or why did the peasant's daughter need a comb? After relishing the story over several days or perhaps a week, lively discussions around these questions may occur. Children have wonderful ideas about how the world works. When they ask you why? Give them the chance to answer first by saying, "Oh, I wonder: tell me what you think."

***The Elves and the Shoemaker***. Read this story in Chapter 8. A kind shoemaker has fallen on hard times. He has faith in something greater than himself. He does not give up. He cuts out the last of his leather, says his prayers—i.e., connects with his higher self or the higher power of goodness in the world—is humble, and is not afraid. The next morning, he finds the shoes are finished. He and his wife share the surprise and the joy. The shoes are so finely made that their lives are transformed.

They eventually discover that two tiny naked elves, have done the work.... for nothing. The wife suggests they give the gift of clothing and shoes to the little men. This kind gift, to keep them warm and comfortable, is given freely. However, once the elves are ***seen*** and then ***clothed*** by the couple at the ***suggestion of the wife*** they are full of joy and set free of the task and never seen again. Meanwhile, the shoemaker and his wife fare well the rest of their lives.

The exchange of gifts follows a test of trust, in which the shoemaker has only enough leather for one pair of shoes, yet he does not let himself fall into despair. He has faith and trusts that something will work out, and it does. Help often comes from a place we know nothing about and from a source we don't expect. Often, we are required to take an inner step rather than do something outwardly in order to experience a change in circumstances. This is a healing message that will live in the heart of the young child like a seed for later in life.

***The Golden Key***. Read this story in Chapter 8. Cold, white snow blankets the earth. A boy is sent forth to fill a sledge with wood. When he tries to build a fire to warm himself after his hard work, he finds a golden key. He marvels at this and wonders what it opens. He digs in the snow and finds an iron box. He wonders if the key will fit? The key fits! He turns the key and now we will have to wait to see what he has found. The story ends!

Let's look at the imagery: no color, a white world, and a boy loads wood onto a wooden sledge and tries to build fire, the image of warmth—a polarity with cold. Finding the key to something beyond the everyday—a treasure box beneath the snow—found when the work is done. Hard work and sacrifice often lead to unexpected treasures in life. One must continue to stay awake in order to notice the hidden treasures around one. These two are common themes in fairy tales.

*The Rescue.* Read this story in Chapter 12. A wise man reading sacred texts is fooled by the moon's reflection to think that the moon has fallen into the well. The child hearing the story knows the saint is seeing the moon's reflection, but loves the humor of the older person being confused by life's enigmas and surprise. It is a childish mistake. Seeing the childlike quality in the adult gives the child a sense of empowerment and enjoyment…so wonderful to be able to laugh at the mistake of the adult! And the joyful wonder of the saint to think he has saved the moon is lovely for the child of this age. The child has the privilege of understanding something that the adult does not! How wonderful!

*The Woodcutter and Hodja Nazrudin.* Read this story in Chapter 12. It's not fair! How often do we hear that exclamation in the life of the child! This story presents a clever set up with an intriguing ending that leaves the listener hanging on the edge of her seat. Hidden under the skin of the story is the question of fairness. This is a question that springs up about age 7/8 and reappears faithfully and regularly ever after! Pondering what is truly fair in this situation and wondering whether the truth of the situation will win out in the end is a complex inner experience perfect for the 8-9 year old who is questioning the world from her newly developing perspective of observing herself as separate from the world. As a judge who is now able to understand and decide what is right and what is wrong and, therefore, what *is fair,* the child of this age will appreciate the twists and turns of this light-hearted tale.

*The Tiger and the Coal Peddler's Wife, A folktale from Korea with a female hero.* Read this story in Chapter 15. This is a perfect story for children who are studying the characteristics of the animals in zoology in school or doing a comparative study of the difference between human beings and animals. This is a story of inner resourcefulness on the part of the wife in her encounter with the tiger. It can be told quite simply for the woman is remarkably calm throughout the adventure. The climax can also be understated as a way of actually punctuating its significance.

It is that remarkable. At this age, the details can carry the drama without need for emphasis. The story raises interesting questions about the relationship between animals and human beings, the question of compassion for other beings, and offers the question of necessity—in its presentation of the necessary sacrifices that one makes to earn a living and survive in the wild.

## Summary

Story language is rich in imagery and deep in meaning. Every culture has such stories that offer the child soul pictures to guide and nourish him or her. Not only does the story itself nurture the child through its meaning and movement, but the language and imagery are archetypal, which means the stories can be interpreted by the child in his or her own unique way. When the story is told openly and without explanation or emphasis on the part of the adult, we can trust that the child's inner wisdom will take what it needs from the story and leave the rest behind. To test this out, tell a story to a group of children. Let a day or two go by and come back and talk to them about it. Perhaps have them draw a picture of the part they liked the best, or have them write something about it. The variety of responses will convince you and encourage you to tell more stories and restore your faith in the diversity of the human experience. We are not all the same!

# Additional stories to address issues particularly pertinent to adolescents

"Feathers" (gossip) [From *Doorways to the Soul*]

"You're Still Carrying Her" (dogmatism) [From *Doorways to the Soul*]

"The Wisdom of Allah" (wisdom) [From *Doorways to the Soul*]

"Dair and Lugne" (physical deformity, acceptance, and love)

"Amaterasu's Light" (betrayal and redemption)

"The Stolen Child" (homelessness, loss of custody of child)

"Sealskin, Soulskin" (friendship, kindness, living in harmony with nature)

"How Old Woman Kytna Brought Her Daughter Home" (abuse, child theft)

"Ixchel and the Dragon Flies" (women's esteem)

"Grandfather Ape" (abandonment of child; recovery & redemption)

"Strong Wind the Mystic Warrior" (jealousy, bullying, betrayal, and redemption)

"The Raven and the Whale" (abuse, death, and seduction)

# Fairy/Wonder Tales, Fables, Myths & Folk Tales – A Comparison

When we begin to tell stories, we discover that here are wondrous tales of all shapes and sizes to explore and tell. While each story is unique, like we are, there are families of stories that naturally go together. There are four particular story genres that have been told to children down through the ages: fairy or wonder tales, fables, folk tales, and myths. These story stepping-stones guide children on the path of life as they mature. They teach, amuse, surprise, delight, challenge, and encourage children.

The fairy or wonder tale is for the youngest children, ages 3 -7. Each fairy or wonder tale is a unique, symbolic expression of the journey through life taken by every individual. Fairy or wonder tales are complex tales that involve a dilemma that sends the hero forth on a journey to find something that is missing in his life, or to solve a problem in the kingdom, or to overcome a challenge or dilemma. Wise helpers appear along the way and offer solutions, which, if taken, lead to a happy ending. Curious characters appear, who try to lead the hero off the path. The hero is active and challenged to prove himself as having a faithful, kind heart and a willingness to help others. The hero is stretched to his limits and becomes a better person as a result of the journey. Sometimes, the hero must serve others for a time and learn humility. Sometimes, the hero must go in search of a specific object or a particular person. Helpers appear, but the hero must be awake to recognize them. Hindrances appear and the hero must rise to the challenge. Inventiveness, kindness, generosity, sympathy for the less fortunate, and steadfastness are common characteristics that these heroes need to accomplish their chosen tasks and return home.

Often, the tale ends with a marriage between the masculine and the feminine, symbolizing the achievement of the integration of the self. Throughout the fairy tale, ordinary life goes on. As an outcome of trials and tribulations, not unlike those of growing up, the fairy tale weaves its way to a conclusion that resolves the central question or dilemma of the story. Whatever happens, the fairy tale presents the ordinary problems human beings experience in the process of growing up in metaphorical imagery.

The fairy tale is the story of every person. The names of the characters in the fairy tale are "youngest daughter or son," girl, boy, princess, prince, sister, brother, king, queen, huntsman, little Red Cap. No one has an individualized name. There are some exceptions. For example, in the story of Cinderella, or Ashputel, the main character has a name. Generally, the characters name corresponds to his position (i.e., King, Queen, huntsman) in the world. Compared to a myth, a fairy or wonder tale is very short. Complete unto itself, it journeys into the imagination returning to the everyday in one story. The problems or challenges faced by the protagonist are met and resolved. Helpful people appear throughout the journey and if the protagonist is kind-hearted and unselfish, help always comes. There is always an element of transformation or "wonder" in a fairy or wonder tale. A frog becomes a prince, a donkey becomes a king, a princess grows her hair from a high tower to the ground and it is as strong as a heavy rope, a sister sits in a tree and sews seven shirts for her brothers who have been transformed into swans. She saves them from the enchantment.

The fable is a cautionary tale. Most often the characters in the fable are animals that portray a particular human characteristic. Often, two animals have an interaction that clearly portrays two diverse or opposite human tendencies. Collections of fables have a moral written in at the end of the story. Children dislike morals. Adults dislike morals. None of us like being told what a story means. We want to let it tell us. We want to figure it out on our own. I have gone through my books of fables and obliterated the "moral" with a black marker. Children will speak a clear and lively expression of the meaning of the story without any help from adults. Children do not need to be preached to; rather, they need to be encouraged to express what they think. In the section on fables, I offer suggestions about how to tell a fable and how to create a conversation with a group children or your own child to discover a succinct and even pithy message within the fable. Children love fables and create remarkably clear and simple phrases that epitomize the fable with no moral overtones.

In the myth, the characters are more individualized. Complex names and relationships are described and embellished as the story unfolds. Gods and Goddesses often play a part. Myths are about specific people with specific parents, who have a heritage, and lineage that is linked to the time and place where the myth occurs. Thus, a myth is the journey of a people. Myths contain many sagas or stories that are strung together like a rope of pearls. They are told over a period of days or even weeks.

Myths share similar themes with fairy tales or wonder tales. One of the key differences is in how they are communicated. The dominant feeling of myth is: this is absolutely unique; it could not have happened to another person or in another setting. The events that occur in a myth are grandiose, awe inspiring, and, therefore, would not happen to an ordinary mortal like you or me. Whereas, the fairy tale events are presented as ordinary, something that could happen to you or me or the person next door. Another contrast is found in the way these two story genres end. Myths are the sagas of a people, while the wonder tale is the story of the individual. Myths nearly always end tragically, while the fairy tale nearly always ends happily. The myth is more pessimistic and the fairy tale is more optimistic. The happy ending and the optimism that lives in the story set the fairy tale apart. Myths challenge the child of 10 to 13 with their complexity, historical perspective, and drama. They are exciting, thought-provoking, and inspiring.

Creation Stories are a particular kind of myth, and are found in every culture. Some involve wondrous gods and goddesses; some involve great spirits or mysterious animal helpers. They, too, have common themes that are colored by the culture out of which they arose. They are wonderful stories to tell to 8- and 9-year-olds who, in the third and fourth grade, are very interested in where things come from and how things work. Creation stories help children understand, on an intuitive level, that we are all connected to one another in mysterious ways and that we are truly, in the end, brothers and sisters all over the earth.

# Story Creating Guide

Now that you've learned the basics of selecting the right story at the right time for your children or students, let's explore the elements for taking the next step. Let's explore what it takes to create your own stories.

## Key Ingredients:

**Metaphor** – create a metaphor for the challenging situation the story will address

**Obstacles** – creating obstacles along the journey, people or animals that lead the hero off the path

**Helpers** and **Guides** – helpful animals and people who support the hero along the way

**Journey** – a journey to find something, or someone that leads to a resolution of the problem

**Resolution** – the satisfying ending that restores the situation and/or moves things forward in a healthy way

### Using a metaphor:

* The use of metaphors builds the imaginative connection for the listener
* A metaphor is a figure of speech in which a term is applied to something to which it is not literally applicable in order to suggest a resemblance. Something becomes something else. Someone suffering from a trauma or nervous breakdown can be called a "wreck", or a "ruin". A child who is nervous or cannot hold still can be a "restless red pony". A child who is often complaining can be a "whining whale" or a "grumpy giraffe".
* Metaphors allow children to see themselves in the animal kingdom, in nature, and because there is no judgment about the specific behavior, they can live into it and see it from another point of view without feeling attacked or judged. They then experience the way out of it through the character in the story.
* Allowing them to experience their behavioral challenge through the eyes of the story nurtures and speaks to their subconscious, which then leads to an inner shift that is reflected in changed behavior.

# Family Evening Routine Guide

Think about your current routine. Where and when do you want to tell a bedtime story? Changing the space lets everyone know what's to come and sets the mood for a story! Here are some ideas that parents have shared with me. Begin right after dinner perhaps with some shared clean up. Follow this with a family activity: an evening walk, a short game, or a discussion. Then it's time for a story.

* Gather the family together on the couch. Snuggle together and tell a story.
* Sit next to your child's bed, light a candle, sing a song and tell a story. Blow out the candle and say goodnight.
* Choose a story invocation or make one up. Here are some old standards:

    "Once upon a time…."

    "When did it happen? When did it not happen…"

    "Once upon a time when pigs spoke rhyme…"

    See Chapter 3 for other examples.
* A simple verse or invocation repeated every time you tell a story announces to all those present that we are leaving the world of the every day and entering another world together: the world of imagination. The invocation gives everyone a moment to relax more deeply, let go of the cares of the day, and open the heart to the wisdom hidden in the tale.
* Story endings are just as important as story beginnings. They finish the story and offer a transition back to the present. See Chapter 3 for a list of story endings. Say goodnight, a short verse, or a prayer and lights out or candle out.

# Part 4

# Indices and Bibliography

# Story Suggestions by Age Group

**Author's Note:** The list below is a guide for choosing age-appropriate stories. By telling these stories, you will experience directly how specific stories are just right for specific age groups. Any story can be told to both its age group and to older children. An asterisk denotes stories available in this book.

## Stories for Children Ages 3–7 (Pre-School through 1st Grade U.S.)

Cummulative Tales, Fairy/Wonder Tales, Nature Stories, Folk Tales
Note: Stories in this book are noted with an asterisk *

### Cumulative Tales
The Rooster and the Bean*
The Little Red Hen*
Hugin and the Turnip
The House That Jack Built*

### Fairy/Wonder Tales
Sweet Porridge (Grimm) ages 3 and up*
The Runaway Pancake–ages 3-4 and up
The Golden Goose – ages 3-4 and up*
The Queen Bee (Grimm) ages 4 and up*
The Roly Poly Rice Ball (Japan) 4 and up
The Golden Key (Grimm) ages 4 and up *
The Donkey (Grimm) ages 5 and up*
The Haughty Princess (Ireland) ages 5-6 and up
Mother Holle (Grimm) ages 5-6 and up*
The Crystal Ball (Grimm) ages 6 and up*
The Shining Loaf*
The Elves and the Shoemaker (Grimm)*
The Three Brothers (Grimm)*

### Nature Stories

*Nature Stories* by Margaret Peckham (order at waldorfbooks.com)

The Littlest Gnome      First Signs of Spring

The Butterfly      And others

*Animal Stories* by Jacob Streit (order at amazon.com)

The Fish and Freshwater Clam*    The Squirrel and the Toad*

The Deer and the Fox      The Cow and the Sparrow

The Owl and the Bat      The Lizard and the Snail*

The Bee and the June Bug

### Folk Tales

The Thick, Fat Pancake*      Stone Soup*

The Frog and the Pail of Cream* The Three Billy Goats Gruff

## Stories for Children Ages 7-8 (Second Grade U.S.)

Fables, Jataka Tales, Legends of the Saints, Object Stories (How things came to be), Native American Stories such as *Indian Why Stories*, by Frank B. Linderman, and stories from the *King of Ireland's Son*

### Fables

The Sun and the Wind (Aesop)

The Fox and the Grapes (Aesop)

The Fox and the Crow (Aesop)*

The Hare and the Tortoise (Aesop)*

The Milkmaid and her Pail (Aesop)*

The Hedgehog and the Hare (Aesop)

The Brave Little Parrot (Jataka Tale)

The Cat Who Came Indoors (Africa)*

Why Hares Have Long Ears (Mansi Tale from Siberia)

How Beetle Got Her Colors (Brazil)

The Lion and Mouse*

The Foolish, Timid Rabbit*

The Three Fishes*

The Flying Squirrel*

### Legends

The Legend of St. Valentine*
Odelia and Alaric
St. Francis and the Birds
The Wolf of Gubbio
The Legend of the Big Dipper*
The Little Red House with the Star Inside*
How Robin Got his Red Breast
The Rescue*
The Woodcutter*

### Folk Tales

Lazy Jack and other Jack Tales*
The King of Ireland's Son (by Padraic Colum)
Native Peoples' Stories from Hawaii and mainland U.S.

### Object Stories

How Paper Came to Be*
How the First Flute Came into the World*
The Magnet, by Leo Tolstoy*

## Stories for Children Ages 8-9 (Third Grade U.S.)

Creation Stories from around the world, Old Testament stories adapted for children, Farming Stories, Native People's stories (e.g., Inuit), Animal Stories

### Creation Stories

The Story of Adam and Eve (The Old Testament of the Bible)
Pangu Creates the World (Chinese)*
The Curious Honeybird (A Bantu Myth from Africa)
Wild Pony and Smoke (Native American)
Crow Brings Light (Inuit)*
Maui Snares the Sun
Maui Fishes up the Islands*, and other stories of Maui

# Stories for Children Ages 9-10 (Fourth Grade U.S.)

Norse Myths, Folk Tales, Geography Stories, Animal Stories

### Norse Myths

Note: If possible, tell them all in order beginning with the creation story as presented in collections such as "The Norse Myths" by Kevin Crossley-Holland, D'Aulaires' "Book of Norse Myths", and "The Prose Edda: Norse Mythology" published by Penguin Classics. I have provided two that can work together in the order they appear in the book.

Norse Creation Story
Thor's Hammer
The Walls of Asgaard*
The Apples of Iduna*

### Folk Tales

The Most Noble Story
Stone Soup*
The Key Flower
Winning without Hands
Coyote and the Frog People
Wee Jack and the Old King*
How Jack went out to seek his Fortune
The Rumor*
The First Marionette*

# Stories for Children Ages 10-11 (Fifth Grade U.S.)

Folk Tales, Creation Stories, Ancient Mythologies from India, Persia, Egypt, Greece

### Folk Tales

The Old Woman and the Rice Fields*
The Maker of Dreams
The Golden Dagger*
The Wise Peasant and the King*
Strong Wind the Mystic Warrior
The Cow on the Roof

The Fisherman and the Seals*
The Leopard, the Jackal and the Ram*
**Myths of Ancient Civilizations**
In order of their origination:
Ancient India, Mesopotamia, Persia, Ancient Egypt, Ancient Greece

**Note:** Charles Kovacs has excellent collections of myths from each ancient culture. Available at bookstores and Amazon.com.

## Stories for Children Age 12 (Sixth Grade U.S.)

Biographies from the Age of Discovery and the Renaissance period, Initiation Stories from all cultures, Folk Tales, Roman Mythology, Native People's Stories

### Initiation Stories
The Boy and the Tiger
The Tiger and the Coal Peddler's Wife*
Amaterasu's Light
Maureen the Red
Raven and the Whale, an Inuit story
Ixchel and the Dragonflies
### Folk Tales
A Grain of Rice*
The Hermit and the Elephant*
That is Good*
The Three Questions*
Being Yourself*
The Wolf and the Gypsy*
The King of the Fish*
Marduk, the Fearless One*
### Roman Mythology and History
Julius Caesar and the Crossing of the Rubicon*

**Note:** Charles Kovacs has excellent collections of myths from each ancient culture. Available at bookstores and Amazon.com.

# Stories for Children Ages 13-14
## (Seventh and Eighth Grades U.S.)

Biographical Tales, especially of people who had to struggle and overcome, and Folk Tales

### Folk Tales

The Chess Game*

Mastering the Sword*

Talk

Teaching by Example*

Mero's Bride*

The Plucky Bride

Hubris, Foolishness and a Lion*

The Forbidden Door

The Old Woman and the Rice Fields*

Winning Without Hands

The Squeaky Bed*

The Origin of Strawberries*

The Warmth of a Fire

### Additional Folk Tale Collections

Folk Tales of India (Pantheon Press)

Arab Folk Tales (Pantheon Press)

Children of Wax: African Folk Tales (Alexander McCall Smith)

The Moon in the Well (Erica Helm Meade)

> **Note:** The author is a psychologist who recommends specific stories for various behavioral problems. She has chosen a great collection of Folk Tales from around the world that work especially well with older children and adolescents.

# Index of Themes and Behavioral Issues

How to use this Index: Find the theme or behavioral issue you are interested in. They are listed below in alphabetical order.

Then read to the right to see suggested stories that will address it. Then to the right of that, you can find out what chapters the stories are in, and for what age-groups they are most appropriate.

| Theme/Issue | Title | Chapt | Age |
|---|---|---|---|
| Adoption | The Flying Squirrel | 13 | 6+ |
| Ambition | Julius Caesar and the Crossing of the Rubicon | 16 | 12 |
| Arrogance | Hubris, Foolishness and a Lion | 17 | 13+ |
| Attitude | The Squeaky Bed | 17 | 13+ |
| Being Observant | The Cat Who Came Indoors | 13 | 7+ |
| Being Present in the Moment | The Three Questions | 16 | 12+ |
| Being Yourself | Being Yourself | 16 | 12+ |
| Boredom | The Little Red House with a Star Inside | 7 | 3-6 |
| | Dolly Duck | 8 | 4-5 |
| | The Bored Little Boy | 8 | 4-5 |
| Bravery | Crow Brings the Daylight | 14 | 9+ |
| | The Tiger and the Coal Peddler's Wife | 16 | 12+ |
| Cleverness | Wee Jack and the Old King | 14 | 9+ |
| | The Leopard, the Jackal and the Ram | 15 | 10+ |
| | One Grain of Rice | 16 | 12+ |
| Community | The Shining Loaf | 8 | 5-7 |
| | Stone Soup | 11 | 6-10 |
| | The Enchanting Song of the Magical Bird | 14 | 9+ |
| Compassion | The Thick, Far Pancake | 7 | 3-6 |
| | The King of the Fish | 16 | 12+ |
| | The Chess Game | 17 | 13+ |
| | The Origin of Strawberries | 17 | 13+ |

| Theme/Issue | Title | Chapt | Age |
|---|---|---|---|
| Concentration | The Legend of the Big Dipper | 13 | 7-9 |
| | The Chess Game | 17 | 13+ |
| Confidence | The Cat Who Came Indoors | 13 | 7+ |
| | | | |
| Cooperation | The Little Red Hen | 7 | 3-7 |
| | The Rooster and the Bean | 7 | 3-7 |
| | This is the House that Jack Built | 8 | 4-6 |
| Courage | The Crystal Ball | 11 | 6-7 |
| | The Frog and the Pail of Cream | 11 | 6-9 |
| | The Legend of Saint Valentine | 13 | 7+ |
| | The Lion and the Mouse | 13 | 7-9 |
| | The Old Woman and the Rice Fields | 15 | 10+ |
| | Marduk, the Fearless One | 16 | 12+ |
| | Mastering the Sword | 17 | 13+ |
| Creation Story | Crow Brings the Daylight | 14 | 9+ |
| | Maui Fishes up the Islands | 14 | 9+ |
| | Pangu Creates the World | 14 | 9+ |
| | Marduk, the Fearless One | 16 | 12+ |
| Creativity | The First Marionette | 14 | 9+ |
| Deception | One Grain of Rice | 16 | 12+ |
| Determination | The Rooster and the Bean | 7 | 3-7 |
| | The Shining Loaf | 8 | 5-7 |
| | The Crystal Ball | 11 | 6-7 |
| | The Donkey | 11 | 6-7 |
| | The Frog and the Pail of Cream | 11 | 6-9 |
| | The Warmth of a Fire | 17 | 13+ |
| Dishonesty | The Wise Peasant and the King | 15 | 10+ |
| | The Warmth of a Fire | 17 | 13+ |
| Distraction | The Milkmaid and Her Pail | 13 | 7-9 |
| Environmentalism | The Queen Bee | 11 | 6-7 |
| | The Fisherman and the Seals | 15 | 10+ |
| Exaggeration | Wee Jack and the Old King | 14 | 9+ |

| Theme/Issue | Title | Chapt | Age |
|---|---|---|---|
| Fairness | The Little Red Hen | 7 | 3-7 |
| | The Woodcutter and Hodja Nazrudin | 13 | 7+ |
| | The Wall of Asgaard | 15 | 10+ |
| Faith | The Elves and the Shoemaker | 8 | 4-7 |
| | The Legend of Saint Valentine | 13 | 7+ |
| Fear | The Foolish, Timid Rabbit | 13 | 7-9 |
| | The Leopard, the Jackal and the Ram | 15 | 10+ |
| | One Grain of Rice | 16 | 12+ |
| Finding One's Place in the World | The Cat Who Came Indoors | 13 | 7+ |
| Flattery | The Fox and the Crow | 13 | 7-9 |
| Focus | The Legend of the Big Dipper | 13 | 7-9 |
| | The Milkmaid and Her Pail | 13 | 7-9 |
| Foolishness | The Foolish, Timid Rabbit | 13 | 7-9 |
| | The Three Fishes | 13 | 7-9 |
| | Hubris, Foolishness and a Lion | 17 | 13+ |
| Forgiveness | The Fisherman and the Seals | 15 | 10+ |
| | The Origin of Strawberries | 17 | 13+ |
| Friendship | The Flying Squirrel | 13 | 6+ |
| | The Lion and the Mouse | 13 | 7-9 |
| | The King of the Fish | 16 | 12+ |
| | The Wolf and the Gypsy | 16 | 12+ |
| Generosity | The Three Brothers | 8 | 4-7 |
| Gossip | The Foolish, Timid Rabbit | 13 | 7-9 |
| | The Rumor | 14 | 9+ |
| Greed | The Wall of Asgaard | 15 | 10+ |
| | The Wise Peasant and the King | 15 | 10+ |
| | One Grain of Rice | 16 | 12+ |
| | The Warmth of a Fire | 17 | 13+ |
| Hard Work | The Golden Key | 8 | 4-7 |
| | Mother Holle | 11 | 6-7 |
| History | The Golden Dagger | 15 | 10+ |

| Theme/Issue | Title | Chapt | Age |
|---|---|---|---|
| Honesty | The Golden Goose | 7 | 3-6 |
| | The Crystal Ball | 11 | 6-7 |
| | The Queen Bee | 11 | 6-7 |
| Hope | The Shining Loaf | 8 | 5-7 |
| | The Donkey | 11 | 6-7 |
| Hubris | The Hare and the Tortoise | 13 | 7-9 |
| | Hubris, Foolishness and a Lion | 17 | 13+ |
| Humility | The Elves and the Shoemaker | 8 | 4-7 |
| Humor | The Rescue | 13 | 7+ |
| Identity | Being Yourself | 16 | 12+ |
| Imagination | The Golden Key | 8 | 4-7 |
| | Iduna and Her Golden Apples | 15 | 10+ |
| Industriousness | Mother Holle | 11 | 6-7 |
| Ingenuity | Lazy Jack | 14 | 9+ |
| Injustice | The Wall of Asgaard | 15 | 10+ |
| Innocence | The Rescue | 13 | 7+ |
| Inspiration | The Golden Dagger | 15 | 10+ |
| Inventiveness | How Paper Came to Be | 9 | 5-8 |
| | How the First Flute Came into the World | 9 | 5-8 |
| Irreversible Decisions | Julius Caesar and the Crossing of the Rubicon | 16 | 12 |
| Kindness | The Rooster and the Bean | 7 | 3-7 |
| | The Three Brothers | 8 | 4-7 |
| | The Fisherman and the Seals | 15 | 10+ |
| Laziness | Mother Holle | 11 | 6-7 |
| | Lazy Jack | 14 | 9+ |
| Loss of Innocence | The Wall of Asgaard | 15 | 10+ |
| Love | The Shining Loaf | 8 | 5-7 |
| | The Legend of Saint Valentine | 13 | 7+ |
| | Mero's Bride | 17 | 13+ |
| | The Origin of Strawberries | 17 | 13+ |
| Lying | Wee Jack and the Old King | 14 | 9+ |
| Magnetism | The Magnet | 15 | 10+ |

| Theme/Issue | Title | Chapt | Age |
|---|---|---|---|
| Manipulation | The Wise Peasant and the King | 15 | 10+ |
| Maturing | The Three Billy Goats Gruff | 11 | 6+ |
| Nature | The Little Red House with a Star Inside | 7 | 3-6 |
| | The Queen Bee | 11 | 6-7 |
| | The Legend of the Big Dipper | 13 | 7-9 |
| | The Fisherman and the Seals | 15 | 10+ |
| | The Fish and the Fresh Water Clam | 8 | 5-7 |
| | The Squirrel and the Toad | 8 | 5-7 |
| | The Lizard and the Snail | 8 | 5-7 |
| Object Story | How Paper Came to Be | 9 | 5-8 |
| | How the First Flute Came into the World | 9 | 5-8 |
| | The First Marionette | 14 | 9+ |
| | The Magnet | 15 | 10+ |
| Optimism | That is Good! | 16 | 12+ |
| Overcoming | The Three Brothers | 8 | 4-7 |
| Overcoming Exclusion | Maui Fishes up the Islands | 14 | 9+ |
| Overcoming Fears | Mastering the Sword | 17 | 13+ |
| Overcoming Limitations | The Donkey | 11 | 6-7 |
| Overcoming Obstacles | The King of the Fish | 16 | 12+ |
| Overcoming Selfishness | Stone Soup | 11 | 6-10 |
| | Mero's Bride | 17 | 13+ |
| Patience | The Golden Key | 8 | 4-7 |
| | The Three Billy Goats Gruff | 11 | 6+ |
| | The Frog and the Pail of Cream | 11 | 6-9 |
| | Mero's Bride | 17 | 13+ |
| Perseverance | The Donkey | 11 | 6-7 |
| Persistence | The Golden Goose | 7 | 3-6 |
| | The Rooster and the Bean | 7 | 3-7 |
| | The Flying Squirrel | 13 | 6+ |
| | The Cat Who Came Indoors | 13 | 7+ |
| | The Squeaky Bed | 17 | 13+ |

| Theme/Issue | Title | Chapt | Age |
|---|---|---|---|
| Pomposity | Wee Jack and the Old King | 14 | 9+ |
| Power of Words | Sweet Porridge | 3 | 3+ |
| Present-Mindedness | The Old Woman and the Rice Fields | 15 | 10+ |
| Prevention | A Drop of Honey | 17 | 13+ |
| Pride | The Hare and the Tortoise | 13 | 7-9 |
| Problem-Solving | The Enchanting Song of the Magical Bird | 14 | 9+ |
| Resourcefulness | The Tiger and the Coal Peddler's Wife | 16 | 12+ |
| Responsibility | Lazy Jack | 14 | 9+ |
| | The King of the Fish | 16 | 12+ |
| | A Drop of Honey | 17 | 13+ |
| Rumors | The Rumor | 14 | 9+ |
| Science | The Magnet | 15 | 10+ |
| Selfishness | Stone Soup | 11 | 6-10 |
| Selflessness | The Thick, Fat Pancake | 7 | 3-6 |
| | Mother Holle | 11 | 6-7 |
| | Pangu Creates the World | 14 | 9+ |
| Self-Sacrifice | The Crystal Ball | 11 | 6-7 |
| | The Legend of the Big Dipper | 13 | 7-9 |
| Sharing | The Thick, Fat Pancake | 7 | 3-6 |
| | Stone Soup | 11 | 6-10 |
| Steadfastness | The Golden Goose | 7 | 3-6 |
| | The Elves and the Shoemaker | 8 | 4-7 |
| | The Frog and the Pail of Cream | 11 | 6-9 |
| | The Legend of Saint Valentine | 13 | 7+ |
| | The Hare and the Tortoise | 13 | 7-9 |
| | Pangu Creates the World | 14 | 9+ |
| | Iduna and Her Golden Apples | 15 | 10+ |
| Stinginess | Crow Brings the Daylight | 14 | 9+ |
| Straightforwardness | The Golden Goose | 7 | 3-6 |

| Theme/Issue | Title | Chapt | Age |
|---|---|---|---|
| Trickery | Crow Brings the Daylight | 14 | 9+ |
| | The Leopard, the Jackal and the Ram | 15 | 10+ |
| | The Wall of Asgaard | 15 | 10+ |
| Waiting for the Right Time | The Three Billy Goats Gruff | 11 | 6+ |
| Wisdom | The Woodcutter and Hodja Nazrudin | 13 | 7+ |
| | The Legend of the Big Dipper | 13 | 7-9 |
| | The Three Fishes | 13 | 7-9 |
| | The Enchanting Song of the Magical Bird | 14 | 9+ |
| | The Three Questions | 16 | 12+ |
| | The Wolf and the Gypsy | 16 | 12+ |
| | Teaching by Example | 17 | 13+ |
| | The Warmth of a Fire | 17 | 13+ |
| Wonder | The Little Red House with a Star Inside | 7 | 3-6 |
| | The Golden Key | 8 | 4-7 |
| | The Legend of the Big Dipper | 13 | 7-9 |

# Further Reading, Story Collections and Resources

*Aesop's Fables.* There are numerous collections of fables, however, be sure to mark out the "moral" that is often written in bold at the end of the fable. There is also a good collection online at www.aesopfables.com. See Chapter 13 to review how to create a pre-story conversation before telling a fable.

*Best-Loved folktales of the World,* published by Anchor, Joanna Cole ISBN 0385189494 Anchor Publishing

*Between Form and Freedom,* by Betty Staley (A master teacher explores the world of adolescence and the psychology of teens.) ISBN 1903458897, Hawthorne Press, 2009

*The Complete Grimm's Fairy Tales* ISBN B004QJXMV0, Pantheon Press

*The Cry for Myth,* by Rollo May (The gifts that myths give us and why we need them.) ISBN 0393331776, W.W. Norton & Co., 1991

*Doorways to the Soul: 52 Wisdom Tales from Around the World,* by

Elisa Davy Pearmin. Great short gems for teenagers (13 +) and adults ISBN 1556357400, Wipf & Stock Pub, 2007

*Fables for Children,* by Leo Tolstoy – various editions available online

*Fearless Girls, Wise Women, and Beloved Sisters: Heroines in Folktales from Around the World,* by Kathleen Ragan and Jane Yolen. A fine collection of stories with female heroines. ISBN 0393320464, W. Norton and Company, 2000

*Favorite Folktales from Around the World,* by Jane Yolen ISBN 0394751884 Pantheon Press

*Healing Stories for Challenging Behaviour,* by Susan Perrow (How to create your own stories to change the behavior of *young* children using metaphors from the animal kingdom and nature.) ISBN 1203458781, Hawthorne Press, 2008

*The Hero with a Thousand Faces*, by Joseph Campbell (Campbell's seminal work comparing the hero's journey throughout the world's literature) ISBN 0691067840, Princeton University Press, 1972, ISBN 1577315936, New World Library, 2008

*The High Deeds of Finn MacCool*, Rosemary Sutcliff (Delightful adventure stories from Ireland – Finn is a bit like Robin Hood) ISBN 0140303804 Puffin Books

*Italian Folktales*, by Italo Calvino, ISBN 0141181346, Penguin Books

*Jataka Tales*, by the Buddha (A fascinating collection of stories from the Far East)

Many stories online, just type in Jataka Tales. Numerous collections available.

*Little House Nine-Book Box Set*, Laura Ingalls Wilder, A beloved series of books about her journey across America in a covered wagon in the 19th century. ISBN 0064400409, Harper Trophy

*The Moon in the Well, Wisdom Tales to Change your Life*, by Erica Helm Meade. Written for adults, but many great stories for children and adolescents; choose the right story based on the advice in this book. ISBN 0812694414, Open Court

*Multiple Intelligences, New Horizons in Theory and Practice*, by Howard Gardner ISBN 0465047688, Basic Books, publisher 2006

*Spirit of the Forest, Tree Tales from around the World* (Just what it says, great stories about trees) ISBN 1845072685, Francis Lincoln Children's Books

*The Storyteller's Way*, by Sue Hollingsworth and Ashley Ramsden (Two master storytellers share their wisdom on how to learn a story by heart and tell it well) ISBN 978-1-907359-19-4, Hawthorne Press, 2013

*Storytelling with Children*, by Nancy Mellon (A charming journey into the world of childhood) ISBN 1907359265, Hawthorne Press, 2013

*Thirteen to Nineteen: Discovering the Light*, by Julian Sleigh ISBN 086315283X, Floris Books

*Winnie the Pooh,* A.A. Milne (In addition to great stories, also a wonderful exploration of the four temperaments: Tigger – sanguine, Pooh – phlegmatic, Eeyore – melancholic, and Kanga – choleric) ISBN 4871873005, Ishi Press, 2011

Books by Charles Kovacs are published by Floris Books. Kovacs was a master teacher who understood the power of stories. He created collections like the following and in so doing did a great service for the next generation.

*Ancient Greece (blend of myth and history)*

*Ancient Rome (blend of myth and history)*

*The King of Ireland's Son*

*Norse Mythology*

Printed in Great Britain
by Amazon.co.uk, Ltd.,
Marston Gate.